CW00502496

Revolts and Rebellions

Revolts and Rebellions

Parliamentary Voting Under Blair

Philip Cowley

First published in Great Britain 2002
by Politico's Publishing
8 Artillery Row
Westminster
London SW1P 1RZ

www.politicos.co.uk/publishing

A catalogue record for this book is available from the British Library.

ISBN 1 84275 029 1

Printed and bound by Creative Print and Design, Wales

For Gwen Pearce (1912–2001)

Contents

Preface

In his 1946 book *Can Parliament Survive?*, Christopher Hollis claimed that it would 'be simpler and more economical to keep a flock of tame sheep and from time to time to drive them through the division lobbies in the appropriate numbers'. Almost identical comments were made with astonishing regularity following the election of the Labour Government in 1997. Labour's MPs – once such a fractious and troublesome group – were said to do little more than flock, sheep-like, through the division lobbies in unthinking support of the Government.

But Hollis's analogy was invalid in the 1940s – rebellion was far more common than he realised – and it remains invalid today. MPs were not sheep-like in 1946, and they are not sheep-like today. This book charts and explains backbench dissent in the House of Commons between 1997 and 2001 and, as will become clear, backbench rebellion under Blair was more substantial than most people realised; moreover, what cohesion did exist was in many cases far from unthinking.

It is usual in prefaces to remark that 'this book could not have been written without the help of . . .'. Researching and writing this book, I benefited hugely from the assistance of many MPs. Almost 70 granted me interviews face to face, another 17 did so over the phone, and more than 80 responded to my inquiries by post. They include Members from all three main parties and none. They range from the most rebellious to the most loyal, from senior members of the Government to backbenchers, and from the newly arrived (some still stunned at their victory in 1997) to long-serving MPs who had seen it all before. This book probably could have been written without their help, but it would not be half as good. MPs get a permanently bad press but, with one or two exceptions (with whom, with any luck, the electorate will eventually catch up), most MPs were extremely helpful and gave generously of their time and knowledge. All the interviewees were granted anonymity, broken only with their permission, and so it is impossible to thank them individually by name – but they know who they are. Many MPs then helped further by reading early drafts of the book and correcting errors. However they helped, I am very grateful to them.

It is true, however, that this book could not have been written without the largesse of the University of Hull's Research Support Fund and, most generously of all, the Leverhulme Trust. Their funding enabled me to employ Mark Stuart as a research assistant. Mark, who is simply the best that money can buy, did all the hard work, enabling me to get the glory, such as it is.

The reader should be warned that, for a book on a fairly dry subject like Parliamentary voting, there is a relatively high swear count in what follows. Just like (almost) everyone else, MPs occasionally say rude words. Faced with a choice between leaving them in, and running the risk of offending people, or taking them out, and making our Parliamentarians sound like Mr Cholmondley-Warner, I've gone for the authenticity of the former.

As well as comprehensive data on almost 1,300 divisions in the House of Commons during the 1997 Parliament, the book benefits by being able to draw on data compiled by other researchers: Darren Darcy and Colin Mellors provided data on Parliamentary backgrounds; Pippa Norris was very generous with the British Representation Survey data; Michael Rush provided me with the data from the Study of Parliament Group's Socialisation Survey. I also draw on two excellent undergraduate dissertations written by students from Hull's Politics Department: Christine Coates (whose dissertation on the Labour Whips Office was very helpful for Chapter 8) and Jon Neal (whose work on the Liberal Democrats in Parliament was equally useful in Chapter 11). Chapter 7 is co-authored with Sarah Childs and also draws on her interviews with many of the newly elected women MPs. I am grateful to all of them for their assistance.

Early versions of parts of this book (in various states of preparedness) were presented at conferences and seminars over the last four years, from Essex to Aberdeen and from Copenhagen to San Francisco, and I am grateful to the participants of each for their comments. Individual chapters were commented on by Ron Johnston, Cristina Leston-Bandeira, Jon Neal, Ed Page, Charles Pattie, Andrew Russell and Matthew Seward, whilst the entire manuscript was read by Matthew Bailey, Sarah Childs, Sally Clark and Mark Stuart. Whilst I am hugely indebted to them for their help, the usual disclaimer applies: all errors of fact or interpretation are mine and mine alone.

Philip Cowley

1. Introduction

On 7 May 1997, six days after Labour's landslide election victory, the new Parliamentary Labour Party crowded into the General Synod's room in Church House. Addressing the massed ranks of Labour MPs, the Prime Minister made it clear what role he envisaged for them. They had been elected to support the Labour Government. There should be no indiscipline:

> Look at the Tory Party. Pause. Reflect. Then vow never to emulate. Day after day, when in government they had MPs out there, behaving with the indiscipline and thoughtlessness that was reminiscent of us in the early 80s. Where are they now, those great rebels?

The answer: not in Parliament.

> When the walls came crashing down beneath the tidal wave of change, there was no discrimination between those Tory MPs. They were all swept away, rebels and loyalists alike. Of course, speak your minds. But realise why you are here: you are here because of the Labour Party under which you fought.[1]

Underlying Blair's comments was a simple point, and one that is the justification for this book. For all the talk of the decline of Parliament – an ever-present complaint of the last hundred or so years – the way MPs behave in Parliament is still important. MPs may not matter as much as they once did, or as much as some would like, but they do still matter. No political party comprises only those who agree wholeheartedly with the leadership, however much its leaders may wish it so, and expressions of dissent are a fact of political life. The main focus of this book is on one of the most public forms of discontent: dissenting votes. As Philip Norton once noted: 'In terms of the expression of dissent within a Parliamentary party, voting against one's party in the division lobby represents only the tip of an iceberg; but, like the tip of an iceberg, it represents the part that is visible.'[2]

Visible or not, MPs' impact on the majority of policy decisions is usually limited. British politics has long been described as 'post-Parliamentary', with public policy formulated in segmented, consensus-seeking policy networks, each network consisting of the relevant organised interests and executive units.[3] Once formulated, such policy is presented to Parliament, where because of strong party discipline and exaggerated government majorities, it is almost always accepted. Even one of its strongest academic defenders admits that Parliament is 'at best a proximate – at worst, a marginal – actor in determining the content of measures of public policy'.[4] It is extremely rare for governments to see their measures defeated within Parliament; even minor amendments are very unlikely to be passed unless supported by the Government. But Parliamentarians do have the potential to act both as a constraint on, or – perhaps more rarely – as a prod to, government action. All but the most technical of decisions are affected by some considerations of party management.[5] This was starkly visible in the preceding Parliament under the Conservatives. John Major was forced to tack and trim for the entire five years, most obviously over Europe, where his freedom of manoeuvre was limited by Conservative Eurosceptic MPs, but also in a range of other areas where the Government withdrew or modified policies in the face of Parliamentary opposition.[6] But to a greater or lesser extent, the same has been true of almost all recent governments. Despite her reputation as an autocrat, Mrs Thatcher was often willing to make concessions to backbenchers.[7] In the 1970s, Heath, Wilson and Callaghan were all repeatedly forced by their own backbenchers to withdraw or amend policy. And as Ronald Butt's 1967 work *The Power of Parliament* showed, this was merely the continuation of a long tradition of backbenchers managing to influence government through overt or covert pressure.[8]

And even if, for the most part, Parliament plays a limited role in policy-making, there are issues where its role is far more significant. These are 'free votes', those on which the party managers do not provide instructions to their MPs. Such votes usually occur on private members' legislation, on many proce-dural or internal House of Commons matters, and occasionally on some aspects of government legislation, especially those dealing with what are commonly referred to as 'issues of conscience'. The 1997 Parliament saw a raft of such votes, often far more high-profile than many of the more conventional political issues, covering such topics as embryo research, capital punishment, euthanasia, gun control, hunting and – most frequently and graphically – homosexuality. Here, the executive remains (ostensibly) neutral, and the issues are left to Parliamentarians to decide according to their own consciences.[9] As a result, rather than being peripheral, the legislature, and the legislators within it, becomes central. If the formulation of British public policy as a whole is post-Parliamentary, when dealing with issues of conscience it remains most firmly Parliamentary.

MPs also matter for symbolic reasons. A party's Parliamentarians are one of its most public manifestations. As Jack Brand noted, 'even the most junior and the least gifted receive media attention'.[10] Again, this was clearly demonstrated during the preceding 1992 Parliament. For much of John Major's premiership, the media focused with searing intensity on the divisions within his Parliamentary party, and the term 'Conservative Party unity' became an oxymoron. The Conservatives lost their reputation for unity (a reputation they had long enjoyed), and the blame for this was laid largely at the feet of the party's MPs. When the Conservatives gathered for their first party conference following defeat in the general election, 'speaker after speaker was loudly cheered whenever they criticised the Parliamentary party and its divisions'.[11] It was a view with which the outgoing Prime Minister was in agreement, claiming that 'divided views – expressed without restraint – in the Parliamentary party made our position impossible'.[12] Parties that want to appear united, therefore, want their MPs to appear united.

So even with his enormous majority – the largest since 1935 and Labour's largest ever – Tony Blair could not afford to be blasé about the behaviour of his MPs. Governments with large majorities are not always immune to defeat – as Mrs Thatcher discovered to her cost on several occasions – and even rebellions that do not inflict defeats have the potential both to influence policy and to be an embarrassment. Blair's desire for a disciplined Parliamentary party was therefore understandable. What Prime Minister would want anything else? But as every child soon learns, wanting is not the same as getting. All previous Labour governments had seen widespread rebellion by their backbenchers. Why should this one be any different?

The rise and fall of party discipline

Party cohesion has been a marked feature of British Parliamentary life since the end of the nineteenth century. In tandem with the development of parties outside the House grew the cohesion of the parties within.[13] Party votes – those in which 90 per cent or more of the members of one party vote one way, facing 90 per cent or more of the members of the other principal party – were the norm by the end of the nineteenth century.[14] Cohesion became even greater in the twentieth century. Voting in the period from 1945 to 1970 was characterised by extraordinary levels of party cohesion.[15] Charles de Remuset once declared that unanimity was almost always an indication of servitude, and by this definition MPs in the immediate post-war period were servile almost to excess. In 1966 Samuel Beer was driven to remark that 'when one makes a statistical study of party voting, the figures are so monotonously 100 per cent or nearly 100 per cent it is hardly worth making the count'.[16] From 1970 onwards, however, things changed. MPs in the three Parliaments of the 1970s voted against their own side on more occasions than before, in greater numbers, and with greater effect.[17] Beer was now to note the 'rise of Parliament'.[18] Another observer talked of the Commons having acquired a 'new role' in policy-making.[19] Such rebellious behaviour continued through the 1980s and into the 1990s. Even with the large majorities enjoyed by the Conservatives in the 1980s, government MPs proved willing to defeat the Government.[20] Mrs Thatcher's governments suffered one clear defeat in each Parliament: on the immigration rules in 1982, on the Shops Bill in 1986 and on the National Health Service and Community Care Bill in 1990.[21] There were also some 67 government defeats in standing committees.[22] The relatively limited number of defeats in this period was primarily a matter of Parliamentary arithmetic: MPs continued to be willing to defeat the Government but found the size of the majorities too great in all but a small number of cases.[23] Once the Parliamentary arithmetic changed in 1992, rebellions were suddenly more significant. The Conservative rebel Nicholas Winterton was once curtly dismissed by a whip with the words: 'I'm too busy to waste my time with a tosser like you.'[24] But during the 1992 Parliament it did not take many such 'tossers' to threaten the Government's majority. The Major Government suffered four defeats as a result of its own backbenchers rebelling and avoided others only by a mixture of threats, concessions and procedural manoeuvres.[25]

Labour MPs had, traditionally, been more troublesome to their party leaderships than Conservatives, especially when in government. (As Simon Hoggart once noted, 'the party of brotherly love is the most vicious of all'.[26]) The record of the Parliamentary Labour Party (PLP) was far from that of a tightly disciplined group, but was one of a rebellious, fractious, and troublesome body. The PLP had form and had regularly given Labour's party managers sleepless nights in the past: the three previous periods of Labour government had all seen significant (and increasing) levels of rebellion.

From the very first Labour government in 1924, Labour MPs had been prepared to defy their party managers in considerable numbers. In 1924, 73 Labour MPs – almost four out of every ten members of the PLP – voted against the MacDonald Government over the right of strikers to claim unemployment benefit. The Government of 1929 saw 64 Labour MPs vote against their party over the appointment of Lord Hunsdon, a prominent opponent of the General Strike, as the first Public Works Loan Commissioner.[27] And whereas Conservative MPs were likely to rebel alone, Labour MPs have always been more likely to hunt in packs. For example, under Conservative governments between 1945 and 1970, nine out of every ten Conservative rebellions involved fewer than ten MPs. By contrast, the majority of Labour rebellions in the same period involved ten or more MPs. Between 1945 and 1951, six per cent of Labour rebellions involved 40 or more MPs, with the largest, in April 1947, seeing 72 MPs vote against the National Service Bill.[28] Between 1964 and 1970 the percentage of Labour rebellions involving 40 or more MPs rose to 10 per cent, with sizeable revolts over 'virtually all of the major policy positions of the Labour Government', including the Industrial Relations White Paper, In Place of Strife, and the Parliament (No 2) Bill to reform the House of Lords.[29] During the 1974–79 period, almost a quarter of all Labour rebellions (23 per cent) involved 40 or more MPs; 45 separate votes saw 50 or more Labour MPs rebel, three times the number in the entire post-war period up to 1974; and one vote, on agricultural rent, saw 110 MPs defy their frontbench.[30]

Moreover, each post-war period of government saw more rebellions than its predecessor. Between 1945 and 1951, there were 84 rebellions by Labour MPs; between 1964 and 1970, there were 110; and the period between 1974 and 1979 saw a remarkable increase to 317 Labour revolts, almost a threefold increase on the preceding period, and almost as many as in every single previous Labour government combined.

The effect of the rebellions also increased. Although previously a government might amend or withdraw its policy as a result of backbench opinion and pressure – as occurred with both In Place of Strife and the Parliament (No 2) Bill, for example – until 1974 no Labour government was ever defeated by its own Members voting with the Opposition.[31] Indeed, while Labour MPs often proved willing to vote against their own government, they mostly rebelled in large numbers on occasions when the Conservatives were either abstaining from voting or else voting with the Labour government.[32] To adapt a canine metaphor once used by Harold Wilson, before 1974 Labour MPs were prepared to bark – sometimes quite loudly – but never to bite.[33]

Between 1974 and 1979, Labour MPs began to bite – and frequently. There was a much greater willingness on the part of Labour rebels to vote in a whipped Conservative lobby. The size of the Government's majority during this period – a minority in February 1974, a majority of just three after October 1974, slipping back to a minority in April 1976 – meant that one or more Labour MPs voting with the Opposition could risk Labour's majority. As a result, the Government suffered 23 defeats caused by its own backbenchers, with a further 36 defeats attributed to its minority status. Given that only 34 defeats had occurred in the 67 years from July 1905 to March 1972, the change was remarkable.[34]

It is, of course, important not to overstate the level of rebelliousness in this period. Both in the 1940s and the 1960s, even the most rebellious MPs exercised considerable self-discipline. Even in the 1970,s cohesion remained the norm, dissent the exception. In the 1974 Parliament, Dennis Skinner, the most rebellious Labour MP, voted against his party whip on 156 occasions, and Nicholas Winterton, the most rebellious Conservative, did so 92 times. Yet this still meant that Skinner voted with his whips in 90 per cent of votes, and Winterton in 94 per cent.[35] As Richard Rose pointed out in 1983: 'The suggestion that the House of Commons is now filled with rebel MPs who roam the jungle freely rather than being caged is grossly misleading'.[36] Yet something had changed. Writing in 1970, Ergun Ozbudun had noted 'occasional deviations' from the norm of party cohesion in Britain.[37] Such deviations were always more common under Labour than under the Conservatives; and by the 1970s they had long ceased to be occasional.

Before the 1997 election, therefore, the very real prospect of a Labour government – the first for almost two decades – prompted renewed interest in the behaviour of Labour MPs, not only amongst academics and journalists, but also within the party's own ranks. Previous Labour leaders used to play down their party's rebellious streak, arguing either that things were not as bad as people thought (probably true), or that some division was a sign of healthy discussion (probably wishful thinking). Blair's strategy was different. He talked up how bad things used to be, in order to talk about how good things had become.[38] As with the creation of so much of New Labour, this involved distorting and exaggerating the historical record, but it allowed the party's supposed cohesion to be presented as an important part of what made it new, and (just as importantly) what made Labour different from the Conservatives, then widely seen by the public as split.[39]

This view was largely shared in the media. In July 1996, the *Guardian* claimed that 'Mr Blair leads a disciplined party where dissent is rare'.[40] The *New*

Statesman, another of the British left's house journals, claimed that 'the prospect of power imposes a discipline of which government whips can only dream'.[41] But empirical analysis of the beliefs and behaviour of Labour MPs before the last election revealed a slightly more complicated picture. In fact, in the 1992 Parliament, Labour MPs had been rebelling in much greater numbers than Conservative MPs and over more issues.[42] The difference – and it was a crucial one – was that whereas Conservative MPs appeared almost suicidally willing to broadcast their differences, even those Labour MPs known to have doubts about the Blairite 'project' had for the most part taken what the *New Statesman* described as 'trappist-like vows'.[43] As Steve Richards wrote:

> Any broadcaster compiling a report of dissent in the Labour Party faces a single over-whelming problem – only a predictable handful of MPs will comment on tape. There are scores of MPs who have private doubts about Tony Blair's leadership, but they won't utter a word in public. Labour MPs are desperate to win. They are more tightly disci-plined than they have been for years.[44]

It was, though, a discipline of voice rather than vote. If it represented a change, it was, in the terminology of Henry Drucker, one of ethos as much as doctrine.[45] And many of those who were keeping quiet were prepared to admit that there was little likelihood of their behaviour continuing once Labour was in office.[46]

Whatever their public pronouncements, the Labour leadership were certainly aware that they had a potential problem. Donald Macintyre claimed that: 'it is the Parliamentary Party, of all the branches of Labour, which has proved most resistant to the Blairite transformation'.[47] By July 1996, stories began appearing in the media about the way that Labour would function in government, stories which raised the possibility of removing the whip from rebellious Labour MPs. The issuing of pagers to MPs to keep them informed of the party's line became standard. The standing orders of the PLP were amended to limit the opportu-nities for expressions of dissent from PLP decisions. MPs were to consult the Chief Whip before tabling 'any motion, amendment or prayer'. And for those who sinned, 'a reprimand may be given by the Chief Whip in writing and reported to the constituency Labour party of the Member concerned'.[48] In August 1996, it was announced that Blair was to launch a 'crusade to win over the doubters' within his own party.[49] In an (supposedly) off-the-record remark, an exasperated John Major had famously referred to some of his rebels as 'bastards', a phrase which was taken up and worn by some as a badge of pride.[50] The prospect of Blair having his own bastards seemed a real one.

The players

The general election of 1997 has variously been described as a 'landslide', 'a political earthquake', 'a massacre', 'stunning', 'a truly seismic shift in the politics of the nation', 'a sea-change' and – somewhat apocalyptically – as 'an asteroid hitting the planet and destroying practically all life on earth'.[51] However you describe it, the electorate's decisive rejection of the Conservatives on 1 May 1997 led to the largest turnover in the composition of the Commons since 1945: 39 per cent of MPs were entering the Commons for the first time. One defeated Conservative MP commented that he did not mind losing his seat 'because he would no longer be able to recognise anyone in the Commons'.[52] On the government benches, the change was even greater: 43 per cent of the PLP was newly elected. The scale of the victory was such that when Nick Brown, then Labour's Chief Whip, first addressed the new PLP, he began by saying: 'Normally I would ask, "How are you?". But this time I should ask, "Who are you?".'[53]

Table 1.1 Party composition, 1997

Party	Seats	%
Labour	418	63
Conservative	165	25
Liberal Democrat	46	7
SNP/PC	10	2
Northern Ireland	18	3
Others	2	–
Total	659	100

The partisan make-up (see Table 1.1) was also very different. There were more Labour MPs than ever before – 'it's like that scene from *Zulu*', said one Conservative MP when he first saw them assembled.[54] The Conservatives were reduced to just 165 MPs, lower than at any time since 1906, and the Liberal Democrats had 46, their best result since 1929.[55] And for the first time since 1950, there was an independent MP totally free of party ties, the former TV journalist Martin Bell.

The changes in the socio-economic composition of the Commons, though, were somewhat less dramatic. The most obvious was the increase in the number of women MPs, which, as Figure 1.1 shows, reached a record 120, or 18 per cent of the Commons.

Figure 1.1 Women MPs, 1945-1997

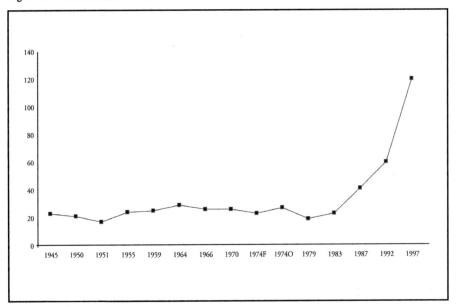

Nearly all of these women sat on the Labour benches. There were just 13 Conservative women, three Liberal Democrats, two SNP, and the Speaker, Betty Boothroyd. The main explanation for the large increase in women elected in 1997 was Labour's policy of all-women short-lists (AWS). Labour adopted sex quotas for internal positions in 1990, followed three years later by the adoption of AWS for parliamentary constituencies.[56] These were to apply in 50 per cent of all vacant Labour-held seats, as well as 50 per cent of all target seats. The process was not exactly problem-free – running into determined local opposition in some seats – and was derailed completely in January 1996 when an industrial tribunal declared the policy illegal.[57] But those parliamentary selections already completed were not re-opened, and the policy had a positive impact in other seats that had already begun to operate AWS.[58] It produced the largest ever increase in the number of women in the Commons. Yet even with this increase less than one in five MPs were women, and women constituted 24 per cent of the governing party, a huge increase, but still a clear minority. Important though it was, it was most certainly not the 'feminisation' of the PLP.[59]

Moreover, this very visible sign of change drew attention away from other areas where change was less dramatic or less positive. For example, there was just another very small increase in the number of Black or Asian MPs, to nine (all Labour), including the first Muslim MP. The sole Conservative Asian MP – Nirj

Deva – lost his seat at Brentford and Isleworth. Similarly, although there was a lot of concentration on the very young Labour MPs swept in by the landslide – such as Claire Ward and Chris Leslie ('He looks just like that guy who used to do Gordon's photocopying', 'Tony, that is the guy who used to do Gordon's photocopying'), the median age of Labour MPs fell by just three years to 48.[60] The median age of Conservative MPs actually rose slightly.[61] The Commons remained an example of middle-aged spread in action. And the middle-class takeover of the Commons continued: just 13 per cent of the PLP elected in 1997 had a manual-worker background, an all-time low.[62] The largest single occupational group in the PLP in 1997 – accounting for 26 per cent of its MPs – was the teaching profession.

By-elections during the Parliament did little to alter the composition of the Commons (see Appendix 1), and although the Parliament was to see a high number of MPs lose their party whips, or face suspension or worse from the House (see Appendix 2), the combination of the various defections and ejections (which largely cancelled each other out), together with an astonishingly successful record in by-elections, meant that Labour began and ended the Parliament with 418 MPs, the first time any government had not seen its representation fall in the course of a Parliament since 1951. Throughout the Parliament, the Government enjoyed the largest majority of any single party since 1935, and Labour's largest ever.

Positive liabilities

Just after the 1966 election, at which Labour leapt from a single-figure majority to one just three seats shy of a hundred, Harold Wilson was interrupted by a visitor while practising his putting at Chequers. 'How's your handicap?' the visitor asked. 'Gone up from three to 97', replied the Prime Minister.[63] He was being typically astute. One academic text described Labour's 1997 majority as a 'luxury', but although they make defeat less likely, large majorities bring problems of their own.[64] What at first glance looks like an overwhelming advantage can soon become a positive liability. A huge Parliamentary majority has the potential to be a huge disciplinary headache.

A large majority means that MPs can break ranks in numbers, safe in the knowledge that they will not defeat the government.[65] To return to that Wilsonian metaphor: they can bark as loud as they want, knowing that they will not bite. Small majorities, by contrast, require self-discipline from MPs. Between

1950 and 1951, and between 1964 and 1966, Labour MPs delivered exactly that self-discipline (as they did, to a lesser extent, between February and October 1974). Indeed, the Parliament of 1964 holds the record for seeing the most cohesive government backbenchers of the post-war period: the entire two years saw just one Labour rebellion, which in turn consisted of just one MP.[66] And, because MPs in large majorities know they can rebel in numbers, it becomes harder to discipline them. Small rebellions invite isolation and punishment. But party managers are virtually powerless to take action after the fact against a significantly large group of dissidents. Once a potential rebellion attracts a critical mass of MPs, it becomes much more difficult to stop other sympathisers joining the fray.

A large majority also reduces the power of patronage. At the most basic level, the larger the Parliamentary party, the smaller the relative size of the 'payroll vote', those hundred or so ministers and Parliamentary Private Secretaries (PPSs) whose votes can be taken for granted. The more MPs there are, therefore, the more MPs need to be persuaded, both within Parliament as a whole and within internal party meetings. Not only that, but the more MPs there are, the lower the chance of any one of them getting a job within government. The number of ministerial (or Parliamentary) carrots that can be dangled in front of ambitious MPs does not expand in proportion to the Parliamentary party.[67] More MPs therefore inevitably means more disappointed and disgruntled MPs. As one party insider said despairingly, shrugging his shoulders, with so many MPs 'what the fuck do you do?'.[68] To begin with, a new MP may be kept in line with the promise of office in the future, but once enough of their colleagues begin the climb up the ministerial ladder, even the most thick-skinned will realise that they are unlikely ever to get their hands on a ministerial red box.

A large majority also has the potential to bring in 'troublesome' MPs. The scale of Labour's victory in 1997 was such that, in addition to winning every one of its target ('key') seats, it won at least 60 that it had not expected to win, right down to the most unlikely Labour MP of all, Gareth Thomas in Harrow West, the doubtless surprised Labour victor of a seat where, just five years before, the Conservatives had enjoyed a majority of almost 33 per cent. Many of these unexpected victors – named 'the unlikely lads' by one of their number – were largely unknown to the central party before their election, bringing fears within the party hierarchy that they might cause trouble. The day after the election, Peter Mandelson ordered every one of Labour's regional press officers to provide the party headquarters at Millbank with a list of 'little-known and potentially troublesome new MPs'.[69] They identified at least 20 'suspect' MPs.[70]

Divisions and dissenters

The main focus of this book is on one of the most public forms of Parliamentary discontent: dissenting votes. These are the occasions when one or more MPs vote against their own party whip or the apparently clear wishes (sometimes implicit) of their own fron bench.[71] But what to call it? Some of those MPs who have voted against their party line do not like their behaviour to be described as 'rebelling', or them as 'rebels'. Tony Benn outlined his objections to some of these phrases in a debate in November 1999. His views are worth quoting at length:

> On welfare reform, I did not vote against the Government; I voted for disabled people. I very much resent the press talking about a rebellion. There was no rebellion. There were Members of Parliament voting according to their convictions, in the interests of their constituents. Some may disagree, as people did, but those who voted for the Government were not actually voting for the Government; they were voting for the changes in the Welfare Reform and Pensions Bill. I greatly resent the current personification of media coverage – the references to the 'awkward squad', the 'mavericks', the 'rebels'.[72]

He was later to describe the use of the phrase 'rebels' as 'the language of Millbank Tower', Labour's party headquarters.[73] Another Labour MP said that he didn't like the term 'rebelling – it's dissenting'.[74] Yet another objected to using the phrase 'mavericks' as a way to dismiss MPs.[75] Others object to the phrase 'loyal' being used to describe those who do not vote against their party, on the perfectly fair grounds that (as discussed above) all British MPs overwhelmingly vote with their party most of the time. Few, if any, MPs therefore are not 'loyal'.

The public's enthusiasm for MPs who defy their whips tends to exist only when the MP's deviations are appealing to them, what Woodrow Wyatt once described as a 'typically hypocritical British afterthought', and there is no doubt that value judgements are frequently made about those who do (or do not) vote with their party.[76] MPs are criticised both when they follow the party line and when they do not. Put at its most technical, and most neutral, the main focus of this book is on those occasions when there is intra-party dissent in the voting lobbies, when MPs dissent from their party's line in the division lobbies of the House of Commons. But, *pace* Benn and others, both because 'intra-party voting dissent' is so convoluted a phrase, and to avoid repetition, the phrase 'rebel' (and its derivatives) is used in what follows to describe those who vote against their party whip. It is a readily understood phrase, used in this context long before the Labour Party moved its headquarters to Millbank Tower. And, at times (and despite appreciating the connotations), 'loyal' (and its various derivations) will be used to describe those who vote with the Government.

But no value judgement is intended: 'rebels' are not better than 'loyalists' or *vice versa*. And in what follows (except where discussing the views of others), there are no references to MPs showing a lack of spine or backbone. Nor are there references to MPs as sheep or clones or poodles or Daleks, or any of the other phrases heaped on the heads of those MPs who, for whatever reason, voted with their party. There are also no references to those who, for whatever reason, voted against their party whips as being brave or independent-minded. Equally, they will not be referred to as mavericks, serial rebels, the usual suspects, or any of the other phrases used to dismiss their behaviour. Voting against the party line is neither a Good Thing nor a Bad Thing. Voting against the party is not necessarily brave (although it can be); nor is voting with the party line necessarily a sign of subservience (although, again, it can be). As should become clear throughout this book, MPs can vote with, or against, the party line for the best or the worst of reasons.

The good news is that the voting procedures in the House of Commons score highly in terms of transparency.[77] In an average year, there will be around 300 divisions (that is, votes), with the names of those voting for or against a motion recorded in the pages of *Hansard*, the record of Parliamentary debates. That is important in terms of democratic accountability – since electors can see how their elected representatives have voted – and it is also invaluable in terms of scholarship: the published records of divisions yield a mass of what David Truman termed 'hard data'.[78] In many other legislative chambers, formal roll-call votes are used more sparingly, making it much harder to analyse the behaviour of Parliamentarians.

Yet the data are not perfect. Printing errors (such as the names of MPs being mixed up) are not frequent, but neither are they rare. Some errors are obvious (such as when a minister votes against their own government, for example), but others have to be resolved by checking with the MPs concerned. MPs suffer from a complex medical condition known as 'questionnaire overload' and are often extremely unwilling to respond to questionnaires and surveys (with Labour MPs being explicitly advised not to do so by their whips), but they are thankfully still very likely to respond to direct queries about their voting.[79] Almost every MP contacted replied to such queries.

For example, in the first session, *Hansard* recorded Phil Woolas (Oldham East and Saddleworth) as voting against the Government in only the third division of the Parliament during the debate on the Queen's Speech. This would have been a remarkable act for any newly elected government MP, but, in fact, *Hansard* had merely confused Phil Woolas with Phil Willis (the Liberal Democrat MP for Harrogate and Knaresborough). Similarly, although *Hansard* records Dan Norris (Wansdyke) as voting for a Liberal Democrat reasoned amendment on the Second Reading of the Social Security Bill, and Russell Brown (Dumfries) as voting against the third reading of the Bank of England Bill, both claim that these 'rebellions' are simply *Hansard* mistakes. Throughout the Parliament, there were another five cases where MPs denied having dissented.

Occasionally, the fault lies with the MPs themselves rather than with *Hansard*. As Paul Flynn notes in his book *Commons Knowledge*, 'outsiders guffaw at the possibility of MPs voting the wrong way. After all the choice is simple, yes or no'. But with around 300 votes each year, there is no way that MPs can know all the details about each vote they cast, especially on the more arcane amendments, so they are 'grateful for the sheepdog herding of the Whips who direct them safely into the lobby of righteousness and truth'.[80] Despite this, mistakes still happen. Voting can be a particular problem for Liberal Democrats and those from minor parties because they often lack both the sight of their party whip to guide them or the equally reassuring sight of masses of their colleagues flocking into one lobby. It can, though, happen to MPs of all parties. One Conservative MP, who retired in 2001, confessed that his eyesight had become very poor. 'I rushed into the Government lobby in some haste, and by a mistake, which I don't think I would have made had I been able to see who my companions were.'[81] 'When it happens', advises Flynn, 'pray that nobody notices'.[82] Unfortunately, anyone writing a book on Parliamentary voting *will* notice, and contact the MP concerned. 'Bugger!', said one MP when contacted, 'I had hoped nobody had noticed'.[83] One common remedy in such situations is to try to cancel out a mistaken vote by rushing around to the other division lobby, to vote both ways. This happened on 22 occasions during the 1997 Parliament. Where an MP has voted against their own party by mistake, or where they have then cancelled that vote out by voting in both lobbies, their votes have not been included in the analysis that follows. The focus here is on MPs deliberately choosing to dissent from their party, not on the dazed, confused, or short-sighted.

A further drawback of divisions in the House of Commons is that, unlike in some legislative chambers (including the Scottish Parliament, for example), abstentions cannot be formally recorded.[84] The party managers (the whips) may formally sanction an absence from a vote, it may be accidental, or it may be deliberate. There is no information on the record that allows us to establish, at least not systematically, the causes of absences. We cannot therefore necessarily read anything into non-voting. For the purposes of systematic analysis over time, therefore, we have to rely on the votes cast. Whilst the text may include reference to the number of MPs believed to have been abstaining on some votes, all the analysis is conducted solely with dissenting votes.

What follows

MPs are not all of equal importance. In an important article on legislative studies in 1976, Anthony King noted that although commentators often talked about 'Parliamentary control' as if Parliament was one entity, there were in fact three groups within Parliament who would try to 'control' the executive. These were the Opposition frontbench, the Opposition back bench, and the Government's own backbenchers. Of these, it was the relationship between the Government's own backbenchers and the executive – what he termed the 'intra-party' relationship – that was crucial. 'As far as the Government is concerned, government backbenchers are the most important Members of the House.'[85] Douglas Hurd, the former British Foreign Secretary, once said that he never lost his 'wholesome respect, even fear, of the House of Commons. I felt it was always there behind my shoulder'.[86] Yet the House of Commons was not just behind his shoulder; it was all around him. Behind his shoulder, and the focus of his concern, were his own backbenchers.[87]

Given this, the main focus of this book is on those behind the Government's shoulder: the PLP, looking at the way Labour MPs voted during the 1997 Parliament. The initial premise of the research was easily put. New Labour claimed to be different. It claimed to be more disciplined and cohesive than its predecessors. But was it? Moreover, as the Parliament progressed, far from being rebellious, the PLP became portrayed in a way that would be unrecognisable to MacDonald, Attlee, Wilson or Callaghan. Backbench MPs were said to be trooping loyally (many said far *too* loyally) through the government lobbies. If the complaint used to be that Labour leaders were not in control of their party, from 1997 it became that they were too much in control. So the focus of the research soon shifted: was this new perception accurate? And if it was, what explained the change?

Part I of the book ('The Absence of War?') describes the backbench Labour rebellions that took place between 1997 and 2001, with each chapter examining a session (that is, roughly a year) of the Parliament. The aim of the chapters is both to provide context for the more analytical chapters that follow, and as to put on record the events of the Parliament. Those who know – or think they know – what happened during the 1997 Parliament can skip or skim these four chapters.

Part II ('Explaining the Absence of War') analyses the behaviour documented in the previous four chapters. Chapter 6 examines why some MPs rebel against the party whips but others do not. Chapter 7 (co-authored with Sarah Childs) looks in detail at the behaviour of the women MPs elected in 1997, who were to come in for especial criticism during the Parliament for not voting against the Government. Chapter 8 discusses the methods the PLP utilised to keep dissent private and to mediate between front and backbenches, between leaders and led. Chapter 9 then draws the analysis together and tries to explain why the Parliament saw so few Labour backbench rebellions.

Part III ('The Opposition') turns attention away from the Government. Chapter 10 looks at the Conservatives. Out of government for the first time since 1979, how did the Conservatives adapt to Opposition? Did the splits seen under John Major continue? Chapter 11 examines the Liberal Democrats. Perhaps understandably, given the small number of MPs involved, most existing studies of Parliament tend to overlook divisions within the third party. The election of a sizeable number of Liberal Democrat MPs in 1997 meant that it was possible for the first time to measure meaningfully how the Liberal Democrats behave in comparison to other parties.

The final chapter discusses the impact of the 2001 election, and the prospects for the forthcoming Parliament. What lessons, if any, can we learn from the 1997 Parliament for the current one?

[1]   Tony Blair, speech to the Parliamentary Labour Party, Church House, London, 7 May 1997.
[2]   Philip Norton, *Dissension in the House of Commons, 1945–1974*, London, Macmillan, 1975, ix.
[3]   Jeremy Richardson and Grant Jordan, *Governing Under Pressure: The Policy Process in a Post-Parliamentary Democracy*, Oxford, Martin Robertson, 1979, p. 191.
[4]   Philip Norton, *Does Parliament Matter?*, London, Harvester Wheatsheaf, 1993, p. 88.
[5]   As the editors of a recent comparative collection conclude, when (as in the UK) Cabinet composition is dependent on party, 'internal party politics and cabinet decision making are intimately intertwined and it is impossible to say where one begins and the other ends'. Michael Laver and Ken Shepsle, 'Introduction', in M. Laver and K. Shepsle (eds), *Cabinet Government and Parliamentary Government*, Cambridge, Cambridge University Press, 1994, p. 7.
[6]   Philip Cowley and Philip Norton, 'Rebels and Rebellions: Conservative MPs in the 1992 Parliament', *British Journal of Politics and International Relations*, 1 (1999).
[7]   See the examples given in Philip Norton, 'Behavioural Changes', in P. Norton (ed), *Parliament in the 1980s*, Oxford, Blackwell, 1985, p. 29.

[8] R. Butt, *The Power of Parliament*, London, Constable, 1967.

[9] The word 'ostensibly' is important, because the executive is frequently able to influence the outcome whilst appearing to remain neutral. See Philip Cowley, 'Moral Issues', in J. Fisher, D. Denver and J. Benyon (eds), *Central Debates in British Politics*, London, Pearson, 2002.

[10] Jack Brand, *British Parliamentary Parties*, Oxford, Clarendon Press, 1992, p. 1.

[11] Peter Riddell, 'Tories have yet to face up to their new status', *The Times*, 9 October 1997.

[12] *The Times*, 8 October 1997.

[13] Although, as Hugh Berrington has shown, the Golden Age of Parliament was not quite as brilliant as traditionally thought, and 'the consequences of backbench independence have been grossly exaggerated by some commentators' ('Partisanship and Dissidence in the nineteenth century House of Commons', *Parliamentary Affairs*, 21 (1967-8), p. 360). And Crommell and Fraser have both argued that any Golden Age had begun to disappear even before the emergence of extra-Parliamentary parties. See Valerie Crommell, 'The losing of the initiative by the House of Commons, 1780-1918', *Transactions of the Royal Historical Society*, 18 (1935); and Peter Fraser, 'The growth of ministerial control in the nineteenth century House of Commons', *English Historical Review*, 75 (1960).

[14] A. L. Lowell, *The Government of England*, London, Macmillan, 1926 (Vol 2).

[15] Norton, *Dissension in the House of Commons, 1945–1974*.

[16] S. H. Beer, 'The British Legislature and the Problem of Mobilising Consent', in E. Frank (ed), *Lawmakers in a Changing World*, Englewood Cliffs, NJ, Prentice-Hall, 1966. See also S. H. Beer, *Modern British Politics*, London, Faber and Faber, 1969, pp. 350-1.

[17] Norton, *Dissension in the House of Commons, 1945-1974*; and Philip Norton, *Dissension in the House of Commons, 1974-1979*, Oxford, Clarendon Press, 1980.

[18] S. H. Beer, *Britain Against Itself*, London, Faber and Faber, 1982, p. 181.

[19] John E. Schwarz, 'Exploring a New Role in Policy-Making: The British House of Commons in the 1970s', *American Political Science Review*, 74 (1980), p. 23.

[20] Norton, 'Behavioural Changes'.

[21] For the Shops Bill, see F. A. C. S. Bown, 'The Defeat of the Shops Bill', in Michael Rush (ed), *Parliament and Pressure Politics*, Oxford, Clarendon Press, 1990; and Paul Regan, 'The 1986 Shops Bill', *Parliamentary Affairs*, 41 (1990).

[22] David Melhuish and Philip Cowley, 'Whither the New Role in Policy Making? Conservative MPs in Standing Committees 1979 to 1992', *Journal of Legislative Studies*, 1 (1995); and Philip Cowley, 'Chaos or Cohesion? Major and the Conservative Parliamentary Party, in P. Dorey (ed), *The Major Premiership*, London, Macmillan, 1998.

[23] Philip Cowley and Philip Norton, 'Rebelliousness in the British House of Commons', unpublished paper presented to the Third Workshop of Parliamentary Scholars and Parliamentarians, Oxford, 1998.

[24] Anthony Seldon, *John Major*, London, Weidenfeld and Nicolson, 1997, p. 286.

[25] Cowley and Norton, 'Rebels and Rebellions'.

[26] Simon Hoggart, 'Foreword', in S. Thomson (ed), *Dictionary of Labour Quotations*, London, Politico's, 1999,

[27] I am grateful to Mark Stuart, whose work on the pre-war Labour governments has been funded by the Nuffield Foundation, for this information.

[28] R. K. Alderman, 'Discipline in the Parliamentary Labour Party 1945-51', *Parliamentary Affairs*, 18 (1964-5), pp. 294, 299; Norton, *Dissension in the House of Commons, 1945-1974*, p. 21.

[29] J. R. Piper, 'Backbench Rebellion, Party Government, and Consensus Politics: The Case of the Parliamentary Labour Party 1966-70', *Parliamentary Affairs*, 27 (1974), p. 385.

[30] Norton, *Dissension in the House of Commons, 1974–1979*, p. 180.

[31] J. J. Lynskey, 'The role of British backbenchers in the modification of Government policy', *Parliamentary Affairs*, 27 (1970).

[32] Norton, *Dissension in the House of Commons, 1974–1979*, p. 439.

[33] Addressing the PLP on 2 March 1967 Wilson had said: 'Every dog is allowed one bite, but a different view is taken of a dog that goes on biting all the time.... He may not get his licence renewed when it falls due'.

34   Norton, *Dissension in the House of Commons, 1974–1979*, p. 439.

35   Richard Rose, 'Still the era of party government', *Parliamentary Affairs*, 36 (1983).

36   Rose, 'Still the era of party government', p. 289.

37   E. Ozbuden, *Party Cohesion in Western Democracies: A Causal Analysis*, New York, Sage, 1970, p. 316.

38   Tim Bale, 'Managing the Party and the Trade Unions', in B. Brivati and T. Bale (eds), *New Labour in Power*, London, Routledge, 1997.

39   By 1993 a mere 19 per cent of the electorate considered the Conservatives to be united. This figure fell into single figures for parts of 1996. 'Not since polls asked the question in the early 1970s has the party been so widely regarded as split', wrote Ivor Crewe in 1996. I. Crewe, '1979-1996', in A. Seldon (ed), *How Tory Governments Fall*, London, Fontana, 1996, p. 432.

40   *Guardian*, 2 July 1996.

41   Steve Richards, 'In search of cracks on tax', *New Statesman*, 26 July 1996.

42   Philip Cowley and Philip Norton with Mark Stuart and Matthew Bailey, *Blair's Bastards*, Hull, Centre for Legislative Studies, 1996.

43   *New Statesman*, 3 July 1996.

44   *New Statesman*, 2 August 1996.

45   Henry Drucker, *Doctrine and Ethos in the Labour Party*, London, Allen and Unwin, 1979.

46   Private information.

47   Donald Macintyre, 'Blair's leftist rebels are out on a limb', *Independent*, 30 July 1996.

48   Philip Norton, 'Parliament', in A. Seldon (ed), *The Blair Effect*, London, Little Brown, 2001, p. 57.

49   Philip Webster, 'Blair embarks on crusade to convert Labour doubters', *The Times*, 12 August 1996.

50   Such as Teresa Gorman, with H. Kirby, *The Bastards*, London, Pan, 1993.

51   The last is from Tony King's commentary on BBC TV on the evening of 1 May 1997; the rest are from various commentaries of the election.

52   Andrew Roth and Byron Criddle, *New MPs of 1997 and Retreads*, London, Parliamentary Profiles Services Ltd, 1997, i.

53   Derek Draper, *Blair's Hundred Days*, London, Faber and Faber, 1997, p. 31.

54   Private information.

55   The death of Sir Michael Shersby, soon after polling, meant that by the time the Parliament resumed the Conservatives were reduced to just 164 MPs.

56   The quotas were not, as is frequently claimed, gender quotas. The quotas applied to biological sex, not to gender.

57   See Sarah Perrigo, 'Gender Struggles in the British Labour Party from 1979 to 1995', *Party Politics*, 1 (1995); and Joni Lovenduski, 'Gender Politics: A Breakthrough for Women?', in P. Norris and N. T. Gavin (eds), *Britain Votes 1997*, Oxford, Oxford University Press, 1997.

58   Byron Criddle, 'MPs and Candidates', in David Butler and Dennis Kavanagh, *The British General Election of 1997*, London, Macmillan, 1997, pp. 189-191.

59   Criddle, 'MPs and Candidates', p. 188.

60   Andrew Rawnsley, *Servants of the People*, London, Hamish Hamilton, 2000, p. 29.

61   Criddle, 'MPs and Candidates', p. 201.

62   Criddle, 'MPs and Candidates', p. 206. Another study put the figure even lower, at six per cent: see Philip Cowley, Darren Darcy, and Colin Mellors, 'New Labour's Parliamentarians', in S. Ludlam and M. J. Smith (eds), *New Labour in Government*, London, Macmillan, 2001, p. 93.

63   Philip Ziegler, *Wilson: The Authorised Life*, London, Weidenfeld and Nicolson, 1993, p. 248.

64   Dennis Kavanagh and Anthony Seldon, *The Powers Behind the Prime Minister*, London, HarperCollins, 2000, p. 261.

65   E. W. Crowe, 'Cross-Voting in the British House of Commons, 1945-1974', *Journal of Politics*, 42 (1980).

66   Norton, *Dissension in the House of Commons, 1945–1974*, p. 257.

67   See Philip Norton, 'Keeping Blair's Troops Amused', *The Parliamentary Monitor*, June 1997.

68   Interview, 6 January 2000.

69   Draper, *Blair's Hundred Days*, p. 8.

70   *Sunday Times*, 23 November 1997. One party insider described some of those elected as 'flotsam and jetsam left-wing candidates' (*Sunday Telegraph*, 4 May 1997).

71   Norton, *Dissension in the House of Commons, 1974–1979*, x. Excluded – as in previous research – are votes on matters of private legislation, private members' bills, matters internal to the House of Commons and other free votes. Included are those who act as 'tellers' – that is, who help count those voting – along with those who vote.

72   HC Debs, 9 November 1999, c. 1041.

73   Letter to author, 6 December 1999.

74   Interview, 3 January 2001.

75   Interview, 11 December 1998.

76   Woodrow Wyatt, *Turn Again Westminster*, London, Andre Deutsch, 1973, p. 100.

77   E. Rekosh (ed), *In the Public Eye: Parliamentary Transparency in Europe and North America*, Washington DC, International Human Rights Law Group, 1995, pp. 229–39, 294–5.

78   D. Truman, *The Congressional Party: A Case Study*, New York, Wiley, 1959.

79   The advice against replying to questionnaires even applies to the spouses and partners of MPs, for whom the Labour Whips Office also think themselves responsible. See Philip Cowley, 'How the Other Halves Live', *Parliamentary Brief*, 6 (1999), p. 21.

80   Paul Flynn, *Commons Knowledge*, Bridgend, Seren, 1997, p. 16.

81   Letter to author, 26 February 2001.

82   Flynn, *Commons Knowledge*, p. 16. In Andy McSmith's *Innocent in the House* (London, Verson, 2001), the newly elected Joseph Pilgrim is given advice from an old hand: 'It's very ill-advised to admit a mistake in this place. I did that in my first year: went through the wrong lobby by mistake, owned up; they made me look a terrible fool: the man who rebelled because he got lost in the lobby. With hindsight, I should have said I was driven by my conscience. Rather be a troublemaker than a chump' (p. 12).

83   Letter to author, 22 March 2000.

84   Proposals in 1998 to allow the recording of abstentions met with a positive reaction from Parliamentarians, although nothing has as yet happened. See The Sixth Report from the Select Committee on Modernisation of the House of Commons, 'Voting Methods', London, The Stationery Office, HC 799, 1998. In order to get around the lack of any formal abstention, some MPs choose to vote twice. Six MPs did so in the 1997 Parliament, casting between them 16 'abstentions': Dr Evan Harris (six times), Martin Bell (five), Ben Bradshaw (twice), and Andrew George, Julie Kirkbridge, and Dr Howard Stoate (once each).

85   Anthony King, 'Modes of Executive-Legislative Relations', *Legislative Studies Quarterly*, 1 (1976). He continued: 'One discounts the disapproval of the other party; the disapproval of one's own is harder to bear' (p. 16).

86   Douglas Hurd, 'The Present Usefulness of the House of Commons', *Journal of Legislative Studies*, 3 (1997), p. 3.

87   For this reason, British Parliamentary politics has been described as 'over-the-shoulder politics'. Anthony King, 'The Implications of One-Party Government', in A. King et al, *Britain at the Polls 1992*, Chatham, NJ, Chatham House, 1997.

Part I

The Absence of War?

The PLP in Government, 1997–2001

2. The Sounds of Silence

1997–98

The first session of the 1997 Parliament was a whopper: it ran from 7 May 1997 until 19 November 1998, the longest session since 1979. It saw the Government successfully pilot 52 bills on to the statute book, implementing a large chunk of its election manifesto in the process. In all that time, and across all those bills, there were just 16 occasions when backbench Labour MPs voted against their whips. In absolute terms this was far from a high level of rebellion. It meant that slightly fewer than one division out of every 20 saw a rebellion – no matter how small – by Labour MPs. The others saw complete cohesion.

This should not have been all that surprising. The first sessions of Parliaments are usually less troublesome than later sessions. It is in the first session that the Prime Minister's authority is usually greatest. The discipline of the election campaign is still strong; and the fact that the Government is implementing its manifesto is usually enough to prevent many MPs, even those who may disagree with the policies, from dissenting. Only in four post-war Parliaments (those of 1955, 1983, 1987 and 1992) has the first session been more rebellious than the rest of the Parliament. In all the others (save for February 1974 when there was only one session in total) the first session has been less rebellious. Importantly, this is true of *all* first sessions following a change of the party in government (again, excluding February 1974) and it is also true of *every* period of Labour government.[1] The first term of a Labour government, then, has always been the calm before the storm.

But even in relative terms, when compared to the first sessions of other Parliaments, 1997–98 was fairly uneventful. As Figure 2.1 shows, there were fewer rebellions by government MPs in the 1997 session than in the first session of six post-war Parliaments (those of 1959, October 1974, 1979, 1983, 1987, and 1992). And the comparison between 1997–98 and the first session of the more recent Parliaments is especially striking. The first session of *every* Parliament from October 1974 onwards saw more rebellions, and usually far more rebellions, than that of 1997. From his position on the Opposition benches, John Major must have looked on enviously: by the end of the first session of the 1992 Parliament Conservative MPs had voted against his Government on 93 occasions, almost six times as often as Labour MPs voted against Tony Blair's.

Figure 2.1 Number of rebellions by government MPs, in first session, 1945–97

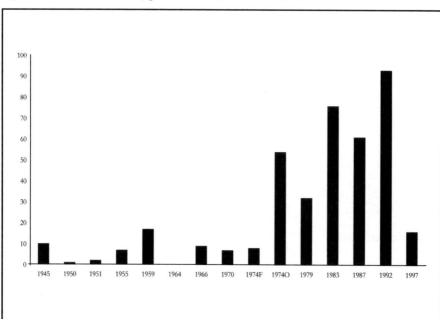

Yet even this relatively high level of cohesion did not mean absolute cohesion. Labour MPs voted against the Government on 16 occasions. As Table 2.1 shows, not all of these 16 rebellions were large. In November 1997 the very first rebellion of the Parliament saw a lone Labour MP, Jamie Cann, vote against the Second Reading of the European Parliamentary Elections Bill, because he believed that the system of proportional representation being proposed breached 'the traditional accountability of member to constituency'.[2] His actions went completely unnoticed outside Westminster and almost completely unnoticed inside Westminster as well.[3] The session saw four other rebellions consisting of a sole MP, together with a further three small revolts of between two and five MPs.

These were not the sort of stuff to cause party managers sleepless nights. But even during this quiet first session, there were more serious rebellions on five separate issues. The most high-profile came over the Government's proposed changes to lone parent benefit, but there were also sizeable revolts over the bombing of Iraq, the introduction of fees for Higher Education (along with the removal of maintenance grants), the provisions contained in the Competition Bill, and the introduction of the Criminal Justice (Terrorism and Conspiracy) Bill. The remainder of this chapter details and explains these rebellions.

Table 2.1 Size of Labour rebellions, 1997-98

Size	N
1 only	5
2–5	3
6–9	0
10–19	3
20–29	3
30–39	1
40–49	1
Total	16

Lone parent benefit

If Jamie Cann's rebellion went unnoticed outside of Westminster, the same could not be said of the next time Labour MPs rebelled. The general source of discontent was social security reform, an issue that would cause disquiet on the Labour benches throughout the Parliament – and beyond. The specific issue was the reform of lone parent benefit contained in the Social Security Bill. Forty-seven Labour MPs voted against the Government together with a large number of deliberate abstentions, and the issue caused the resignation of four MPs from the Government.

As part of its commitment to keep within the previous Conservative Government's spending limits in its first two years in office, in July 1997 the Government announced that it was pressing ahead with some £60 million of reductions in lone parent benefit. The proposals – which applied to new claimants only – sought to remove top-up benefits for lone parents in order to equalise rates of benefit for lone parent and couple families. Evidence of backbench concern soon appeared. Fifty-five Labour MPs signed a critical Early Day Motion (EDM

333) put down by Audrey Wise. A similarly critical round-robin letter organised by Chris Mullin attracted 120 signatures.[4] Many Labour MPs also contacted Gordon Brown, the Chancellor of the Exchequer, and Harriet Harman, the Social Security Secretary, directly. The issue came up at a full meeting of the PLP on 19 November where Harman received what *The Times* described as a 'grilling'.[5] It was also discussed in the PLP's various backbench groups – there were 60 present at the Social Security Committee when it discussed the topic – and it was raised at the Parliamentary Committee on several occasions.[6]

The Government insisted that its plans would proceed unaltered. In part, this was because they did not take the rebels particularly seriously. The lack of previous backbench rebellion (Jamie Cann's lone revolt not withstanding) meant that the strength of backbench concern was not fully appreciated. The leadership, said one senior Labour backbench MP 'didn't really see it coming'.[7] Those MPs who approached members of the Government found their concerns falling on deaf ears. One concerned backbencher wrote to both Gordon Brown and Harriet Harman in July. It took Harman five weeks to reply. Brown never bothered.[8] Another wrote to ministers several times, making clear his concerns, but also pointing out that he had no desire to cause trouble and could (in his words) be 'bought off' fairly easily. He found the Government totally unbending.[9] In the view of a former minister, the Government adopted an 'ostrich approach': 'if we don't think about it, it'll go away'.[10] To make matters worse the Prime Minister was not giving the matter his full attention. Whereas normally the members of the PLP's Parliamentary Committee found Blair willing to listen whenever they raised concerns ('He's very willing to get into dialogue') this time he was not.[11] Blair's attention was distracted by the Bernie Ecclestone affair, the controversy about donations to the Labour Party that had blown up at the time, and he appeared not to appreciate the seriousness of the lone parent benefit issue.[12]

Even when it became clear that there was deep unhappiness over the issue, political machismo intervened. Gordon Brown was unwilling to give way on the matter. He was said by one insider to be 'up for a fight', believing that any potential rebels 'needed to learn a lesson sharp and hard'.[13] Blair similarly believed that to give way would be to appear weak. 'If the choice was between being seen as weak and dithering or harsh and unbending, then he would choose to be seen as Margaret Thatcher rather than John Major. The cut was going to proceed.'[14]

Nor were things helped by the personnel involved. The strained relations between the two senior ministers involved at the Department of Social Security, Harriet Harman and Frank Field have been well recounted in Andrew

Rawnsley's *Servants of the People* (Harman: 'I can't work with someone who thinks I'm a liar'; Field: 'I can't work with someone who *is* a fucking liar').[15] Field believed in the policy. Harman did not, but had been forced by Brown into choosing between two ways of saving expenditure, and had chosen lone parent benefit as the lesser of two evils, despite having previously expressed sentiments that ran counter to the measure. In her book *The Century Gap* she had said that she hoped that 'taking time out of paid employment to care for small children will come to be considered as valuable an occupation as any other in society'.[16] This quote and other previous statements of hers were to be used against her.[17] Perhaps unsurprisingly, therefore, she proved to be an ineffective advocate of the policy. Initially she appeared to accept that the changes were Treasury driven cuts (as, indeed, they were). Then she shifted her ground, and argued that the Government did not want to treat lone parent families any differently from other groups. She ended up arguing against everything she (and the Labour Party) had ever said before on the subject.

Things were made even worse by the debate itself. Harman was left to defend the cuts alone. No Cabinet minister joined her on the Government front bench during the debate. Amongst her backbenchers too she was practically friendless. During her speech, Harman experienced no fewer than 13 hostile interventions, plus two points of order. Labour backbenchers argued that the economy was in good shape and there was no need for the cuts. They reserved especial scorn for the fact that the Government was implementing the previous Conservative administration's spending plans: the cut was 'a wrong, Tory policy', these were 'Tory cuts', and the Bill was described as 'the Peter Lilley Memorial Bill'.[18] Others argued that the proposals hit the poorest children and families, and expressed concern that the Government's childcare and other New Deal reforms were not yet in place, and therefore the Government was gambling on the 'flawless implementation' of its welfare-to-work reforms in order to counter the effect of the cut.[19] A number of Labour backbenchers highlighted the fact that a lone parent would lose benefit if he (or, more usually, she) lost a job and then returned to work. Finally, several Labour MPs stressed the Government's arrogance and lack of consultation. As Ken Livingstone put it: 'If the leadership are not prepared to honour their side of the deal about honest and open consultation before decisions are made, I do not have the slightest intention of honouring their rules that I should not vote against them'.[20] In dealing with these issues, Harman's was not a confident performance. One Labour MP went into the debate not knowing how to vote, but thought that Harman's performance was so poor that she had to oppose.[21]

As well as the most publicised rebellion there were two smaller rebellions. One Labour MP, Dennis Canavan, backed a Liberal Democrat amendment that would have reversed the cuts, and the final vote of the night saw five Labour MPs vote against the entire Bill at Third Reading.[22] But the main rebellion came on an amendment that sought to remove the power to reduce child benefit for lone parents.[23] In the immediate run-up to the vote, the Conservatives announced that they would be voting with the Government, believing that this would maximise the size of any rebellion. It would allow Labour MPs to vote against the measure without having to vote with the Conservatives, something that many Labour MPs would find unpalatable. And it would mean that those who were uneasy about the measure but minded to give the Government the benefit of the doubt would find themselves voting with the Opposition party.[24] Some 47 Labour MPs voted for the amendment, along with at least twenty abstentions.[25] The rebels included four members of the Government, all of whom had to resign their positions.[26] The rebellion was much larger than the whips, the hard core of rebels, or the media had expected. On the morning of the vote *The Times* had predicted that at least 20 Labour MPs would vote against the cut, with between 25 and 30 predicted to abstain. The *Telegraph* claimed similar figures. The *Guardian* headline the next day rightly described the size of the revolt as a 'surprise'.[27] It was to be the largest rebellion of the session.

The party tried to shrug off the rebellion as being little more than the 'usual suspects'. A fortnight before the vote, Blair had been shown a list of those threatening to rebel. 'This is the same bunch who opposed everything I've done to reform the party', he said.[28] But the rebels included 14 of the 1997 intake and Blair failed to appreciate the extent to which the policy was deeply unpopular even with those who voted with the Government.[29] Perhaps the most striking feature about the rebellion was that there was only one MP (Ann Cryer) from the 65 women who had entered the Commons in 1997 (although several others abstained). Given that the cut in lone parent benefit disproportionately affected women, the 'failure' of more of the new women MPs to rebel provoked much media comment, nearly all of it critical of the women.[30] This was to be a trend seen throughout the Parliament, and which is discussed in more detail in Chapter 7. But as well as criticising the new women MPs, the media taunted the Government – which until then had prided itself on control and discipline – for losing control.[31]

In one sense, the lone parent revolt was a textbook example of How Not To Do It. Even amongst those who voted with the Government it has been variously described since as a 'shambles' and a 'disaster'.[32] But the scale of the rebellion – 'There were more of us than they expected' – shocked the party leadership.[33] Threats to discipline those who voted against the cut were soon dropped, once the scale of the revolt became clear. As *The Times* said: 'The size of the revolt stunned the leadership and made severe punishment impossible'.[34] During the debate, Clive Soley, the Chair of the PLP, argued that lessons needed to be learnt from the way the issue had been handled:

> We should all learn the importance in government ... of identifying difficult policy decisions well in advance and alerting the Parliamentary party and ministers to those difficulties. That is not an easy lesson, because there are bound to be areas of difficulty when we have been in government for only a short time.[35]

There is a near-consensus among Labour backbenchers, of all persuasions, that to some extent lessons *were* learnt from the lone parent rebellion, and that it led to a change in attitudes amongst the executive. Government ministers began to make themselves more available for consultation with concerned MPs. Even if they varied in their willingness to make concessions (as will become clear in later chapters), ministers were almost all more ready to listen and discuss than they had been before.

Just as importantly, the Government faced a significant group of loyal MPs who had very reluctantly voted for the measure (some famously doing so in tears), and felt that the leadership owed them a favour. One MP, who had voted with the Government despite grave misgivings, was told by his whip, 'Trust us, it'll get sorted'.[36] And it was. Brown responded in his Budget statement in March 1998 by increasing child benefit by £2.50 a week above the rate of inflation, the largest ever single increase. Labour MPs claim a direct linkage between the Government's shock over the lone parent revolt and this massive increase in child benefit. At no point did the Government concede the principle of cuts for new lone parent claimants, but the establishment of the Working Families' Tax Credit included a childcare tax credit of up to £100 a week for the first child and £150 for two or more children.

Although the lone parent rebellion did not lead to any immediate changes in policy – the measure was not defeated, and lone parent benefit was cut for new claimants – it led to some medium-term changes in policy that more than compensated. Most importantly of all, however, it resulted in a change in relations between the front and backbenches of the PLP. The executive was forced to realise it could not rely on coercion or self-discipline alone to deliver cohesion. Labour backbenchers realised both that the sky would not fall in if they voted against the Government and that they could achieve policy change if they pressed for it.[37] One long-serving MP therefore described it as 'the most effective rebellion of the Parliament'.[38]

Iraq

The next rebellion had considerably less impact. Following the failure of the United Nations weapons inspectors (UNSCOM) to gain access to Iraqi weapons sites the Foreign Secretary, Robin Cook, supported the threat of Anglo-American air strikes against Iraq, designed to cripple its chemical and biological weapons capability.[39] Backbench concerns over the policy had been raised for several weeks.[40] During a statement on Iraq by the Foreign Secretary on 10 February four long-standing critics of the Government's foreign policy, Tony Benn, George Galloway, Tam Dalyell and Bernie Grant, all expressed criticism, while Alan Simpson, Secretary of the Campaign Group, and Tony Benn gave media interviews throughout the day voicing the pacifist line. A week later, when the Commons debated a motion that supported the Government using 'all necessary means', four Labour backbenchers (three of them the same as a week before) spoke against the Government, raising both legal and moral objections to bombing Iraq. Benn argued that the proposed bombing was illegal under the United Nations Charter: 'The Foreign Secretary clothes himself with the garment of the world community, but he does not have that support. We are talking about an Anglo-American preventative war'.[41] Galloway argued that 'there is no such thing as precision bombing. There is no such thing as a smart bomb – bombs do not have brains, still less hearts'.[42] Dalyell emphasised the potential effects of biological and chemical weapons if they were released into the atmosphere as a result of the bombing and claimed that Iraq might also retaliate with SCUD missiles.[43] And both Dalyell and Harry Barnes supported the lifting of sanctions, believing that Saddam Hussein had 'a bunker mentality'.[44]

Cook's line was simple: Saddam would respond to 'the twin tracks of intensive diplomatic efforts, backed by the pressure of military preparations'.[45] He failed to convince 22 Labour MPs, who voted against the motion.[46] The rebels were joined in the noe lobby by four Plaid Cymru MPs, and the Government, supported by the Conservatives and the Liberal Democrats, easily won the vote by 493 to 25. In the event, a last-minute mission by the UN Secretary-General, Kofi Annan, succeeded in a temporary truce, but Saddam's continued failure to comply with UN resolutions led to Operation Desert Fox – an Anglo-American bombing of Iraq – in December 1998 (see Chapter 3).

Higher Education

In July 1997, following the publication of the Dearing Report into Higher Education, the Government announced that it was introducing tuition fees of £1,000 for Higher Education students, and removing (what remained of) the maintenance grant.[47] David Blunkett, the Secretary of State for Education and Employment, argued that the expansion of Higher Education could not be afforded, and that since graduates benefited by seeing their earnings rise, they should contribute to the funding of their own education.[48] Labour back-benchers immediately expressed their objections. Dennis Canavan asked why a Labour Cabinet that included so many beneficiaries of Harold Wilson's comprehensive system of university grants should 'even contemplate kicking away the ladder of opportunity from so many present and future students'.[49] John Cryer failed to see how the measures would widen participation in Higher Education 'mainly because they mean an end to free universal Higher Education – an idea for which the Labour party and the labour movement fought for decades'.[50] An Early Day Motion introduced by Ken Livingstone, and signed by 19 Labour MPs, expressed the view that the Government's policy would 'create a system within which ability to pay took precedence over academic ability'.

In an attempt to allay these backbench concerns, the Government initially tried to buy off the rebels, with David Blunkett announcing a £143 million package of support for Higher Education. But once it was clear that this had not worked the Government tried instead to stifle discussion of the issue. Before the debate on the Teaching and Higher Education Bill started, ministers made three consecutive statements to the House, all eating into the time available. Then, in the course of the debate, five newly elected loyalist MPs made lengthy (and seemingly pre-arranged) contributions supporting the Government line, swamping the two contributions from the rebels – Dennis Canavan (the mover of an amendment on maintenance grants) and Tony Benn. These delaying tactics meant that the last two amendments to be selected, both on tuition fees, could not be debated (and thus voted on) as time had run out.

One of those two amendments, tabled by John McDonnell, had proposed that tuition fees should be payable only 'where a grant in the same amount has been made available for that purpose to that student'. Thirty-five Labour MPs had put their name to McDonnell's amendment, including Tony Benn, who penned an article in the *New Statesman* in which he wrote, 'Some of us will be voting against it because we believed that taxation should be based on wealth and not educational qualifications'.[51] Llew Smith, another rebel, agreed: 'Both I and a lot of my colleagues refuse to be part of a process which will destroy the principle of free education'.[52] In the run-up to the vote, Margaret Hodge, the chair of the Commons Select Sub-Committee on Education, tried to play down the likely size of rebellion, claiming: 'They may get 10 to 15 people voting at most'.[53] In the event, with MPs denied a vote on the tuition fees amendment, the revolt on an amendment on maintenance grants was more than double Hodge's highest estimate. Thirty-four Labour MPs voted for an amendment to retain maintenance grants for students from low-income families.[54] There were also around fifteen abstentions.[55] The amendment was defeated by 313 to 176.

The maintenance grants rebellion was notable both for its size – it was the second largest Labour rebellion of the first session – and also because of its direction: because, unlike the two previous significant Labour rebellions, the Labour rebels went into the same lobby as the Conservatives.

Newspaper ownership

The fourth sizeable revolt of the first session came over the issue of newspaper ownership. Chris Mullin, Chair of the Home Affairs Select Committee, moved an amendment to the Competition Bill to prevent newspaper owners engaging in predatory pricing.[56] In effect, this was a debate about Rupert Murdoch; as one Labour MP admitted, 'we all know that we are debating the Murdoch clauses'.[57] For five years, claimed Mullin, News International had used the profits from the *Sunday Times* and other businesses to sell *The Times* and the *Sun* below the costs of production. This 'war of attrition' had brought newspapers like the *Independent* to the brink of extinction, and it was 'deeply damaging to our democracy to limit or threaten to limit the diversity of our national press'.[58] Mullin's amendment was supported by three other Labour MPs. David Winnick argued that the loss of newspapers such as the *Independent* would be a 'serious blow to the broadsheet market, to British politics and to British democracy'.[59] Bob Marshall-Andrews argued that 'no other commercial undertaking is owned for the express and specific purpose of obtaining and using political power and influence'.[60] And Diane Abbott argued that a special case needed to be made for newspapers in relation to competition policy because newspaper proprietors sought political influence, not profits.[61] The Government's view was that the amendment 'smacked of fixing the legislation to catch *The Times*'. Ian McCartney, the Minister of State at the Department of Trade and Industry, argued that the test of market dominance in the Bill was soundly based and consistent with European competition law, whereas the amendment would have only catered for domestic (UK) competition law.[62] But when Mullin's amendment was put to a vote, 25 Labour MPs voted against the Government.

Criminal Justice (Terrorism and Conspiracy)

In September 1998, Parliament was recalled in the middle of the summer recess to debate the Criminal Justice (Terrorism and Conspiracy) Bill. The Bill was predominantly a response to the Real IRA bombing in Omagh on 15 August, but it was also a response to the international terrorist bombings of United States embassies in Nairobi (Kenya) and Dar es Salaam (Tanzania), and the bombing of US nationals in a restaurant in Cape Town, South Africa. The legislation, which was introduced in tandem with legislation in the Irish Republic, targeted members of specified proscribed organisations – the Real IRA, the Continuity IRA, the Irish National Liberation Army and the Loyalist Volunteer Force – who were not observing a ceasefire. It also removed immunity from prosecution for conspiracy to commit offences overseas while based in the United Kingdom, subject to the safeguard of 'dual criminality', namely that the offence had to be an offence in both countries involved.[63]

Even before the debate, Jack Straw, the Home Secretary, tried to placate back-bench critics by offering a series of concessions. He had originally proposed that the word of a senior police officer alone would be sufficient to secure conviction for membership of a proscribed organisation. After consultation, the proposal in the Bill was that statements by senior police officers of the rank of superintendent or above would be admissible as evidence in court, but not sufficient to secure a conviction. Similarly, whilst the Bill allowed courts to draw inferences from the failure of a suspect to answer questions about membership, in the face of criticism Straw conceded that no inferences could be drawn unless the suspect had first had the opportunity to consult a solicitor. And Straw's original plan to include incitement to commit offences abroad – a much wider offence than conspiracy – was withdrawn from the Bill. Despite this, one senior back-bencher, Robin Corbett, thought that the Government was going down a 'dreadfully mistaken' road, and the Bill attracted four large Labour rebellions.[64]

First, MPs objected to the fact that all stages of the Bill were to be completed in one day.[65] Tony Benn claimed that the Commons was 'being treated as though we were the Supreme Soviet, simply summoned to carry through the instructions of the Central Committee'.[66] Gwyneth Dunwoody expressed 'grave reservations' about the speed with which the Bill was to be debated, and had 'misgivings about legislation that is rushed and probably will not in the final analysis be capable of doing that which is demanded of it'.[67] An amendment objecting to the Business of the House motion was backed by 16 Labour MPs, along with 40 backbench Conservatives.

The second rebellion occurred over a Labour backbench reasoned amendment on Second Reading moved by Kevin McNamara, a former Shadow Northern Ireland Secretary. The amendment (which typically for McNamara ran to some 152 words) argued that the Bill contravened international conventions including the European Convention on Human Rights, left too much power in the hands of senior police officers, and failed to discriminate between countries abroad that respected human rights and democracy and those that did not.[68] Tony Benn argued that the Government's handling of the Northern Ireland issue up until then had been 'absolutely brilliant' but the Bill returned to the failures of past anti-terrorist legislation, infringed civil liberties, and had been introduced in haste in response to media pressure.[69] Robin Corbett was worried that the silence of a defendant and the opinion of a senior police officer would be sufficient to convict a suspect, leading to miscarriages of justice: 'Short cuts with justice lead inevitably to miscarriages of justice'.[70] The Home Secretary, he predicted, would be found to be in breach of the European Convention on Human Rights. At the end of the Second Reading debate, 19 Labour MPs voted in favour of McNamara's amendment.

Then Labour MPs moved on to detail. The third rebellion occurred on an amendment moved by Chris Mullin, making the implementation of the Bill conditional on the audio recording of suspects. Mullin argued that there was a lack of confidence in the rule of law amongst the Nationalist community in Northern Ireland, because suspects lacked the right to have a solicitor present during interviews and because of the absence of jury trials. Audio recording of evidence was therefore vital to the credibility of the legislation. The necessary hardware was already installed in police stations and holding centres, but there was no political willingness to use it. Pressing his amendment to a vote, he claimed that there had been 'a great deal of foot-dragging on this matter'.[71] Mullin was supported by Diane Abbott and Audrey Wise.[72] Straw claimed that the Bill would be delayed by 'some weeks' if audio recording had to be in place before the Bill could have effect. He pointed out that Ronnie Flanagan, the Chief Constable of the RUC, would introduce the arrangements 'as soon as humanly possible'.[73] These assurances proved insufficient to prevent the largest rebellion on the Bill, when 29 Labour MPs supported Mullin's amendment.

The fourth rebellion concerned the Bill's application to cover conspiracy to commit offences outside the United Kingdom. An amendment, in the name of Tony McWalter, a newly elected Labour MP, effectively attempted to remove the provisions in the Bill (clauses 5-7) relating to conspiracy to commit terrorist offences abroad, while preserving those clauses (1-4) specifically related to Northern Ireland terrorism. McWalter argued that it was 'no way to treat new Members to say that the proposals have been coming for some time and that we talked about the issues 17 months ago and reached agreement, so now we just want to ram the measures through'.[74] The conspiracy issues in the Bill, he believed, should be dealt with at a later date. Straw responded by claiming that, not only had he removed the provisions relating to incitement (mentioned above), but he was also accepting a Conservative amendment that would make the provisions of the Act require renewal after a year. These concessions proved insufficient to prevent 18 MPs voting against the Government.

The four rebellions together involved a total of 37 Labour MPs. But as Table 2.2 shows, there was considerable variation between the personnel involved. This was not the same group of MPs voting repeatedly. Instead, the composition of the rebels shifted from vote to vote. For example, one MP, Gwyneth Dunwoody, rebelled solely over the business of the House motion. Another, Bob Wareing, voted only for the deletion of the overseas clauses. Another three, Robin Corbett, John Cryer, and Brian Sedgemore, rebelled solely over the Second Reading vote. Some nine MPs – overwhelmingly new MPs – voted just for Mullin's amendment, whilst eight MPs – nearly all longer-serving ones – took part in all four revolts.

Table 2.2 Labour rebels over Criminal Justice (Terrorism and Conspiracy) Bill

Name	Business of the House	Second Reading	Audio recording	Conspiracy to commit offences overseas
Irene Adams	X	X	X	–
Tony Benn	X	X	–	–
Roger Berry	–	–	X	–
Harold Best	–	X	X	X
David Borrow	–	–	X	–
Christine Butler	–	–	X	–
Dennis Canavan	X	X	X	X
Martin Caton	–	–	X	–
Ann Clwyd	X	–	X	X
Robin Corbett	–	X	–	–

cont'd

Name	Business of the House	Second Reading	Audio recording	Conspiracy to commit offences overseas
Jeremy Corbyn	X	X	X	X
James Cousins	–	–	X	–
Ann Cryer	–	X	X	X
John Cryer	–	X	–	–
Tam Dalyell	X	X	X	X
Ian Davidson	–	–	X	X
Gwyneth Dunwoody	X	–	–	–
William Etherington	–	X	X	–
Maria Fyfe	–	–	X	X
Ian Gibson	–	–	X	–
Bernie Grant	X	X	–	–
Kelvin Hopkins	–	–	X	–
Brian Iddon	–	–	X	–
Lynne Jones	X	X	X	X
Robert Marshall-Andrews	X	X	–	–
John McAllion	X	X	X	X
John McDonnell	X	X	X	X
Kevin McNamara	X	X	X	X
Tony McWalter	–	–	X	X
Christopher Mullin	X	–	X	–
Kerry Pollard	–	X	X	X
Gordon Prentice	–	–	X	X
Brian Sedgemore	–	X	–	–
Dennis Skinner	X	X	X	X
David Taylor	–	–	X	–
Robert Wareing	–	–	–	X
Audrey Wise	X	–	X	X

Note: X indicates that the MP voted against the party whip.

Dogs that didn't bark

As much as for the rebellions detailed above, the session was also notable for the issues that did not cause any overt backbench discontent. The first, and most obvious, absentee was Europe. There were just two small rebellions over Europe, both during the European Parliamentary Elections Bill. The first was Jamie Cann's (noted at the beginning of this chapter). The second came on 24 February 1998 when two Labour MPs – Austin Mitchell and Andrew Mackinlay – voted for an amendment to extend the right to vote in European elections to

Gibraltarians. But with these limited exceptions – and neither of these rebellions was directly related to the European issue *per se* – the question of Britain's future role in Europe was a Parliamentary dog that failed to bark. Compare that to the preceeding Parliament, in which Labour MPs had rebelled on 40 occasions over the Maastricht Bill alone, casting a total of almost 1,300 dissenting votes.[75] Or, indeed, compare that to the last time Labour was in power, when there were enormous splits over the EEC. In April 1975, the issue of continuing membership of the EEC had split the PLP right down the middle: 138 Labour MPs voting in favour of the Labour Government's renegotiation of the Treaty of Rome, 145 Labour MPs voting against.[76]

Similarly, compare the (successful) passage of the Government's devolution legislation with its (unsuccessful) passage between 1974 and 1979. Despite introducing a raft of legislation, including delivering devolved government to Scotland, Wales and Northern Ireland, the first session saw only one rebellious vote cast by a Labour MP on any aspect of that legislation. On 11 November 1998, during a discussion of the Lords amendments to the Scotland Bill, Dennis Canavan supported the Lords proposal to set the number of Members of the Scottish Parliament at 129 irrespective of future boundary changes at Westminster. Compare Canavan's lone stand to the splits within Callaghan's PLP over the same matters: in the 1977–78 session alone, there were 58 separate rebellions by Labour MPs on the Scotland Bill and the Wales Bill, averaging 11 MPs per division.

Nor were there any large rebellions over the rest of Labour's constitutional agenda. The Human Rights Bill, which incorporated the European Convention on Human Rights into British law, saw only one small rebellion: on 2 July 1998 Jeremy Corbyn supported a Liberal Democrat clause on the guaranteeing of non-discrimination. A significant number of members of the left-wing Campaign Group were opposed to granting independence to the Bank of England, but no Labour MPs voted against the Bank of England Bill's Second Reading.[77] At the beginning of the Parliament, the Campaign Group had agreed informally that rebellions would take place only if a substantial number of MPs intended to rebel and if there was public understanding of the issue.[78] The Bank of England Bill fulfilled neither of these criteria.

Conclusion

By the end of the 1997–98 session, the PLP had already begun to attract criticism for being too acquiescent. Jokes about sheep, clones and Daleks were already becoming commonplace.[79] Given the relatively infrequent rebellions during the session, this was perhaps understandable. But these jibes missed two important points. The first was the size of those rebellions that did take place. The average (mean) rebellion during 1997–98 comprised 14 Labour MPs. As Figure 2.2 shows, only four other post-war Parliaments (1945, 1966, and the two of 1974) witnessed larger mean rebellions in the first session. And the largest rebellion of the session (47) was larger than that seen in all but another four Parliaments (1966, February and October 1974, and 1979). To be sure, Labour MPs were rebelling infrequently (and less frequently that government MPs in most of the more recent Parliament) but when they did rebel they did so in numbers, or at least numbers that were on a par with, or greater than, most recent Parliaments.

Figure 2.2 Average size of rebellion by government MPs, in first session, 1945–97

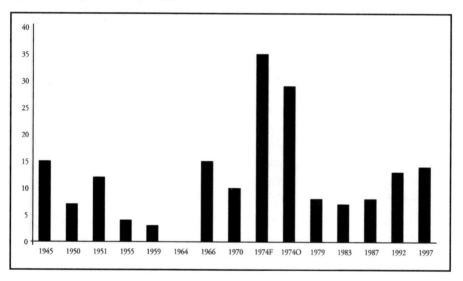

Secondly, the quips about sheep and clones missed the extent to which individual Labour MPs had been prepared to break ranks. The composition of each of the rebellions may have been similar, but they were far from identical; and so by the end of the first session a total of 77 Labour MPs had voted against their party whips at least once. (See Appendix 3 for details of the 77). Admittedly, most had not done so very often: 26 cast just one dissenting vote, another 41 had cast between two and five dissenting votes, with just 10 casting more than five. But the figure of 77 is still important, because it showed that the tendency (or ability) to rebel was not to be found solely amongst a small handful of the Party. Rather, even by the end of one of the quietest first sessions for a generation, almost one in five members of the PLP (that is, around one in four of backbenchers) had already shown that they were willing, if necessary, to defy the whips. Most of them showed exactly that in the next session too.

[1] Philip Cowley, 'The Absence of War?' New Labour in Parliament', *British Parties and Elections Review*, 9 (1999), Table 2.

[2] Letter to author, 4 February 1998.

[3] The whips, however, did notice. Cann was called in to see the Chief Whip Nick Brown, who (with a smile on his face), said: 'Jamie, you've been a naughty boy and I've got to tell you off'. Private information.

[4] *Daily Telegraph*, 30 July 1999.

[5] *The Times*, 21 November 1997.

[6] Interview, 15 February 2000.

[7] Interview, 28 March 2000.

[8] Interview, 15 February 2000.

[9] Interview, 15 February 2000.

[10] Interview, 21 March 2001.

[11] Interviews, 28 March 2000, 6 January 2000.

[12] Interview, 6 January 2000.

[13] Interview, 6 January 2000.

[14] Andrew Rawnsley, *Servants of the People*, London, Hamish Hamilton, 2000, p. 114.

[15] Rawnsley, *Servants of the People*, p. 109.

[16] Harriet Harman, *20th Century Man. 21st Century Woman. How Both Sexes Can Bridge The Century Gap*, London, Vermillion, 1993, p. 71.

[17] See for example the intervention by Dr Lynne Jones, HC Debs, 10 December 1997, c. 1085. Also interviews, 2 August 1999, 21 March 2001.

[18] HC Debs, 10 December 1997, cc. 1052, 1040, 1142.

[19] HC Debs, 10 December 1997, c. 1081.

[20] HC Debs, 10 December 1997, c. 1057.

[21] Interview, 4 July 2000.

[22] The rebellion on Third Reading also almost certainly saw a number of abstentions, including Alan Simpson, Neil Gerrard and Maria Fyfe.

[23] The vote on amendment No. 1 was separated from the debate, meaning that it had to be debated together with the earlier Liberal Democrat new clause.

[24] *The Times*, 21 November 1997. They were to be welcomed into the lobby by Peter Lilley, a former Conservative Social Security Secretary, and author of the cuts, gleefully shouting 'This way for the cuts' (Rawnsley, *Servants of the People*, p. 115).

[25] *The Times* (12 December 1997) claimed 25 deliberate abstentions, of whom they identified ten: Julie Morgan, Rhodri Morgan, George Galloway, Chris Mullin, Harry Cohen, Diana Organ, William Rammell, Tony McWalter, John Naysmith and Huw Edwards. The *Guardian* (11 December 1997) listed 13, of whom Gerry Steinberg, Andrew Bennett, Lawrence Cunliffe and Jim Marshall were identified in addition to those listed in *The Times*.

[26] Malcolm Chisholm, a junior Scottish Office minister; Michael Clapham, PPS to Alan Milburn, the Health Minster; Alice Mahon, PPS to Chris Smith, the Culture Secretary; and Gordon Prentice, PPS to Gavin Strang, the Minister for Transport. Three of the four voted against the government; Clapham abstained.

[27] *Guardian*, 11 December 1997.

[28] Rawnsley, *Servants of the People*, p. 113.

[29] *The Times* inaccurately listed the number as 12, omitting Ann Cryer and Jonathan Shaw.

[30] See, for example, Leader ('Are Blair's babes dumb?'), *Independent on Sunday*, 4 January 1998; Libby Purves, 'Blair's babes in the wood', *The Times*, 2 December 1997; and Austin Mitchell, 'Why I am sick of women MPs', *Independent on Sunday*, 18 January 1998.

[31] See, for example, *The Times*, 12 December 1997.

[32] Interviews, 15 February 2000, 6 January 2000.

[33] Interview, 4 May 1999.

[34] 'Labour's rebels threaten second protest over cuts', *The Times*, 12 December 1997.

[35] HC Debs, 10 December 1997, c. 1055.

[36] Interview, 7 March 2000.

[37] As one newly elected MP said: 'It gave us a confidence that they are not infallible'. Interview, 25 October 2001.

[38] Interview, 25 October 2001.

[39] See John Kampfner, *Robin Cook*, London, Phoenix, 1998, pp. 210-211.

[40] See, for example, Tam Dalyell's interventions (HC Debs, 26 January 1998, cc. 21-31; and 3 February 1998, c. 859).

[41] HC Debs, 17 February 1998, c. 926.

[42] HC Debs, 17 February 1998, c. 939.

[43] HC Debs, 17 February 1998, cc. 953-955.

[44] HC Debs, 17 February 1998, c. 964.

[45] HC Debs, 17 February 1998, c. 906.

[46] They were joined by Mohammad Sarwar, suspended from the PLP, and casting just his eighth vote in the House since his election.

[47] The National Committee of Inquiry into Higher Education (the Dearing Inquiry), *Higher Education in the Learning Society*.

[48] HC Debs, 23 July 1997, cc. 949-962.

[49] HC Debs, 23 July 1997, c. 955.

[50] HC Debs, 23 July 1997, c. 961.

[51] Tony Benn, 'Diary', *New Statesman*, 5 June 1998.

[52] BBC News Online, 5 June 1998.

[53] BBC News Online, 5 June 1998.

[54] There were two other rebellions during the passage of the Bill, both on the so-called 'Scottish anomaly' – the differentiation in fees paid by Scottish residents who go to Scottish universities (where fees are paid for all four years of the honours programme) and other UK residents who go to Scottish universities (who are only entitled to funding for the three years that is the norm in English universities). The first rebellion, on 8 June saw no dissenting votes but 13 abstentions (according to BBC News Online) including Ken Livingstone, Tony Benn, Jeremy Corbyn, Audrey Wise and Dr Lynne Jones. The second, on 1 July 1998, when the Lords insisted on eliminating the Scottish anomaly, saw Dennis Canavan vote against his party whip. In addition, education policy also saw one other small rebellion during the Schools Standards and Framework Bill, when, on 24 March 1998, two MPs – Tony Benn and Jeremy Corbyn – voted in favour of a Liberal Democrat amendment that sought to end partial selection on the basis of ability in schools.

[55] BBC News Online, 9 June 1998.

[56] A similar amendment to Mullin's was moved at the beginning of the debate, but subsequently withdrawn by its mover, Giles Radice, Chairman of the Treasury Select Committee.

[57] HC Debs, 8 July 1998, c. 1146.

[58] HC Debs, 8 July 1998, c. 1146.

[59] HC Debs, 8 July 1998, cc. 1150-1151.

[60] HC Debs, 8 July 1998, c. 1149.

[61] HC Debs, 8 July 1998, cc. 1155-1557.

62 HC Debs, 8 July 199, cc. 1161-1166.
63 HC Debs, 2 September 1998, cc. 744-757.
64 Philip Webster, 'Anti-terror Bill modified to meet MPs' concerns', *The Times*, 2 September 1998.
65 Michael Cunningham, *British Government Policy in Northern Ireland*, Manchester, Manchester University Press, 2000, p. 135.
66 HC Debs, 2 September 1998, c. 717.
67 HC Debs, 2 September 1998, c. 716.
68 HC Debs, 2 September 1998, cc. 779-780.
69 HC Debs, 2 September 1998, cc. 810-811.
70 HC Debs, 2 September 1998, c. 830.
71 HC Debs, 2 September 1998, cc. 869-870.
72 HC Debs, 2 September 1998, c. 873, c. 874.
73 HC Debs, 2 September 1998, cc. 874-877.
74 HC Debs, 2 September 1998, c. 928.
75 Philip Cowley, "Europe' in the House of Commons', Brunel University European Affairs Unit Discussion Paper, 99/5, p. 16.
76 HC Debs, 9 April 1975, cc. 1365-1370. Labour Members were permitted a free vote, although the official Government advice was to support the motion. Philip Norton, *Dissension in the House of Commons 1974–1979*, Oxford, Clarendon Press, 1980, pp. 58-61.
77 A number of Labour MPs abstained, including Diane Abbott, Tony Benn, Jeremy Corbyn and Alan Simpson.
78 Interview, 25 May 1999.
79 See, for example, *Sunday Times*, 29 March 1998.

3. Not so Roughly, Darling

1998–99

At his Christmas Party in December 1998, Jack Cunningham told his guests 'that there was no risk of contracting CJD from BSE-infected sheep: "You see, they have their skulls and spines removed". This provoked one wit to reply: "Just like Labour backbenchers".'[1] For by December 1998 there was little evidence that the second session would bring with it any increase in the rebelliousness of Labour MPs. Anyone expecting (or hoping) that the passage of time would inevitably lead to the onset of civil war on the Labour benches appeared to be disappointed. The first two months of the new Parliamentary year had passed off without a single revolt. By the end of the session, though, things looked slightly different. Not only was there an eventual (slight) increase in the number of rebellions by Labour MPs, but the session was also to see the most concerted spell of backbench opposition of the whole Parliament, as yet again Labour MPs objected to their Government's proposals for the reform of the social security system.

The overall increase in the *number* of revolts was, admittedly, slight. Compared to the 16 revolts in the first session, the second saw 19; by the end of the second session in November 1999, there had therefore been just 35 revolts by Labour MPs in the first two and a half years of the Government. As Figure 3.1 shows, the behaviour of Labour MPs continued to be significantly out of line with that seen in other post-war Parliaments, especially the more recent ones. Of the full-length post-war Parliaments, just three (those of 1951, 1955 and 1966) had seen fewer revolts by government MPs by this stage of their life.[2]

The increase in the *size* of the revolts, though, was noticeably more dramatic. As Table 3.1 shows, almost half of the revolts in the session consisted of 30 MPs or more. The average (mean) size of the rebellions almost doubled, from 14 MPs

(1997–98) to 26 (1998–99), larger than in any other second session since the war.[3] The majority of these revolts – and nearly all of the more sizable ones – occurred on just one bill: the Welfare Reform and Pensions Bill. But there were also sizable revolts over the House of Lords Bill, the bombing of Kosovo, the Access to Justice Bill, and the Immigration and Asylum Bill.[4] The remainder of this chapter details and explains these rebellions.

Figure 3.1 Number of rebellions by government MPs, by end of second session, 1945–99

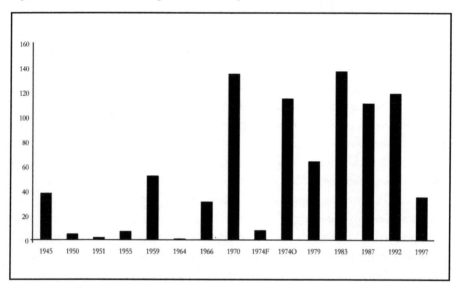

Table 3.1 Size of Labour rebellions, 1998–99

Size	N
1 only	3
2-5	3
6-9	1
10-19	2
20-29	1
30-39	2
40-49	4
50-59	2
60-69	1
Total	*19*

House of Lords reform

Labour MPs were nearly as united on issues of constitutional reform in the second session as they had been the year before. The House of Lords Bill was the only constitutional Bill to provoke dissent; even it saw just two rebellions. The first, and only substantial, revolt came in February when, in the first rebellion of the session, 35 Labour MPs – along with eight Conservatives and five Liberal Democrats – supported an amendment moved by Bob Marshall-Andrews to remove a government's right of patronage to appoint members of the reformed House. Marshall-Andrews described patronage as 'the curse and the blight of the British political system', and his amendment managed to unite unicameralists like himself with those who believed in a wholly elected chamber.[5] Labour back-benchers also expressed doubt that there would ever be a second stage to House of Lords reform, a view disputed by the Government.[6]

The issue saw a free vote on the Conservative side, meaning that turnout was likely to be low (as, indeed, it was).[7] The Labour whips were therefore less concerned than usual about the outcome of the vote, resulting in what one of those involved described as 'almost a free-vote atmosphere, even though it was a three-line whip'.[8] This helps explain the size of the revolt – which, at 35, was then the second highest of the Parliament. The revolt failed, by 51 votes to 269, as did the Bill's second rebellion right at the end of the session, in November 1999, when two Labour MPs – Tony Benn and Mark Fisher – voted against the so-called Weatherill amendment that retained 92 hereditary peers.

The most striking feature of these rebellions, though, was not how many Labour MPs rebelled – but how few. In the 1966 Parliament, faced with concerted opposition from its own ranks (in an unholy alliance with the Conservative right), the Wilson Government had been forced into withdrawing its similar attempt at reforming the Lords.[9] By contrast, the Blair Government (almost entirely) removed the hereditary principle and created an (almost entirely) appointed upper chamber – and just 35 MPs objected.

Foreign affairs

The Government similarly managed to avoid any large rebellions over foreign affairs. This was not because of any lack of events – the session encompassed both the Anglo-American bombing of Iraq in December 1998 and the NATO bombing of Kosovo in March and April 1999 – or because of harmony amongst the ranks of the PLP. Rather, it was because of a combination of procedural shenanigans from the Government (combined with a lack of effective opposition from the rebels), allied with splits within the left, especially over Kosovo.

In his statement to the Commons the day after the bombing of Iraq (known as Operation Desert Fox) on 16 December 1998, the Prime Minister argued that the raid aimed '[t]o degrade the ability of Saddam Hussein to build and use weapons of mass destruction . . . and to diminish the threat Saddam Hussein poses to his neighbours by weakening his military capability.[10] It was not a view shared whole-heartedly on the benches behind him. George Galloway speculated whether:

> . . . as bleeding women and children were carried into hospitals . . . those who were diminished and degraded were not the Iraqis, but us? We are diminished and degraded by being reduced to the tail on this verminous and mangy Desert Fox.[11]

Tony Benn was 'deeply affronted' by the bombing, describing it as 'a return of Victorian imperialism. The only difference is that Britain is so weak that we have to piggyback on top of an American military superpower'.[12] Tam Dalyell found the bombing 'nauseating', and was 'ashamed that it should be endorsed by a Labour Government'.[13] Alice Mahon described it as 'a hideous action', and questioned its timing – in the middle of impeachment proceedings against the President of the United States.[14]

But, despite the passions aroused on the Labour benches, at the end of the debate, the Government deliberately failed to put up tellers for the motion that 'The House do now Adjourn'. Procedurally, this meant that the motion lapsed, ending the debate. Robbed of a division on the bombing and realising that they had been outmanoeuvred, several opponents of the bombing – including George Galloway, Tam Dalyell, Tony Benn and Dennis Canavan – engaged in a series of heated points of order with the Deputy Speaker.[15] But as the loyalist MP Dale Campbell-Savours pointed out in another point of order, the only motion on the Order Paper was for the Adjournment of the House and that motion had now lapsed. The would-be rebels had 'simply misread the procedures of the House of Commons'.[16] One rebel later admitted that the 'vote that never was' was 'a balls-up'.[17] But it was a balls-up deliberately engineered by the Labour whips, and one which prevented any rebellion taking place.

The NATO bombing of Kosovo in April 1999 also divided the PLP.[18] During the main set-piece debate on Kosovo on 19 April, ten Labour MPs spoke in favour of the Government's line, five spoke against, while Gwyneth Dunwoody expressed 'some unease' about the possible use of ground troops.[19] Robert

Wareing, suspended earlier in the Parliament for his failure to register links with a Serbian company (see Appendix 2), warned that ground troops would have to be used, not just in Kosovo, but also across the whole of Yugoslavia. He argued that the NATO bombing had created a spirit in Belgrade similar to that in London during the Blitz.[20] Tony Benn was in favour of using force to counter the ethnic cleansing, but believed this should be run by the United Nations, not NATO. Alice Mahon, who had just returned from a trip to Yugoslavia without the permission of the Labour whips, condemned the war being waged by NATO on the people of Yugoslavia.[21] Tam Dalyell believed that the only option was to enter into 'unpalatable and unpopular' talks with President Milosevic, and that 'Parliament had been insufficiently considered in all this'.[22] And George Galloway claimed that the Serbian people would not voluntarily succumb to dismemberment. Milosevic was a brute, he said, 'but he is not Hitler'.[23]

But unlike Iraq – on which the Labour left were united in their opposition – the conflict in Kosovo divided the left.[24] (It also created splits within the Conservative ranks: see Chapter 10). Of the 22 MPs who opposed the bombing of Iraq in the preceding session, only 12 also opposed the bombing of Kosovo. Many of the fiercest critics of the bombing of the former were amongst the strongest supporters of the bombing of the latter. Left-wing MPs such as Tam Dalyell, George Galloway and Alice Mahon were vehemently opposed to the bombing, whilst Dennis Skinner, Ken Livingstone and Ann Clwyd were in favour.[25] Clwyd even went further than the Government by calling for the deployment of ground troops to back up the air campaign.[26] The bitterness of the split among the left was demonstrated when Clare Short, the International Development Secretary, described Tam Dalyell as 'an absolute disgrace to the Party'.[27] She later said that she was 'ashamed' that Labour MPs could have voted against the bombing.[28]

Just like the Falklands division back in 1982, MPs were denied a chance to vote on the adjournment, and instead had to force a vote by moving for the closure of the House.[29] The Government, realising that the rebels would not attract the 40 MPs required to secure closure, put up two tellers, while abstaining from the division.[30] When the vote eventually came, those rebelling numbered only 13. The result was that the question – 'That the House do now adjourn' – was never put.

Given the limited opposition to the policy within the PLP, the Government felt no need to negotiate with the rebels. Many of those who were unhappy with the Government's stance found Foreign Office ministers, especially the Foreign Secretary, aloof and unresponsive. Robin Cook was not at his best when dealing with backbench MPs. One rebel described him as 'quite inaccessible', another described him as 'stubborn', whilst his biographer makes clear the extent to which Cook became detached from feeling within the PLP.[31] 'Many a back-bencher has complained of feeling deflated after being given short shrift by him'.[32] That may have mattered for Cook's own career (because it meant that he had no power base to support him) but in terms of quelling backbench discontent over foreign policy it was of little importance (because there was little discontent to quell).

Incapacity Benefit

The same was not true of the next issue to cause trouble on the Labour benches. As in the preceding session the general source of the disquiet was again the Government's attempts to reform the social security system, but this time the specific source of complaint was its proposals for incapacity benefit (more widely known as disability benefit). During the debates over lone parent benefit in 1997, some Labour MPs had raised concerns that the next stage of any benefit reform would be changes to incapacity benefit, and they were right to worry. In February 1999 the Government introduced its Welfare Reform and Pensions Bill. Labour MPs supported the majority of the Bill, but many objected to the proposals on Incapacity Benefit. The Government planned to restrict new claimants to means tested benefits if they had been unable to make national insurance contributions in the previous two years, and to reduce payments for new claimants with private pensions or private health insurance. MPs' concerns had been conveyed to ministers quietly behind the scenes since the end of 1997, but backbench discontent became public in March 1999 with an Early Day Motion (EDM 375), put down by Roger Berry, a Labour backbench MP and Secretary of the All-Party Disablement Group.[33] The latter half of the EDM noted:

> . . . the concerns within disability groups regarding the possible effects these changes [in incapacity benefit] may have on the genuinely disabled; and calls upon Her Majesty's Government to give more consideration to a more generous set of arrangements for those recipients of incapacity benefit who draw upon occupational pensions.

Sixty-eight Labour MPs signed the motion, the majority of them (37) from the new intake of MPs. In May, Berry moved an amendment during the Bill's

Report Stage to drop from the Bill the introduction of means testing for incapacity benefit, as well as to excise proposals to remove benefit entitlement from those who had made no national insurance contributions in the previous two years.[34] Again, 68 Labour MPs signed his amendment. Alistair Darling, Harriet Harman's replacement as Secretary of State for Social Security, made it clear that he had no intention of reaching any compromise with the rebels before the vote.[35]

But although he was keen to appear stern and unbending in public, in private Darling was more consultative and was willing to meet with potential rebels. Learning the lesson from the lone parent revolt, the Government was keen at least to be seen to be listening to the anxieties of backbenchers. In the run-up to the vote, unlike before the lone parent benefit vote, MPs were seen individually by at least one minister if they requested a meeting. Even some of those who did not request a meeting often found themselves having meetings with senior ministers – one or more of the Social Security Secretary, the Chancellor and the Deputy Prime Minister – in an effort to make them back the Government's position.[36] One concerned MP went to see Darling, who, in effect, asked him 'What's your price?'[37] Another organised a group of MPs ('normally loyal people, disturbed at what the Government was doing, and willing to negotiate') who sent to see Darling *en masse*. The negotiations were 'tough, serious, prolonged and 11th hour, but I got everything I wanted'.[38]

Darling's room for manoeuvre was, however, somewhat limited because the Government was intent on winning the case for its welfare reform programme, shifting the emphasis away from universal benefits to targeted help for those in the greatest need. 'Ministers agreed early on it was important not to concede ground on the main principles of welfare reform. If they back off over this, they would be signalling weakness and this would mean further problems in the future with other welfare reform.'[39] The Government claimed that they were trying to change the culture of the benefits system and any adverse publicity created by the rebellions had to be set against the need to move 'forward' on welfare reform.[40] Concessions therefore could be only minor.

Throughout the debate, the Labour rebels argued that by in effect taxing occupational pensions at 50 pence in the pound on incomes over £50 a week, the Government was penalising disabled people who had saved throughout their working lives. As Tom Clarke, the former Labour spokesperson on disabled people's rights, argued, occupational pensions were 'nest eggs, not luxuries'.[41] He was later to vote against the Government, saying that for the first time in his sixteen years as an MP he was unable to support 'the party that I love'.[42] Some

Labour backbenchers were also opposed to the whole idea of means testing. Audrey Wise argued that the Government's proposals would 'materially alter' the balance between contributory benefits (such as pensions), non-contributory benefits (child benefit, severe disablement allowance) and means-tested benefits.[43] Those with degenerative illnesses or those who intended to return to work after illness would have no incentive to carry on working because they might not qualify for benefit if their work period was interrupted. Finally, both Roger Berry and Frank Field (now returned to the backbenches) expressed their disbelief that Labour should be behaving like the Conservatives on this matter. Berry asked: 'What on earth could be the justification for doing so [cutting incapacity benefit] again? I do not know; perhaps the Tories did not cut enough'.[44]

Unable fully to negotiate the rebellion away, the Government then tried to pressurise MPs into cohesion. MPs – especially those that were not frequent rebels – later complained of pressure being applied by the whips over this issue, in a way that they did not on other issues.[45] The Government also resorted to procedural devices. At 4.47 on the morning of 17 May, after more than 12 hours of debate, the Government drew back from a confrontation with backbench critics, and postponed the debate until a later date.[46] The aim was to give more time to pacify potential rebels. When the debate resumed three days later, in answer to a prearranged intervention from Chris Mullin about the threshold at which the 50-pence-in-the-pound reduction in incapacity benefit would start to bite, Darling claimed that 'it was always within my contemplation that it [the threshold] would have to be increased'.[47] Darling claimed this was not a concession, that he was just making his existing intentions clear (and the threshold was later raised), but the point of making it clear was to try to pacify backbenchers. It did not work. When the vote on Berry's amendment eventually came, 67 Labour MPs voted against the Government, and there were also a significant number of abstentions, although the exact number was unclear.[48] The Government's majority was reduced to just 40. This was, and was to remain, the largest Labour backbench rebellion of the Parliament. Of the 68 signatories to Berry's amendment, 52 voted against the Government, 13 did not vote, and just three had been persuaded to vote with the Government.[49]

Nor was that the end of the story. In November, when the Bill returned from the Lords, the Government offered more concessions. It announced changes to the pensions threshold (raising it from £50 per week to £85 per week, exempting another 100,000 people from the proposals) and to the contribution conditions.[50] It also agreed to take into account the position of those suffering from degenerative illnesses like multiple sclerosis or Parkinson's disease, and that national insurance contributions in the previous three tax years – not the previous two, as originally proposed – would count.[51] However, these concessions were as much, if not more, about placating opinion in the Lords than overcoming resistance from the Government's own backbenchers.

They certainly did not satisfy the Bill's critics in the Commons and there were a further nine rebellions. There were six consecutive revolts on 3 November. The first, which would have removed the clause restricting entitlement to incapacity benefit to people in recent employment, attracted the support of 54 Labour MPs. The second, which would have removed the clause on the means testing of people who drew on occupational pensions as early retirement income, was supported by 53. The third – an attempt to reverse the abolition of the Severe Disablement Allowance (SDA) – was backed by 47. Two Labour MPs – Harry Barnes and Tony Benn – then supported a clause that would have entitled war widows to a pension even if they subsequently remarried or cohabited; 34 Labour backbenchers then supported an attempt to give bereaved spouses two years of bereavement allowance rather than the 26 weeks proposed by the Government. Finally, John McAllion was the only Labour MP to support an amendment that would have relieved contract workers from paying national insurance contributions.

At this point, with time running out in the session – and facing the possibility of the Bill shuttling back and forth between the Commons and the Lords – the Government offered yet another concession, extending the amount of time for which bereavement allowance could be claimed from six months to a year.[52] But when the Bill then returned from the Lords six days later, Darling made it clear that he would move no further.[53] His concessions had been enough to bring some MPs back on board, although they did not satisfy the majority of those concerned with the legislation.[54] When the Government then rejected amendments to the Bill introduced in the Lords by the veteran Labour campaigner for the disabled, Lord (Jack) Ashley, there were another three large rebellions. The first, which would have qualified disabled people for incapacity benefit if they had worked at some point in the previous seven years, rather than in the previous two, was supported by 45 Labour MPs. Another Ashley amendment that would have set the means test taper (at which occupation pensions would become taxable) at the standard rate of income tax (23 per cent), rather than at 50 per cent, attracted the support of 46 backbenchers; and an attempt to set the level of the Disability Income Guarantee at £128 rather than £85 was supported by 45 backbenchers.

These nine revolts saw an average of 36 Labour MPs rebelling on each vote, with the rebellions reaching 54 at their peak. This was by far the most sustained bout of dissent by Government MPs in the entire Parliament. As Table 3.2 shows, the rebels formed a reasonably cohesive grouping. With the exception of the two very small revolts, there was far less variation between the votes than there had been in the rebellions over the Criminal Justice Bill. There was some slight attrition, as MPs who had initially opposed the Government splintered off. The first vote in May saw 67 MPs vote against the Government. The largest revolt on 3 November consisted of 54 MPs. Six days later, the largest revolt consisted of 46. But there were also seven MPs who had not voted against the Government on the initial vote who joined the rebellion later. Taken together, the rebellions involved a total of 74 MPs.

Table 3.2 Labour rebels over Welfare Reform and Pensions Bill

Name	Berry amend't	Recent employ't	Occ. pen's	SDA	Berv'd spouses	Seven years	23% taper	DIG of £128
Diane Abbott	X	X	X	X	X	X	X	X
John Austin	–	X	X	X	X	–	–	–
Harry Barnes	X	X	X	X	X	X	X	X
Tony Benn	X	X	X	X	–	X	X	X
Andrew Bennett	X	X	–	–	–	–	–	–
Roger Berry	X	X	X	X	X	X	X	X
Harold Best	X	–	–	–	–	–	–	–
Ronald Campbell	X	X	X	X	X	–	–	–
Jamie Cann	X	–	–	–	–	–	–	–
Martin Caton	X	X	X	X	X	X	X	X
David Chaytor	X	X	X	–	–	X	X	X
Malcolm Chisholm	–	–	–	–	–	X	X	X
Michael Clapham	X	X	X	X	–	X	X	X
Tom Clarke	X	X	X	X	X	X	X	X
Tony Clarke	X	X	X	X	–	X	X	X
Ann Clwyd	X	X	X	X	X	X	X	X
Michael Connarty	–	X	X	X	X	X	X	X
Jeremy Corbyn	X	X	X	X	X	X	X	X
James Cousins	X	X	X	X	X	X	X	X
David Crausby	X	–	–	–	–	–	–	–
Ann Cryer	X	–	–	–	–	X	X	X
John Cryer	X	X	X	X	–	X	X	X
John Cummings	X	–	–	–	–	–	–	–
Tam Dalyell	X	X	X	X	–	X	X	X
Ian Davidson	X	X	X	X	X	–	–	–
Denzil Davies	X	X	X	X	–	X	X	X
James Dobbin	–	X	X	X	–	X	X	X
Gwyneth Dunwoody	X	X	X	X	X	X	X	X
William Etherington	X	X	X	X	–	–	–	–
Frank Field	X	X	X	X	X	X	X	X

cont'd

Name	Berry amend't	Recent employ't	Occ. pen's	SDA	Berv'd spouses	Seven years	23% taper	DIG of £128
Mark Fisher	X	–	–	–	–	–	–	–
Paul Flynn	X	X	X	X	X	–	–	–
Maria Fyfe	X	–	–	–	–	X	X	X
Neil Gerrard	X	X	X	X	–	X	X	X
Ian Gibson	X	X	X	–	–	–	–	–
Norman Godman	X	X	X	X	X	X	X	X
David Hinchliffe	X	–	–	–	–	–	–	–
Kelvin Hopkins	X	X	X	X	X	X	X	X
Brian Iddon	X	–	–	–	–	–	–	–
Eric Illsley	X	X	X	–	–	–	–	–
Jenny Jones	X	–	–	–	–	–	–	–
Lynne Jones	X	X	X	X	X	X	X	X
Tess Kingham	X	–	–	–	–	–	–	–
Terry Lewis	X	X	X	X	X	–	–	–
Ken Livingstone	–	X	X	–	–	X	X	X
Andrew Mackinlay	X	–	–	–	–	–	–	–
Alice Mahon	X	–	–	–	–	X	X	X
John Marek	–	X	X	X	X	–	–	–
David Marshall	X	X	X	X	X	X	X	X
James Marshall	X	–	–	–	–	–	–	–
Bob Marshall-Andrews	X	X	X	–	–	X	X	X
John McAllion	X	X	X	X	X	–	X	X
Christine McCafferty	X	–	–	–	–	–	–	–
John McDonnell	X	X	X	X	X	X	X	X
Kevin McNamara	X	–	–	–	–	–	–	–
Bill Michie	X	X	X	X	X	–	–	–
Julie Morgan	X	X	X	X	X	X	X	X
Denis Murphy	X	X	X	X	–	–	–	–
Kerry Pollard	X	-	–	–	–	–	–	–
Gordon Prentice	X	X	X	X	–	X	X	X
Edward Rowlands	X	X	X	X	X	X	X	X
Brian Sedgemore	X	X	X	–	–	X	X	–
Alan Simpson	X	X	X	X	X	X	X	X
Dennis Skinner	X	X	X	X	X	X	X	X
Llewellyn Smith	X	X	X	X	X	X	X	X
George Stevenson	X	–	–	–	–	–	–	–
Roger Stott	X	–	–	–	–	–	–	–
Desmond Turner	X	X	X	X	X	X	X	X
Robert Wareing	X	X	X	X	X	X	X	X
Betty Williams	X	X	X	X	X	X	X	X
David Winnick	X	X	X	X	–	X	X	X
Audrey Wise	X	X	X	X	X	X	X	X
Michael Wood	X	X	X	X	X	X	X	X
Tony Worthington	–	X	X	X	–	X	X	X

Note: X indicates that the MP voted against the party whip. The two smallest revolts – detailed in the text – are not shown.

The importance of the incapacity benefit revolt lies in what happened when ministers did not (or, for whatever reason, felt they could not) fully take on board the views of the PLP over an issue about which many of them felt strongly. Just as with the lone parent revolt a year before, and contrary to the popular image, Labour MPs were clearly willing to rebel in substantial numbers when their concerns were not taken seriously. Coercion alone was insufficient. Negotiation was required to bring them into line. This was best exemplified during the next revolt: over benefits for asylum-seekers.

Immigration and asylum

Press reports during the summer of 1998 highlighted the dramatic growth in the number of asylum-sekers arriving in Britain. Local authorities, especially those in Kent and London, claimed they were not able to cope with the increased numbers, and there were tensions between residents and asylum-sekers, especially in Dover. In February 1999 the Home Secretary, Jack Straw, introduced legislation in response to the failure of these locally based arrangements and to deal with a growing backlog in applications. Straw proposed a national system that would include an element of dispersal of asylum-sekers to other parts of the UK. Asylum seekers waiting for their claim to be processed would no longer be given cash benefits but would instead receive vouchers worth 70 per cent of income support payments. Adult claimants would receive £1 a day in cash, with an additional 50 pence a day for each child over the age of three.

The Immigration and Asylum Bill received its Second Reading on 22 February 1999 without any dissenting votes being cast by Labour MPs, although at least two abstained.[55] There were, however, critical speeches from five Labour MPs, including three normally loyal to the Government.[56] The full extent of Labour backbench concerns about the Bill were revealed a month later when 61 Labour Members signed an Early Day Motion (EDM 465) put down by Diane Abbott. The EDM focused on the issue of asylum seeker children, argued that 'no mother can meet the needs of a young child, over and above food and accommodation on 50 pence a day', and urged 'the Government to reconsider this proposal'.

Discontent crystallised around an amendment moved by Neil Gerrard, a backbench Labour MP and Chair of the All-Party Group on Refugees. Gerrard's amendment sought to remove families with children from the voucher system altogether. Exactly half of the 24 signatories to Gerrard's amendment were Labour MPs elected for the first time in 1997, who were described in the press as 'flexing their muscles'.[57] The BBC's *On the Record* programme ran a piece in which four Labour backbenchers – three of them members of the 1997 intake – outlined their objections to the Bill. The *Observer* claimed to have learned from Government business managers that the Bill had 'aroused more opposition among backbenchers than any other legislation before Parliament, including welfare state reforms'.[58] Gerrard's own estimate of support for his amendment was slightly less dramatic, but he still thought it numbered 50 or so backbenchers.[59]

However, backbenchers found the minister responsible, Jack Straw, willing to listen to their concerns. Almost every section of the PLP acknowledged that Straw is good at meeting and negotiating with MPs. He is, said one member of the party hierarchy, 'very adept at sounding hardline and consulting like mad with anyone who'll talk, making it difficult for anyone to rebel'.[60] One persistent Labour backbench critic described Straw as 'intellectually strong' and 'willing to engage in discussion and confront arguments head-on'.[61] Straw seemed to attend almost any meeting at which his proposals were to be discussed, in order to present his point of view and debate with MPs. He was a regular visitor to meetings of the Campaign Group, sometimes at his own invitation. During one week in early June 1999, Straw was meeting with MPs 'all over the place' to discuss the issue. One Labour MP bumped into Straw at six or seven different meetings where the issue was to be discussed.[62] A London Labour MP saw Straw on eight separate occasions during the passage of the Bill.[63] Other ministers may consult and negotiate, said another MP, 'but no-one else is in Jack's league'.[64]

As a result of these discussions, by the time the Bill returned to the floor of the House from Committee, Straw had sought to address concerns that children of asylum-sekers might not be afforded protection by the Children Act 1989. A new clause placed upon the Home Secretary a statutory duty to provide such children with accommodation and living needs if these were not being met.[65] Straw also announced several other concessions immediately before the Report Stage debate. He increased the proportion of cash payments as against voucher payments for a typical family from £21 to £40 of the total (£90.80). Cash allowances for adult asylum-sekers were increased from £7 to £10 a week, while children's cash payments rose from £3.50 a week to £10 a week. Straw also increased the number of immigration officers by 300, in order to speed up the claims process, and declared that the processing of family cases would be fast tracked from April 2001 to April 2000. Finally, he introduced 'a presumption for bail' for asylum-sekers.[66]

Yet further concessions were announced during the debate itself. In response to an intervention from one Labour backbench MP, Straw promised to review payments for larger families so that they did not fall below 90 per cent of income support levels.[67] He also promised not to implement the new support arrangements unless he was satisfied that targets for processing claims could be met.[68] Straw mentioned a target of around 70 per cent of claims, although he was shrewd enough not to tie himself to this target.

Seeing how little support he now had as a result of Straw's concessions, Gerrard decided not to press his amendment to a vote.[69] Straw had conceded enough to placate the rebels without fundamentally altering the Bill. The voucher system, which was central to the Bill, remained. Financial support for asylum-sekers remained at 70 per cent of income support levels (although Straw sought to make it appear 90 per cent by including the provision of utensils, utility bills and bed linen in his calculations). His other concessions amounted to fairly minor changes. The only substantive change was to place on the Home Secretary a duty of care for the children of asylum-sekers, while his promises on larger families and targets were just that: promises. One Labour critic of the proposals said despairingly: 'I think that we have reached a pretty pass when, after one minister had consulted and produced some relatively minor concessions, there is dancing within the Parliamentary Labour Party'.[70] Another critic viewed such concessions on Bills as amounting to little in reality and saw Straw as the 'arch exemplar' of giving 'the minimum they can get away with'.[71]

Yet it had been enough. *The Times* had earlier claimed that the Government would have suffered its first Commons defeat had the level of child asylum cash payments remained at £3.50.[72] In the event, the Bill saw just four rebellions, all of them small. A few hours before the Third Reading vote, Mike Wood was the only Labour MP to vote against the Government over the repeal of Section 8 of the Asylum and Immigration Act, which it was claimed led British universities to discriminate against people from overseas seeking employment. The Third Reading of the Bill saw just seven Labour MPs vote against their party line.[73] When the Bill returned from the Lords, the Government (successfully) attempted to overturn a defeat on an amendment that sought to restore social security benefits until the average targets for processing asylum claims had been met. Sixteen Labour MPs joined the Liberal Democrats in voting against the Government.[74] Five Labour backbenchers then also voted in favour of a Liberal Democrat amendment limiting the length of time that asylum-sekers could be detained to ten days.[75] In total, taking all four revolts together, just 17 Labour backbenchers voted against any aspect of the Bill. Of these, only three were new

MPs, those said earlier to have been flexing their muscles (and only one of those, Iain Coleman, was voting against the Government for the first time). If the revolt over lone parent benefit was How Not To Do It, this was a textbook example of How To Do It, a classic example of how government can negotiate itself out of trouble.

Legal aid

The only other sizeable rebellion of the second session occurred during the Report Stage of the Access to Justice Bill, which removed the right to legal aid for most civil cases.[76] Twenty-one Labour MPs supported an amendment moved by Bob Marshall-Andrews that sought to restore legal aid for cases relating to damages for personal injury to children under eighteen, persons held under the Mental Health Act 1983, those with disabilities and those in receipt of income support. Legal aid, Marshall-Andrews argued, had been a core part of the welfare state, designed to give the poor access to the best available legal advice. He claimed that even the minister responsible – the Lord Chancellor, Lord Irvine – had supported the retention of legal aid for personal injury cases in 1996. Now, Irvine was engaging in 'a conspicuous *volte-face*'.[77] The Government's view was that the vast majority of legal aid cases would be covered by conditional fees ('no win, no fee') and that legal aid would still be available for exceptionally expensive cases or if the wider public interest applied. Moreover, Marshall-Andrews' amendment, which would have extended legal aid to all disabled people, regardless of their means, was unacceptable to the Government.[78]

Marshall-Andrews did not speak to the Lord Chancellor over the issue and, in any event, relations between them would have been rather strained, after he called for the post of the Lord Chancellor to be abolished following the £650,000 refurbishment of his official residence.[79] The position was not improved by the fact that the senior minister was in the House of Lords and informal contact was, therefore, precluded. The Government won the vote easily, by 291 votes to 173, with Marshall-Andrews' amendment backed by 21 Labour MPs.

Conclusion

As with the criticisms of the preceding session, comments that Labour MPs had had their 'skulls and spines removed' did not tally with what actually happened on the Labour benches. For sure, Labour MPs were rebelling infrequently, but when they did break ranks, they continued to do so in numbers. Of the 846 rebellions in the first two sessions of *all* the post-war parliaments, only ten were larger than the 67 MPs who broke ranks over Incapacity Benefit. And, as Figure 3.2 shows, by the end of the second session the average (mean) size of all the rebellions in the Parliament stood at 21, topped by only three other parliaments (and only two if we exclude February 1974, which only had one session). It is also striking how all three are from periods of Labour government. All the periods of Conservative government saw smaller rebellions (if sometimes more rebellions) than were occurring under Blair.

Figure 3.2 Average size of rebellions by government MPs, by end of second session, 1945–99

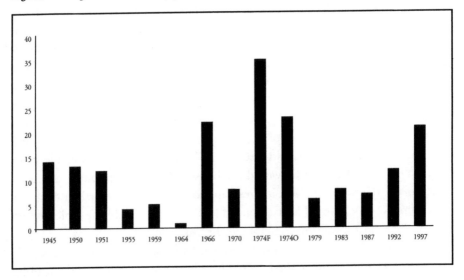

Complaints about clones also failed to appreciate how many Labour MPs had rebelled. By the end of the second session, a full hundred of the PLP had voted against their party whips at least once. The media would frequently describe those voting against the Government as 'the usual suspects', a slightly dismissive phrase meant to indicate that they were just serial troublemakers, but even the West Midlands Crime Squad did not have 100 usual suspects.

Of course, most of those MPs who had voted against the party had done so infrequently. As Table 3.3 shows, 17 of the 100 had cast just one vote against the party line, and another 54 had cast between two and nine dissenting votes. But by the end of the second session, there were 29 Labour MPs who had voted against the party line on 10 or more occasions. Four had done so 20 or more times: Jeremy Corbyn (24 votes), Tony Benn (23), John McDonnell (23) and Dennis Skinner (20).

Table 3.3 Rebellious votes cast by Labour MPs, by end of second session

Number of votes	N
1 only	17
2–5	26
6–9	28
10–19	25
20–29	4
Total	100

But the third reason that the label of 'clones' was so inappropriate was that on several occasions the Government had been forced to negotiate with its back-benchers to prevent them from rebelling. It was a tactic they would be forced to employ frequently in the coming session.

[1]   *Sunday Times*, 20 December 1998.

[2]   That is, excluding the short Parliaments of 1950, 1964 and February 1974.

[3]   Indeed, this was the third-largest average seen in all 57 sessions since the war, beaten only by the first session of the October 1974 Parliament and the last of Major's 1992 Parliament (which saw isolated but extremely large rebellions over gun control legislation). Philip Cowley and Philip Norton, 'Rebels and Rebellions: Conservative MPs in the 1992 Parliament', *British Journal of Politics and International Relations*, 1 (1999), p. 93.

[4]   In addition to the revolts detailed below, there was one other rebellion by a Labour MP during the session: on 13 May 1999 Dennis Skinner voted against a Conservative amendment criticising the Liberal Democrats for using an Opposition Day to attack the failure of the Conservatives to hold the executive to account.

[5]   HC Debs, 16 February 1999, cc. 785-793. Compare, for example, the views of Marshall-Andrews with those of Mark Fisher (HC Debs, 16 February 1999, cc. 817–819).

[6]   See the comments of Tony Benn (HC Debs, 16 February 1999, cc. 798-802), Andrew Mackinlay (HC Debs, 16 February 1999, cc. 810-815), and, for the Government, Paddy Tipping (HC Debs, 16 February 1999, cc. 824-827).

[7]   Only 324 MPs (including tellers) voted in the division.

[8]   Interview, 14 March 2000.

[9]   Harold Wilson, *The Labour Government 1964-70. A Personal Record*, Harmondsworth, Penguin, 1974, pp. 678-680.

[10] HC Debs, 17 December 1998, c. 1097.

[11] HC Debs, 17 December 1998, c. 1107.

[12] HC Debs, 17 December 1998, c. 1129.

[13] HC Debs, 17 December 1998, c. 1143.

[14] HC Debs, 17 December 1998, cc. 1172-1173.

[15] HC Debs, 17 December 1998, cc. 1189-1193.

[16] HC Debs, 17 December 1998, c. 1190.

[17] Interview, 25 May 1999.

[18] As Robin Oakley noted, 'The nods that greeted Sir Peter Tapsell's assertion that the air strikes had united the Serbs behind Milosevic without saving the life or home of a single Kosovan Albanian refugee were not all on the Tory benches'. *The Parliamentary Monitor*, May 1999.

[19] HC Debs, 19 April 1999, c. 592.

[20] HC Debs, 19 April 1999, cc. 599-600.

[21] HC Debs, 19 April 1999, cc. 616-619. See Andrew Pierce, 'Party shocked by MP's secret trip', *The Times*, 21 April 1999.

[22] HC Debs, 19 April 1999, cc. 624-626.

[23] HC Debs, 19 April 1999, cc. 632-634.

[24] See Roland Watson, 'Labour divided by passions of war', *The Times*, 21 April 1999; Simon Hoggart, 'Argument bogs down as dinosaurs of the left battle it out', *Guardian*, 26 March 1999.

[25] Ken Livingstone, 'Why we are not wrong to compare Milosevic to Hitler', *Independent*, 21 April 1999. See Peter Riddell, 'Time for Politicians to reveal their true aims', *The Times*, 31 March 1999; and 'MPs dig in for long and bloody battle', *The Times*, 14 April 1999.

[26] HC Debs, 19 April 1999, cc. 603-605.

[27] *The Times*, 21 April 1999. Ms Short's comments were not recorded in *Hansard*. The next morning she compared her opponents to the appeasers of Hitler. 'Week in Westminster', *The House Magazine*, 26 April 1999.

[28] On BBC Radio 4's Women's Hour. See *Telegraph*, 21 April 1999.

[29] The Government of the day had refused to move the motion, 'That the House do now Adjourn', forcing the 33 Labour rebels to engineer another motion, suspending the proceedings of the House by moving a closure of the House.

[30] The Conservative and Liberal Democrat front benches also abstained from the vote. HC Debs, 19 April 1999, c. 668.

[31] Interview, 4 July 2000.

[32] John Kampfner, *Robin Cook*, London, Phoenix, 1998, p. 209.

[33] HC Debs, 20 May 1999, c. 1242.

[34] HC Debs, 20 May 1999, c. 1243.

[35] Interview, 2 August 1999. Although Darling was careful in his choice of words: no compromise before the vote did not necessarily rule out compromise after the vote.

[36] Interviews, 25 May 1999, 15 February 2000.

[37] Interview, 7 March 2000.

[38] Interview, 25 October 2001.

[39] *Guardian*, 3 November 2000.

[40] HC Debs, 20 May 1999, c. 1284-1291.

[41] HC Debs, 20 May 1999, c. 1254.

[42] HC Debs, 20 May 1999, c. 1252.

[43] HC Debs, 20 May 1999, cc. 1263-1263.

[44] HC Debs, 20 May 1999, c. 1246.

[45] Interview, 2 August 1999.

[46] *The House Magazine*, 24 May 1999.

[47] HC Debs, 20 May 1999, c. 1290.

[48] The *Independent* and *Guardian* said 14 (although a later *Guardian* article, 3 November 1999, claimed 14-15); the *FT* said 15; *The Times* put the numbers higher than 15; and the *Telegraph* claimed nearer 20. One of the leading rebels claims 20 (interview, 2 August 1999).

[49] A further 15 who had not signed the amendment joined the rebels.

[50] HC Debs, 3 November 1999, cc. 308-311.

[51] HC Debs, 3 November 1999, c. 311.

[52] HL Debs, 8 November 1999, c. 1180.

[53] HC Debs, 9 November 1999, c. 934.

[54] Interviews, 15 February 2000, 7 March 2000. See also the comments of Tony McWalter (HC Debs, 9 November 1999, c. 940) and Nick Palmer (*The House Magazine*, 29 November 1999).

[55] Tony Benn and Jeremy Corbyn.

[56] HC Debs, 22 February 1999, cc. 37-130. See also 'Straw faces critics over asylum plans', *The Parliamentary Monitor*, March 1999.

[57] *Independent*, 21 May 1999, *Telegraph*, 22 May 1999.

[58] *Observer*, 2 May 1999.

[59] Interview with Neil Gerrard, 29 February 2000.

[60] Interview, 6 January 2000.

[61] Interview, 25 May 1999.

[62] Interview, 29 February 2000.

[63] Interview, 19 January 2000.

[64] Interview, 28 March 2000.

[65] HC Debs, 16 June 1999, c. 410.

[66] *Independent*, 9 June 1999.

[67] HC Debs, 16 June 1999, c. 473.

[68] HC Debs, 16 June 1999, c. 475.

[69] Interview, 29 February 2000.

[70] HC Debs, 16 June 1999, c. 450.

[71] Interview, 11 July 2000.

[72] *The Times*, 10 June 1999.

[73] Diane Abbott, Tony Benn, Jeremy Corbyn, Neil Gerrard, Ken Livingstone, John McDonnell and Alan Simpson.

[74] Dennis Canavan also voted against the Government, but by this stage he had been suspended from the PLP for standing as an independent candidate at the Scottish Parliamentary Elections in May 1999. See Appendix 2.

[75] Tony Benn, Jeremy Corbyn, Dr Lynne Jones, John McAllion and John McDonnell.

[76] *The House Magazine*, 19 April 1999.

[77] HC Debs, 22 June 1999, c. 1002.

[78] HC Debs, 22 June 1999, cc. 1007-1009.

[79] Interview, 14 March 2000; *Sunday Times*, 6 September 1998.

4. Shots Across the Bow

1999–2000

By the standards of the 1997 Parliament, the third session saw a veritable explosion in dissent – although, by the standards of most previous Parliaments, it was not exactly anarchy. From the start of the session in November 1999 to its conclusion a year and thirteen days later there were a total of 48 revolts by Labour MPs, more than in the first two sessions of the Parliament put together.

In part this was because there was plenty to rebel over. The Government introduced a raft of legislation characterised by both complexity and controversy. Substantial omnibus Bills – such as that reforming transport policy – sat alongside controversial legislation, such as that restricting the right to trial by jury or introducing freedom of information. According to one backbench Labour MP, the (relative) explosion in the level of revolt was therefore due to 'subject not season'.[1] But the season was important too. The middle sessions of Parliaments usually see more rebellions than those at either end, not least because any legislation is increasingly likely not to have been part of the election manifesto, making it much easier for government MPs to object to.[2]

Especially noticeable in this session was the increasing number of small rebellions. There were still large revolts – as Table 4.1 shows, 13 of the rebellions comprised 20 or more Labour MPs – but there was also a growing number of smaller revolts. Fifteen of the 48 rebellions consisted of between two and five MPs; the proportion of revolts involving between two and five MPs (or between two and nine) was the largest of the three sessions.[3] To borrow some concepts from military studies, there continued to be the big set-piece battles, but there was also a definite increase in the number of low-intensity conflicts.

And it could have been worse. The bulk of the legislative burden fell on the Home Office, which was responsible for nine of the 28 Bills announced in the

Queen's Speech (and three of the further 12 to be introduced as the session progressed).[4] The Home Secretary, Jack Straw, repeatedly employed the tactics deployed during the passage of the Immigration and Asylum Bill the year before – offering enough concessions to ease the passage of a Bill – and in most cases the numbers rebelling were cut substantially as a result.

Table 4.1 Size of Labour rebellions, 1999–2000

Size	N
1 only	6
2–5	15
6–9	7
10–19	7
20–29	5
30–39	3
40–49	5
Total	48

Despite this, the session saw large revolts over six separate issues: the Terrorism Bill, the Criminal Justice (Mode of Trial) (No 2) Bill, the issue of pensions up-rating, the Freedom of Information Bill, the Transport Bill, and the Football (Disorder) Bill. The remainder of this chapter details and explains these rebellions, as well as the issues involved in the increasingly frequent small rebellions.

Terrorism

The Government's Green Paper *Legislation Against Terrorism* published in December 1998 advocated extending the definition of terrorism to include domestic organisations such as animal rights extremists and militant environmentalists, as well as preventing international terrorist groups using Britain as a base for activities in other countries.[5] It also agreed with the findings of Lord Lloyd's 1996 report that existing anti-terrorism laws – the Prevention of Terrorism Act and the Northern Ireland (Emergency Provisions) Act – which were subject to annual renewal, should be made permanent.[6] A year later, Straw published a series of responses to his consultation document, and the Terrorism Bill was given its Second Reading on the same day. Throughout the Bill's passage, the Government adopted a conciliatory tone, with Straw stressing at the outset that 'it is the role of the House to examine with particularly great care that which we are proposing' and that if there were ways in which the Bill could be improved 'it is our duty to accept those suggestions'.[7] The Liberal Democrats moved that the Bill be sent to a special standing committee (SSC) – a hybrid of a standing committee and a select committee – but the previous consultation process allowed Straw to argue that the Bill had been part of a 'long, open and deliberative process', and that therefore there was no need for an SSC to look into the issue yet further.[8] He was able to point out that he had already made changes to the Bill as a result of the consultation exercise, having added a right of appeal to an Appeals Commission for all newly proscribed organisations. During the debate, Straw accepted eight hostile interventions from backbench Labour MPs, engaging in a genuine debate with them on the merits of the Bill, and making another small concession in the process, announcing that the Secretary of State for Northern Ireland would review the arrangements for non-jury trials in the Province.[9] And Charles Clarke, the Minister of State at the Home Office, announced that the Government would be willing to listen in standing committee to the best means of scrutinising the work of the legislation, whether by renewal every Parliament or by annual reports.[10] In the subsequent division, only seven Labour MPs voted with the Liberal Democrats.[11]

There were a further five Labour rebellions during the Bill's Report stage, but like the first, they were all small in number. The largest occurred over the definition of 'terrorism'. The Government wished to include organisations committing violence against property. Kevin McNamara tried to restrict the definition to organisations putting the public in fear or coercing the institutions of democratic government, and 13 Labour MPs backed his amendment. One Labour MP, Audrey Wise, then also supported a Liberal Democrat amendment seeking to withdraw the word 'property' from the definition of terrorism. Four Labour MPs backed another Liberal Democrat amendment on the offence of 'possession for terrorist purposes', believing that this aspect of the Bill breached the European Convention on Human Rights.[12] Yet another Liberal Democrat amendment to review the legislation after five years, rather than making it permanent, attracted the support of six Labour MPs.[13] At the Bill's Third Reading, just three Labour MPs voted against the Government.[14]

In all, only 14 Labour MPs voted against any part of the Bill.[15] Compared to previous years, when Labour MPs had regularly rebelled in sizeable numbers against anti-terrorist legislation, this was a stunningly low figure.[16] The rebels refused to give much credit to the Government, and instead blamed what they saw as the illiberal nature of the PLP, especially among the new intake. One Labour MP complained that there were 60 or 70 Labour MPs who would not object to the murder of the first born.[17] But even by the standards of other rebellions in the Parliament, this was a very small revolt, consisting almost entirely of MPs who had already rebelled frequently.[18]

Trial by jury

Criminal offences in England and Wales are categorised according to the severity of the crime. Serious offences such as rape and murder are tried before a jury in a Crown Court, while 'summary only' offences are tried by a magistrate. In between are 'either way' offences such as stealing from shops or absconding from bail where the defendant can choose whether to be tried in a Magistrates' Court or a Crown Court. Evidence presented to the Runciman Royal Commission on Criminal Justice appeared to show that one of the key reasons why defendants chose trial by jury was that they thought that they would receive a lighter sentence at a Crown Court than at a Magistrates' Court.[19] Believing it was wrong for defendants to work the system in this way, the Government's Criminal Justice (Mode of Trial) Bill sought to give magistrates the power to decide where defendants would be tried in 'either way' cases.

The proposal met with hostility from sections of the legal profession, including the Bar Council and the Law Society, as well as the civil liberties group, Liberty.[20] The barrister and backbench Labour MP Bob Marshall-Andrews called on the Government to think again, and 24 Labour MPs signed a hostile EDM put down by Tom Cox (EDM 105).[21] In response, Straw described his critics as 'Hampstead liberal lawyers', not themselves the victims of crime.[22] Straw's view was shared by some Labour MPs, who saw the issue as one of concern largely to lawyers and barristers.[23] Like freedom of information (discussed below), some Labour MPs saw trial by jury as what one called 'a *Guardian* reader's issue'.[24] Another described them as 'chattering classes' issues on which he had received no letters.[25] One MP was even more blunt: these were 'wanky middle-class issues'. 'No one comes to my surgeries worrying about jury trials . . . they want people locked up'.[26]

Wanky middle-class issue or not, the Bill was introduced into the Lords, where on 20 January 2000 the Government was defeated on an amendment that effectively negated the Bill. The defeat both raised the media profile of the issue and increased the level of backbench Labour anxiety in the Commons. Whereas

Cox's EDM had gathered 24 signatures, a new EDM (406) in the name of Marshall-Andrews, calling on the Government to postpone legislation until the publication of the review into the Criminal Justice System then being conducted by Sir Robert Auld, gathered 69 signatures.[27]

In response both to the defeat in the Lords and to this increased backbench pressure in the Commons, Straw strengthened the safeguards in the Bill to include a right of appeal to a High Court judge against a magistrate's decision.[28] He also made concessions following criticisms that defendants from ethnic minorities or poor backgrounds might be discriminated against, and in March 2000 the Bill was reintroduced into the Commons as the Criminal Justice (Mode of Trial) (No. 2) Bill. Bob Marshall-Andrews promptly moved a reasoned amendment to the Second Reading (attracting a total of 19 signatories) arguing that the Bill failed 'to safeguard or maintain the right to trial by jury in either-way offences which may result in serious punishment and loss of livelihood'.[29] He was backed by Harold Best, who described the right to trial by jury as 'wonderful'; by Mark Fisher, who thought it 'very precious'; and by Brian Sedgemore who claimed that the Bill was 'all about money' and suggested that for daring to introduce it the Home Secretary should be 'stripped bare, whipped to the bone and sent to a land governed by tyrants'.[30]

Marshall-Andrews found Straw willing to meet to discuss the issue, only for there to be very little to discuss. Unlike the issue of immigration and asylum in the previous session, the nature of the issue left little room for manoeuvre on either side.[31] When the vote on Marshall-Andrews' reasoned amendment was taken at the end of the Second Reading debate, 29 Labour MPs voted against the Government. Immediately afterwards, one Labour MP, David Kidney, who had described the Bill as emanating from 'a mighty Government to weaken one of the bulwarks of our liberties that protect us from the act of some future over-mighty Government' also voted against the Second Reading itself.[32] Five Labour MPs then supported a Liberal Democrat motion that called for the Bill to be committed to an SSC.[33]

Table 4.2 Labour rebels over Mode of Trial Bill

Name	Reasoned amend'	2nd treading	SSC	Time-table	3rd reading
Diane Abbott	–	–	–	X	X
Harry Barnes	X	–	–	–	X
Tony Benn	X	–	–	–	–
Andrew Bennett	X	–	–	–	X

cont'd

Name	Reasoned amend'	2nd treading	SSC	Time-table	3rd reading
Harold Best	X	–	–	–	–
Michael Clapham	X	–	–	–	–
Ann Clwyd	X	–	–	–	–
Harry Cohen	X	–	–	–	X
Jeremy Corbyn	X	–	–	X	X
John Cryer	X	–	–	–	X
Denzil Davies	X	–	–	–	X
Terence Davis	–	–	–	–	X
Gwyneth Dunwoody	X	–	–	–	X
William Etherington	X	–	–	–	–
Frank Field	–	–	X	–	–
Mark Fisher	X	–	X	X	X
Paul Flynn	X	–	–	X	X
Neil Gerrard	X	–	–	–	X
Kelvin Hopkins	X	–	–	X	X
Alan Hurst	X	–	–	–	X
Jenny Jones	–	–	–	–	X
Lynne Jones	X	–	X	–	X
David Kidney	X	X	–	–	X
Andrew Mackinlay	–	–	–	–	X
Alice Mahon	X	–	–	–	X
Robert Marshall-Andrews	X	–	X	X	X
Christine McCafferty	–	–	–	–	X
John McDonnell	X	–	–	X	X
Kevin McNamara	X	–	–	–	X
Austin Mitchell	X	-	–	–	–
Gordon Prentice	–	–	–	–	X
Brian Sedgemore	X	–	–	X	X
Alan Simpson	X	–	–	–	X
Dennis Skinner	X	–	–	X	X
Llewellyn Smith	X	–	–	–	–
Robert Wareing	–	–	–	–	X
Audrey Wise	X	–	X	–	–

Note: X indicates that the MP voted against the party whip.

The Bill attracted more dissent on 25 July, when nine Labour MPs voted against the Government's timetable motion on the Bill's Report stage. In the subsequent Third Reading vote, a further 28 Labour MPs voted against the Government. A total of 37 MPs, listed in Table 4.2, rebelled over the issue at any point. (Of these, all but one voted against either Second and/or Third Reading). None of this was enough to stop the Bill in the Commons. But when it reached the Lords in September 2000, it was defeated for a second occasion, this time at Second Reading.

Pensions

In November 1999, in what was later seen as one of its worst political decisions of the Parliament, the Government confirmed that, from April, the basic pension would rise by the rate of inflation, meaning an increase of just 75 pence per week.[34] The announcement led to huge dissatisfaction within the extra-Parliamentary party and beyond. Trade union groups joined forces with pensioner charities such as Age Concern and Help the Aged, together with Baroness Castle of Blackburn and Jack Jones of the National Pensioners' Convention, arguing that linking pensions to prices – particularly with low inflation – had seen the value of the pension fall as society became richer. The issue caused the Labour leadership to suffer their first Party Conference defeat since 1994, when a motion which called for an 'immediate and substantial increase' in the basic state pension and to link it to 'average earnings or inflation, whichever was the greater', was carried by 60 per cent.[35] After a poor perform-ance in the local council elections in May 2000 a survey by *The Times* found that three quarters of ousted Labour councillors believed that they had lost their seats because of the pensions issue.[36]

The issue also played very badly within the Parliamentary party, and was the subject of four rebellions.[37] On 17 January 2000, a lone Labour MP, Hilton Dawson, voted for a Liberal Democrat motion describing the 75-pence-a-week increase as 'inadequate'. And during the debate several backbench Labour MPs, although not voting against the Government, flagged up their hostility to the measure by pointing out that they had signed EDM 73 which called on the Government to restore the link between earnings and the basic state pension, and which had attracted 73 Labour signatories. The EDM was organised by Paul Flynn, who made a special effort to put down the first EDM of each year calling for the restoration of the link between pensions and average earnings. He succeeded in the first three sessions, although at the beginning of the fourth 'some treacherous Liberal got up before me'.[38]

The further rebellion presaged by the EDM duly occurred during the passage of the Child Support, Pensions and Social Security Bill later in the year. Eight Labour MPs supported a Liberal Democrat amendment that proposed an age addition to the basic state pension of £5 per week for pensioners over the age of 75.[39] Four Labour Members also supported a second Liberal Democrat amendment that would have speeded up the introduction of the Government's new state second pension.[40] But the largest rebellion by far – numbering 40 Labour MPs – was in support of a new clause moved by John McDonnell that sought to increase the basic retirement pension in line with earnings or the retail price index, whichever was greater.[41]

Labour MPs were only one part – and perhaps only a small part – of the pressure placed on the leadership over the issue. But the result of that pressure was seen that November. In his pre-Budget statement, Gordon Brown chose to focus the bulk of his £4.8 billion package of concessions on giving more money to pensioners: the basic state pension was to rise the following year by £5 for single pensioners and £8 for couples; the winter fuel allowance was increased by £50 to £200; and as well as increasing the level of the minimum income guarantee to £92.15 a week by 2001, its level would rise to £100 by 2003.[42]

Freedom of information

Labour had promised freedom of information legislation in its election manifesto of 1974 but in the view of many MPs the eventual legislation was not worth the 25-year wait.[43] The original White Paper had been drawn up by David Clark, who 'had addressed it with wide-eyed enthusiasm and paid the penalty for doing so'.[44] Following Clark's sacking, the responsibility for the Bill itself passed to the Home Office, where Jack Straw – who used to boast at Home Office ministerial meetings that he would 'sort out' freedom of information – heavily watered it down.[45] One Cabinet minister described Straw as the 'most reactionary man I've ever met in the Labour Party', and the Bill's numerous critics complained that the eventual legislation was even weaker than the ministerial code it had replaced.[46]

The Freedom of Information Bill introduced a statutory right of access to information from government and public authorities but with several important blanket exemptions, including defence, government policy-making, national security, commercial secrecy and international relations. The new Information Commissioner could adjudicate on, but crucially not override the decisions of government departments to withhold documents.

Opposition to the Bill was somewhat ad hoc, but Dr Tony Wright and Mark Fisher were both in the van. David Clark was also involved, but he kept a slightly lower profile, in case his involvement gave the impression of sour grapes on his part.[47] They were joined by the *Guardian*, which launched an 'Open Up' campaign, supported by civil liberties groups such as Liberty and the Campaign for Freedom of Information. One of the Bill's strongest critics saw the *Guardian's* campaign as counter-productive because (just like trial by jury, discussed above) it meant that the issue became seen as a 'middle-class issue', as another *Guardian* newspaper issue that prevented other newspapers from coming onside.[48] And again, this perception was shared by some Labour MPs, who saw Freedom of Information as an issue 'for intellectuals, not for the majority of my constituents'.[49] Or as another put it, 'no one cares about it outside the beltway of the M25'.[50]

Despite this, the Bill saw six rebellions by Labour MPs. All centred on the extent to which policy information could be separated from policy advice and the former revealed to the public without hampering the internal workings of government. On 5 April 2000, in the largest rebellion of the Bill, 36 Labour MPs voted in favour of an amendment moved by Dr Tony Wright that sought to require public authorities to disclose such factual information.[51] A Liberal Democrat amendment that would have allowed the withholding of information by police regulators only if disclosure would prejudice an investigation – the Government had proposed a blanket exemption – attracted 23 Labour MPs.[52] Twenty-eight Labour MPs also supported a Liberal Democrat amendment to disclose data used to inform government decision-making, as opposed to revealing the private discussions between ministers and civil servants. Another Liberal Democrat amendment, backed by 18 Labour MPs, sought to eliminate the test of harm being determined by reference to the 'reasonable opinion' of a qualified person.

Throughout its passage, Straw agreed to meet critics of the Bill (who in turn sent normally loyal Labour MPs to see ministers, believing this would have more impact), and at one point Straw offered critics of the legislation the sight of the contents of his ministerial red boxes in order to illustrate the difficulty of distinguishing between factual information and policy advice.[53] Straw also attended an open meeting organised by the Campaign Group at which Maurice Frankel, director of the Campaign for Freedom of Information, was also speaking.[54]

Table 4.3 Labour rebels over Freedom of Information Bill

Name	Factual info'	Police	Gov't data	R'able opinion	Min'rial veto	Public inq'
Tony Benn	X	–	–	–	–	–
Ronald Campbell	X	–	X	–	–	–
David Clark	X	X	X	X	–	X
Ann Clwyd	X	X	X	X	X	–
Harry Cohen	X	–	–	–	–	–
Frank Cook	X	X	X	X	X	–
Robin Corbett	X	–	–	–	–	X

cont'd

Name	Factual info'	Police	Gov't data	R'able opinion	Min'rial veto	Public inq'
Jeremy Corbyn	X	X	X	X	X	X
James Cousins	X	X	X	X	X	–
Tam Dalyell	X	–	X	X	X	–
Gwyneth Dunwoody	X	X	X	X	X	–
Mark Fisher	X	X	X	X	X	–
Derek Foster	X	–	X	X	X	–
Neil Gerrard	X	X	X	–	X	–
Patrick Hall	X	–	X	–	–	–
David Hinchliffe	X	X	X	X	–	–
Kelvin Hopkins	X	X	X	X	X	–
Jenny Jones	–	–	–	–	–	X
Jon Owen Jones	X	X	X	X	X	–
Lynne Jones	X	–	X	X	X	X
Andy Love	X	–	–	–	X	–
Andrew Mackinlay	X	–	–	–	X	–
Alice Mahon	X	X	X	–	X	·
James Marshall	X	X	X	–	X	–
Robert Marshall-Andrews	X	X	X	X	X	–
John McDonnell	X	X	X	X	X	X
Kevin McNamara	–	–	–	–	–	X
John McWilliam	–	X	X	–	X	–
Bill Michie	X	X	X	–	–	–
Austin Mitchell	–	–	–	–	–	X
Julie Morgan	X	X	X	–	X	–
Gordon Prentice	X	X	X	X	X	–
Alan Simpson	X	X	X	X	X	X
Dennis Skinner	X	–	–	–	–	X
Llewellyn Smith	X	–	–	–	–	–
Rudi Vis	–	–	–	–	–	X
Betty Williams	X	X	X	–	X	–
David Winnick	X	–	–	–	–	–
Michael Wood	X	–	–	–	–	–
Tony (Dr) Wright	X	X	X	X	X	X
Derek Wyatt	X	X	X	–	–	–

Note: X indicates that the MP voted against the party whip.

He carried this consultative approach into the debate itself. The Government had originally intended that the Information Commissioner could recommend, but not order, disclosure. After redrafting, the Information Commissioner held the power of disclosure, subject to large areas of exemption. However, the Government wanted ministers to be able to over-ride the Commissioner. Straw compensated for the introduction of this executive over-ride by deciding that only a Cabinet minister (rather than junior ministers) could prevent disclosure, and that guidance for this power would be written into the ministerial code. What was remarkable about his concession was that it was negotiated while Straw was on his feet in the chamber of the Commons.[55] As Steve Richards of the *New Statesman* reported: 'Straw conducted what was, in effect, a seminar with MPs'.[56] Mark Fisher, a backbench critic of the Bill, said 'He [Straw] has moved a great deal and it has been an extraordinary experience for the House to see a Home Secretary reshaping a central part of the Bill while on his feet'.[57] Despite this, some MPs pushed the new clause to a vote and 24 Labour MPs voted against the Government. When the Bill returned from the Lords, there was another rebellion, numbering just 12 Labour MPs, in support of a Liberal Democrat amendment on the disclosure of information by public inquiries. In total 41 Labour MPs (listed in Table 4.3) voted against some part of the Bill. Just three took part in all six revolts; another nine took part in five of the rebellions.

Air traffic control

The Transport Bill introduced to the Commons in December 1999 covered four huge aspects of transport policy, of which by far the most controversial was the partial privatisation of National Air Traffic Services (NATS).[58] Arguing that the existing public sector framework was inadequate to deal with the expected growth in the volume of air traffic, the Government proposed an agreement with a private sector partner, in which the Government would control 49 per cent of the shares, the private sector partner 46 per cent, and employees five per cent. The Secretary of State, John Prescott, tried to reassure backbenchers by stressing that the Government's golden share would ensure that the private sector element would not be allowed to dominate and that safety would remain paramount.[59]

Despite these assurances, 50 Labour backbenchers signed a reasoned amendment on Second Reading put down by the former transport minister, Gavin Strang, arguing that government ownership and control of NATS was 'necessary for national security', that the UK's air traffic control system was 'recognised internationally as the safest and most reliable in the world' and that 'the introduction of the private profit motive could jeopardise safety standards in the future'.[60] To Strang's surprise, the Conservatives did not put down a reasoned amendment of their own and his amendment was therefore selected for debate, forcing him to fly back from Germany for the debate.[61] He stressed that he was 'speaking for more than 50 Labour MPs . . . and I hope that the Government will listen'.[62]

The Second Reading debate, supposedly on a large omnibus Bill, was dominated by discussion of NATS. Of the 11 Labour backbenchers who spoke, nine expressed concerns about NATS.[63] Only Rosie Winterton and Peter Snape, both political allies of John Prescott, supported the NATS plans in the debate. Snape was scathing about the rebels, claiming that:

> . . . most of the signatories to the amendment have been voting against Labour govern-
> ments for most of their political careers . . . One or two of them do not need any excuse
> to vote against their party – and it helps them to prove that they are better socialists
> than the rest of us.[64]

Gwyneth Dunwoody, the formidable chair of the Transport Sub-Committee of the Select Committee on Environment, Transport and the Regions, argued that the NATS sell-off was not the same as previous 'bricks and mortar' privatisations such as the sale of the British Airports Authority, because the newly privatised company could not generate more profit by opening more shops or outlets; and that NATS employees would not offer the same high quality of service after privatisation because the primary aim would be to increase profits for share-holders.[65]

Strang decided not to press his amendment to a vote, only for the Conservatives to force a vote. Several Labour MPs wanted to vote for the amendment anyway, but Strang stopped them, arguing 'We either all vote or none of us vote'.[66] Some of the rebels were later critical of Strang's tactic of moving a reasoned amendment on Second Reading, because they knew that he would have to withdraw it, making the rebels' case look weak.[67] One thought that Strang had 'bottled it'.[68] But (as should be clear from earlier chapters) most of the other rebellions in the Parliament had taken place at Report or Committee stage, rather than at Second Reading. Except where they opposed the entire thrust of a Bill (as with jury trials) MPs tended to use Second Reading debates to flag up issues of concern, moving specific amendments at Report stage only if the Government had not responded.[69] Yet some ministers did read the wrong signs from the lack of any revolt, believing that the issue would be resolved without a huge rebellion, and that stories in the press of sizeable revolts were 'wide of the mark'. As one minister said dryly: 'It's only now that I'm discovering how unreliable the *Guardian* is'.[70] In the event, the *Guardian* proved prescient: the issue produced the largest revolts of the year.

The rebels' case was bolstered by a Select Committee on Transport report published in February 2000 describing the Government's plans as the 'worst possible option'.[71] By now, the potential number of rebels was estimated to be somewhere between 60 and 70, with the key rebels meeting fortnightly to discuss their opposition to the Government.[72] Prescott addressed a full meeting of the PLP to try to take the heat out of the issue and a group of three leading NATS rebels – including Alice Mahon and Martin Salter – also went to see him on several occasions. According to one of those present, Prescott was unyielding and just 'told them what was what'.[73] Another described the meeting as like hitting a 'Treasury brick wall'.[74] One MP believes that throughout the issue Prescott behaved like 'a bull in a china shop', 'making him extremely difficult to deal with'.[75]

As was clear from earlier chapters, on most issues the Government would make a number of (often small) concessions to its backbenchers that would succeed in reducing the size of any putative rebellion. NATS was different, as Martin Salter, one of the leading rebels, complained:

> In my short time in this place, various bills have received a bumpy ride ... because of the legitimate anxieties of the Government's supporters. I am thinking in particular of lone parent benefit, welfare reform, the Freedom of Information Bill and the Immigration and Asylum Act 1999. In almost every case, the ministers in charge listened carefully to the concerns and, after due modification, we ended up with better legislation and a happier Parliamentary party.

Salter contrasted that with the situation regarding NATS. 'I regret that I am unable to report any such substantial progress on the private-public partnership for National Air Traffic Services'.[76] In some respects, the lack of willingness to compromise over NATS was understandable, since there was little room for compromise. It was essentially an either/or issue. For most of the rebels, the issue was essentially one of ownership: they were ideologically opposed to any form of privatisation, making them less amenable to compromise. As Dr Norman Godman, a NATS rebel, put in a later debate: 'It is a question not of safety but of ideology and mistrust of privatisation, whether part or whole'.[77] But Prescott appeared to go out of his way to seem uncompromising. He laid into critics of the plans, describing fears over safety as 'a lot of tosh' and said that those worried about safety were the sort of people who felt better on reading the old local authority notices that stated 'This is a nuclear-free area'. 'It is a load of nonsense.'[78]

However, even here the Government was not completely unyielding. It made a number of concessions on NATS, partly as a result of a defence of constituency interests by Sandra Osborne, the MP for Prestwick, and partly as a result of House of Lords pressure and the need to secure the Government's legislative programme. Even before the end of the Second Reading debate, there were some signs that the Government appeared to be willing to give ground where it could. Keith Hill, the Parliamentary Under-Secretary of State at the DETR, left room for compromise by saying that there was nothing to stop NATS management or a not-for-profit group from submitting a bid by competitive tender. Such a bid would have to meet the Government's criteria, but there was 'no reason why it should not be considered on an equal footing with any commercial bid'.[79] During the Report Stage, Sandra Osborne moved an amendment seeking assurances from the Government that it was committed to a two centre strategy for air traffic control, one centre to be located in her Prestwick constituency in addition to the one proposed at Swanwick in England.[80] At the end of the debate, Prescott announced that he was accepting her amendment.[81] According to one rebel, the Government believed that Osborne's position was 'pivotal' and that the vote might have tipped over into a larger rebellion, especially among Scottish Labour MPs, had it not conceded the two-centre strategy. Six of the 12 Labour MPs to speak at a full meeting of the PLP on 3 May 2000 were from Scottish seats, where the SNP was said to be running Labour 'ragged on the issue'.[82]

Despite this, the Report stage debate still saw the Government heavily criticised by its backbenchers. Ten Labour MPs spoke against the Government's plans (five of them from Scottish seats) with only four speaking in favour. Dr Desmond Turner argued that the objection to public-private partnerships 'boil down to safety, safety and safety again'.[83] He said that although he would be voting against the Government, 'most of us are extremely loyal Government backbenchers and it is a matter of great pain to us to find ourselves forced into doing so'.[84] There were then three sizeable Labour rebellions. The two largest saw some 46 Labour MPs support amendments which would have ensured either that any new company would be owned by the Crown or that the transfer would be made to a not-for-profit company. A third rebellion, which would have required any transfer scheme to a new company to be subject to Parliamentary approval, attracted 45 Labour MPs. There were also at least 20 abstentions.[85] As Table 4.4 shows, these first three revolts saw very cohesive opposition from critics of the Government's plans.

The Bill then went to the Lords, where a series of defeats forced further concessions from the Government. The Lords amended the Bill to delay any public-private partnership until after the general election, and when the

Commons rejected this amendment 37 Labour MPs voted against the Government, nine fewer than at Report stage.[86] In a later division, the Government rejected an amendment guaranteeing the pension entitlement of employees of NATS, with 17 Labour MPs voting against the Government. The Bill was then sent back to the Lords, but in an attempt to avert defeat the Government added a provision similar to the one that they had just rejected, safeguarding the pension entitlement of NATS employees. These concessions proved insufficient and the Lords again voted to delay the sell-off. With the Government running out of time before the end of the session and facing the prospect of losing other important transport measures (especially those affecting the railways), a last-minute compromise was cobbled together, with the Government promising to undertake a three-month consultation before proceeding with the sale. But first, the original Lords amendment delaying the sell-off until after the general election was formally rejected by the Commons, provoking another sizable rebellion, this time involving 43 Labour MPs. Immediately after that division, the Lords' compromise was put to the Commons and accepted, although 38 Labour MPs voted against even this compromise. This brought the number of Labour MPs to have voted against the Transport Bill to 65. The issue was formally resolved the following day when, on the last day of the session, the Government won the vote in the Lords by 157 votes to 57.

Table 4.4 Labour rebels over NATS

Name	Crown ownership	Not-for-profit	Par'tary app'val	Delay I	Pensions	Delay II	Lords com'mise
Diane Abbott	–	–	–	–	–	X	X
Harry Barnes	X	X	X	X	X	–	–
Tony Benn	X	X	X	–	–	–	–
Andrew Bennett	X	X	X	–	–	–	–
David Chaytor	X	X	X	X	X	X	X
Michael Clapham	X	X	X	X	–	X	X
Ann Clwyd	X	X	X	–	–	–	–
Michael Connarty	X	X	X	X	–	X	X
Frank Cook	–	–	–	X	–	X	X
Jeremy Corbyn	X	X	X	X	X	X	X
Ann Cryer	X	X	X	X	–	X	X
John Cryer	X	X	X	X	–	X	X
Tam Dalyell	X	X	X	X	X	X	X
Ian Davidson	X	X	X	X	X	X	X
Denzil Davies	–	–	–	X	–	X	X
Terence Davis	–	–	–	-	-	X	X

cont'd

Name	Crown ownership	Not-for-profit	Par'tary app'val	Delay I	Pensions	Delay II	Lords com'mise
Janet Dean	X	X	X	–	–	–	–
Andrew Dismore	X	X	–	–	–	X	–
James Dobbin	X	X	X	X	–	X	X
Brian Donohoe	X	X	X	–	–	–	–
Gwyneth Dunwoody	X	X	X	X	X	X	X
William Etherington	–	–	–	X	–	–	–
Frank Field	X	X	X	X	X	X	X
Paul Flynn	X	X	X	–	–	–	–
Maria Fyfe	X	X	X	–	–	–	–
Neil Gerrard	–	–	–	–	–	X	X
Norman Godman	X	X	X	X	X	X	X
Llin Golding	X	X	X	–	–	–	–
Eileen Gordon	X	X	X	–	–	X	X
Kelvin Hopkins	X	X	X	X	X	X	X
Eric Illsley	–	–	–	X	–	–	–
Jenny Jones	–	–	-	–	–	X	–
Lynne Jones	X	X	X	X	–	X	–
Alan Keen	X	X	X	–	–	–	–
Peter Kilfoyle	–	–	–	–	–	X	–
Tess Kingham	–	–	–	X	–	–	–
David Lepper	X	X	X	–	–	–	–
Terry Lewis	X	X	X	–	–	X	X
Alice Mahon	X	X	X	X	X	X	X
John Marek	X	X	X	–	–	–	–
R. Marshall-Andrews	–	X	–	X	–	X	X
Christine McCafferty	–	–	–	–	–	X	X
John McDonnell	X	X	X	X	X	X	X
Kevin McNamara	–	–	–	–	–	X	X
Bill Michie	X	X	X	X	X	X	X
Gordon Prentice	X	X	X	X	–	X	X
Gwyn Prosser	X	X	X	–	–	–	–
Edward Rowlands	–	–	–	–	–	X	X
Martin Salter	X	X	X	X	–	X	X
Jonathan Shaw	–	–	–	X	–	X	–
Alan Simpson	X	X	X	X	–	X	X
Dennis Skinner	X	X	X	X	X	X	X
Llewellyn Smith	X	X	X	X	X	X	X
George Stevenson	X	X	X	X	–	–	–
Gavin Strang	X	X	X	X	X	X	X
David Taylor	X	–	–	X	–	X	X
Desmond Turner	X	X	X	X	–	X	X
Rudi Vis	–	–	–	–	–	X	X
Robert Wareing	X	X	X	X	X	X	X
Betty Williams	X	X	X	–	–	–	–
David Winnick	X	X	X	X	–	X	X
Michael Wood	X	X	X	X	X	–	–

Note: X indicates that the MP voted against the party whip.

Football (Disorder) Bill

The Football (Disorder) Bill was introduced following violent disorder during the European Football Championships ('Euro 2000') both prior to and during England's matches. It made it easier to use banning orders against known or suspected hooligans, preventing them from travelling abroad. The Government announced the legislation on 4 July 2000 and, despite an already overcrowded legislative programme, aimed to get it speedily onto the statute book before England's next away fixture on 2 September.

Many Labour MPs, including some not known for openly criticising the Government, expressed anxieties about the rushed nature of the legislation (there was, for example, no pause for reflection between the Bill's Committee and Report stages), the civil liberties implications and the power of the police to detain people on the most limited evidence. However, again, Jack Straw was willing to make concessions, both to appease his own backbenchers and also to keep the Conservative front bench happy, whose tacit support he needed to ensure the Bill's speedy passage. On 10 July, Straw held an all-party meeting of peers and MPs to discuss the draft Bill, which had been published the previous Friday. He accepted a suggestion that a police officer would have to give reasons in writing for detaining someone and promised to set a time when the legislation would expire, unless the House decided to continue it. He set this at five years, with a review of the legislation to take place after its first year.

As a result, the six Labour rebellions on the Bill were very small indeed. The Bill's Second Reading on 13 July saw only one Labour MP, Jeremy Corbyn, vote against the Government. A guillotine motion four days later saw just two Labour MPs, Corbyn and Paul Flynn, rebel. The largest Labour rebellion during the Bill saw 11 Labour MPs support a Liberal Democrat amendment that would have removed the power of a police constable to stop someone from travelling abroad if they were likely to cause trouble. Another Liberal Democrat amendment, which sought to remove the power to detain a person if they 'had caused and contributed to violence and disorder' and to replace it with a requirement that they had to have 'been convicted of an offence involving violence or any other relevant offence' attracted the support of only four Labour MPs.[87]

More concessions were announced when the Bill was in committee. The Government now required the police to have 'reasonable grounds' for suspecting that a person had been involved in violence or disorder before that person could be prevented from travelling and they also reduced the length of time – from 24 hours to four hours – that the police could hold an individual for questioning.

The subsequent Third Reading of the Bill saw a mere three Labour MPs vote against the Government.[88] Finally, when the Bill returned from the House of Lords, only two dogged opponents of the measure, Corbyn and Flynn, voted against a second guillotine motion.

Other rebellions

For the first time in the Parliament, the 1999-2000 session saw isolated or low-level revolts (usually completely unnoticed by the media) over a wide range of issues. For example, the Local Government Bill saw three rebellions. Six Labour MPs supported a Liberal Democrat clause to allow local authorities to choose their own executive arrangements, rather than having to select from the Government options of a cabinet or mayoral system.[89] The second and third rebellions related to the Government's plans to repeal Section 28, the law that forbids the 'promotion' of homosexuality by local councils. On 5 July three Labour MPs objected both to the abolition of Section 28 and to the fact that the division was whipped. One of the rebels, Geraldine Smith, felt that 'the intolerant way in which the party whips are being used for this debate on a topic that is essentially a matter of conscience leads me to believe that the major parties in this place have much to learn about tolerance'.[90] On 25 July 2000, when the Government announced it was dropping its plans to repeal Section 28 following its defeat in the Lords over the issue, four Labour MPs voted in favour of sending the issue back to the Lords. One, John McDonnell, asked 'Why do we not draw a line in the sand on this fundamental issue of human rights?'[91] McDonnell and fellow rebel Jeremy Corbyn both sought, but failed to get, assurances from Hilary Armstrong, the Minister for Local Government and the Regions, that the Government would introduce a fresh Bill in the fourth session of the Parliament.[92]

Northern Ireland produced four rebellions on the Labour benches, rebellions that reflected both wings of opinion in the party. On 8 February 2000 the decision of Peter Mandelson, the Secretary of State for Northern Ireland, to suspend the Northern Ireland Executive due to the failure of the IRA to decommission any of its weapons provoked two rebellions by a total of ten Labour MPs sympathetic towards the Nationalist point of view in the Province. Nine Labour MPs voted against the Second Reading of the Northern Ireland Bill, with eight Labour Members opposing the Bill at Third Reading. The future of policing in Northern Ireland caused two further rebellions. Frank Field was the sole Labour

MP to voice his opposition to aspects of the Patten Report into reform of the Royal Ulster Constabulary. By contrast, the perceived watering down of Patten's proposals in the subsequent Police (Northern Ireland) Bill, caused five Labour MPs sympathetic to the Nationalist viewpoint, to support a Liberal Democrat amendment urging that the new policing board's plan should include training for police staff that included paying attention to human rights.

On 15 December 1999, three Labour MPs supported a Liberal Democrat amendment during the Committee Stage of the Representation of the People Bill that would have reduced the voting age from 18 to 16. On 28 February 2000, ten Labour MPs supported an amendment moved to the Government's Defence White Paper, largely, but not exclusively in protest at the Government's failure to adhere to the United Nations Charter when bombing in Iraq and Kosovo.[94] During the spillover, on 7 November 2000, there were two rebellions related to the introduction of programming motions for all government bills and deferred divisions. Although the two issues were themselves subject to free votes, a number of Labour MPs objected to the lack of time to debate the procedural changes. Two Labour MPs voted against a closure motion and five Labour Members opposed a guillotine motion limiting the debate on the new proposals.[95] On 16 November 2000, Austin Mitchell was the only Labour MP to support a new clause to the Insolvency Bill that would have placed a duty on company directors to involve their employees when their firms went into administration. A day later 17 Labour MPs backed a Liberal Democrat prayer that sought to revoke the £500 charge placed on immigrants who wished to appeal against the rejection of their visa application.

Conclusion

By the end of the third session, some 131 Labour MPs had voted against their party whips at least once. This was a small, but noticeable, increase on the situation at the end of the previous session: after 48 more revolts, the total number of Labour rebels had increased by 31, an increase of less than one new rebel per rebellion. (Those MPs to rebelled during the session are listed in Appendix 5). With a few exceptions, the third session saw those who had already rebelled being prepared to do so again – just more frequently. This is clear from Table 4.5, which shows the number of dissenting votes cast by Labour MPs by the end of the session. Whereas by the end of the second session, just four Labour MPs had rebelled 20 or more times, by the end of the third, the comparable figure was 23. The most rebellious Labour MP by the end of the second session was Jeremy Corbyn, who had voted against his whips on 24 occasions. By the end of the third session Corbyn's tally had risen to 62.

Table 4.5 Rebellious votes cast by Labour MPs, by end of third session

Number of votes	N
1 only	20
2–5	42
6–9	16
10–19	30
20–29	15
30–39	6
40–49	0
50–59	1
60–69	1
Total	131

Figure 4.1 Number of rebellions by government MPs in 'middle sessions', 1945–2000

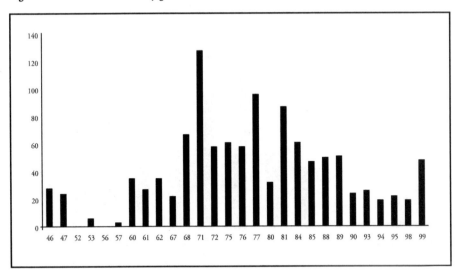

Relative to the rest of the Parliament, this was a noticeable increase in rebelliousness. But relative to previous parliaments, the session was not atypical. Excluding sessions at the front and back of parliaments (which are usually less rebellious) and ignoring the three short post-war parliaments, there were 28 'middle' sessions between 1945 and 2000. As Figure 4.1 shows, although the session of 1999–2000 saw fewer rebellions than the comparable sessions of the 1970s, it saw more rebellions than 17 other middle sessions, including all of those from the 1940s, 1950s and 1990s, as well as most of those from the 1960s, and it was on a par with most of those from the 1980s. By 1999, then, the behaviour of Labour MPs had become similar to the behaviour seen in many other parliaments.

Of course, given the two preceding and relatively quiet sessions (as Figure 4.1 shows, the 19 rebellions in the preceding session meant that it was the joint least rebellious middle session since 1957) the cumulative total number of rebellions seen throughout the Parliament remained low. As Figure 4.2 shows, even after the increase in the number of rebellions between 1999 and 2000, the number for the Parliament as a whole (83) was the lowest of any full-length Parliament since that of 1959. At the end of the session, one (normally reasonably astute) commentator was able to write that 'Barring disasters – and they would need to be real humdingers – this Government is almost certain to go to the election having faced fewer revolts than any recent government'.[96]

Figure 4.2 Number of rebellions by government MPs, by end of third session, 1945–2000

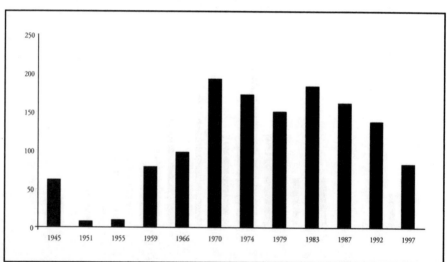

The size of those revolts remained high, however. Although the increasing tendency of Labour MPs to rebel in small numbers meant that the average size of the revolts in the third session was lower than that in the preceding session (14, compared to 26), a figure of 14 still constituted an above average rebellion. Of the 28 middle sessions analysed above, just six had larger average rebellions.[97]

And, as Figure 4.3 shows, by the end of the third session the average size of rebellion in the Blair Government numbered 17 MPs. Of the 12 full-length Parliaments since the war, just two had seen a higher average revolt by government MPs by this point in their life.

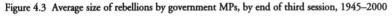

Figure 4.3 Average size of rebellions by government MPs, by end of third session, 1945–2000

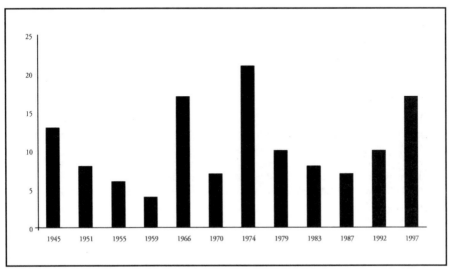

[1]   Interview, 13 March 2001.

[2]   The average number of revolts by government MPs in the middle sessions is higher than the overall average in eight of the 11 full-length post-war parliaments prior to 1997. The exceptions are the parliaments of 1955, 1959 and 1992.

[3]   Some 31 per cent of this session's rebellions comprised between two and five MPs, compared to 19 per cent for the first session and 21 per cent for the second. Comparable figures for rebellions of between two and nine MPs are 46 per cent, compared to 19 per cent and 21 per cent.

[4]   Philip Cowley and Mark Stuart, 'Parliament: A Few Headaches and a Dose of Modernisation', *Parliamentary Affairs*, 54 (2001).

[5]   *Legislation Against Terrorism*, Report, Cm 4178, London, TSO, 1998.

[6]   *Inquiry into Legislation Against Terrorism*, Report, Cm 3420, London, TSO, 1996.

[7]   HC Debs, 14 December 1999, c. 161.

[8]   HC Debs, 14 December 1999, c. 154.

[9]   HC Debs, 14 December 1999, c. 166.

[10]   HC Debs, 14 December 1999, c. 225.

[11]   Tony Benn, Jeremy Corbyn, Dr Lynne Jones, Ken Livingstone, John McDonnell, Bob Marshall-Andrews and Audrey Wise.

[12]   Jeremy Corbyn, Dr Lynne Jones, John McDonnell and Kevin McNamara.

[13]   Paul Flynn, John McDonnell, Kevin McNamara, Jim Marshall, Alan Simpson and Audrey Wise.

[14]   Jeremy Corbyn, Paul Flynn and John McDonnell.

[15] The 13 to vote for McNamara's amendment, plus Ken Livingstone.
[16] In 1988, for example, 44 Labour MPs voted against the Labour front bench's policy of abstaining on the Second Reading of the Prevention of Terrorism Bill.
[17] Interview, 14 March 2000.
[18] When the Bill returned from the House of Lords, an amendment in the name of John McDonnell that sought to restrict the definition of terrorism was not voted on. Had this been selected, it might have increased the number of rebellions on the Bill, but it seems unlikely that it would have resulted in many more Labour MPs voting against the measure. *Telegraph*, 11 July 2000; interview, 11 July 2000.
[19] Royal Commission on Criminal Justice, *Report*, Cm 2263, London, TSO, 1993.
[20] Frances Gibb, 'Bar fights Straw over jury trial curb', *The Times*, 11 October 1999.
[21] Claire Dyer, Michael White and David Hencke, 'Fury at Straw jury plans', *Guardian*, 20 November 1999.
[22] Frances Gibb, 'Lawyers attack jury reforms', *The Times*, 11 January 2000.
[23] Interviews, 7 March 2000, 6 February 2001, 13 March 2001.
[24] Interview, 29 February 2000.
[25] Interview, 7 March 2000.
[26] Interview, 13 February 2001.
[27] Alan Travis, 'Straw's concession on jury trial change', *Guardian*, 23 February 2000. Marshall-Andrews later claimed that 80 Labour MPs had signed his EDM. Interview, 14 March 2000.
[28] HC Debs, 7 March 2000, c. 892. The appeal process would normally be completed within 48 hours and magistrates would also be required to give reasons for their decisions.
[29] HC Debs, 7 March 2000, c. 917. Marshall-Andrews claimed that 28 signed the amendment. Interview, 14 March 2000.
[30] For Best, see HC Debs, 7 March 2000, c. 942; for Fisher, c. 947; and for Sedgemore, cc. 929-930.
[31] Interview with Bob Marshall-Andrews, 14 March 2000.
[32] HC Debs, 7 March 2000, c. 959.
[33] Frank Field, Mark Fisher, Dr Lynne Jones, Bob Marshall-Andrews and Audrey Wise.
[34] At the same time, Gordon Brown increased the minimum income guarantee in line with earnings in an (unsuccessful) attempt to head off criticism. *The Times*, 10 November 1999.
[35] *Telegraph*, 28 September 2000.
[36] *The Times*, 15 May 2000.
[37] See, for example, 'Government criticised over 'obscene' pensions rise', *The House Magazine*, 25 October 1999.
[38] Interview with Paul Flynn, 6 February 2001.
[39] Diane Abbott, Tony Benn, Jeremy Corbyn, Frank Field, Lynne Jones, John McDonnell, Alan Simpson and Michael Wood.
[40] Tony Benn, Jeremy Corbyn, Dr Lynne Jones and John McDonnell.
[41] A total of 41 Labour MPs rebelled over the Bill – the 40 who backed McDonnell's amendment, plus Frank Field, who backed only the extra £5 for the over 75s.
[42] *Guardian*, 9 November 2000.
[43] Matthew Flinders, 'The Politics of Accountability: A Case Study of Freedom of Information Legislation in the United Kingdom', *Political Quarterly*, 71 (2000).
[44] *Your Right to Know*, Cm 3818, London, TSO, 1997; Robin Oakley, 'Week in Westminster', *The House Magazine*, 31 May 1999.
[45] Private information.
[46] Private information.
[47] Interview, 23 October 2001.
[48] Interview, 21 March 2000; also 23 October 2001.
[49] Interview, 6 February 2001.
[50] Interview, 13 February 2001.

51 In a rare appearance in the division lobbies, Tommy Graham, the expelled Labour MP, also voted against the Government.

52 Tommy Graham also voted against the Government.

53 Private information.

54 Interview, 19 January 2000.

55 HC Debs, 4 April 2000, cc. 917-934.

56 *New Statesman*, 24 April 2000.

57 HC Debs, 4 April 2000, cc. 927-928.

58 In addition to the NATS rebellions, there was one other Labour revolt during the Bill's passage: on 10 May 2000 Hilton Dawson, David Drew and Bob Laxton supported a Liberal Democrat clause that would have required the Secretary of State to draw up a strategy to reduce road traffic by ten per cent by 2010.

59 HC Debs, 20 December 1999, cc. 534-537.

60 HC Debs, 20 December 1999, c. 557.

61 Interview with Gavin Strang, 7 March 2000.

62 HC Debs, 20 December 1999, c. 561.

63 Apart from Strang and Dunwoody, the seven other Labour MPs to express concern over NATS during the Second Reading debate were Sandra Osborne, whose Ayr constituency included the airport of Prestwick, John McDonnell, whose Hayes and Harlington seat included Heathrow and the terminal control centre at West Drayton, Martin Salter, a former Heathrow shop steward, as well as Gordon Prentice, Paul Goggins, Jim Dobbin and George Stevenson.

64 HC Debs, 20 December 1999, c. 567. For an alternative view ('it is not the 'usual suspects' who're critical, there's a large range of opinion across the party concerned about it') see Gwyneth Dunwoody, *The House Magazine*, 14 February 2000.

65 HC Debs, 20 December 1999, cc. 553-555.

66 Interview with Gavin Strang, 7 March 2000.

67 Interviews, 28 March 2000, 11 July 2000. One MP took an entirely different view: she had signed thinking it was an EDM and had been shocked to discover that it was an amendment to Second Reading.

68 Interview, 21 March 2000.

69 Interview, 11 July 2000.

70 Interview, 28 March 2000.

71 Environment, Transport and Regional Affairs Select Committee, *The Proposed Public-Private Partnership for National Air Traffic Services Ltd*, Third Report, HC 35 (1999-2000). Also see Keith Harper, 'Air control sell-off "worst option"', *Guardian*, 18 February 2000.

72 Guardian, 4 May 2000, *Telegraph*, 3 May 2000.

73 Interview, 13 March 2001.

74 Interview, 13 March 2001.

75 Interview, 13 March 2001.

76 HC Debs, 9 May 2000, c. 684.

77 HC Debs, 15 November 2000. See also the comments of Michael Connarty, HC Debs, 9 May 2000, cc. 702-704.

78 HC Debs, 9 May 2000, c. 714.

79 HC Debs, 20 December 1999, cc. 624-625.

80 HC Debs, 9 May 2000, cc. 678-679.

81 HC Debs, 9 May 2000, c. 711.

82 Interview, 11 July 2000. See also Patrick Wintour, 'Prescott fights to convince air traffic sell-off rebels', *Guardian*, 4 May 2000.

83 HC Debs, 9 May 2000, c. 680.

84 HC Debs, 9 May 2000, c. 682.

[85] *The Times* (10 May 2000) referred to 'dozens' of abstentions, as did the *Telegraph* (10 May 2000).

[86] *The Times* (16 November 2000) claimed that a similar number who voted against – 37 – also abstained.

[87] Diane Abbott, Harry Barnes, Jeremy Corbyn and John McDonnell.

[88] Jeremy Corbyn, John McDonnell and Bob Marshall-Andrews.

[89] Denzil Davies, John McDonnell, Alan Simpson, Dennis Skinner, Llew Smith and Mike Wood.

[90] HC Debs, 5 July 2000, c. 346. The two other Labour MPs were Joe Benton and Denzil Davies.

[91] HC Debs, 25 July 2000, c. 1047.

[92] The other two Labour dissenters were Diane Abbott and John McAllion.

[93] Tony Benn, Jeremy Corbyn and John McDonnell.

[94] The amendment was tabled by Tony Benn, Jeremy Corbyn, John McDonnell, Kelvin Hopkins, Alan Simpson and Robert Wareing. Eight of the ten Labour MPs who voted against the White Paper also voted against the Government over Kosovo in April 1999.

[95] The former: Jeremy Corbyn and Llin Golding. The latter: Harry Barnes, Jeremy Corbyn, Gwyneth Dunwoody, Llin Golding and Ian Pearson.

[96] Philip Cowley, 'They huff and puff, but Labour MPs are the tamest since 1945', *Independent*, 18 December 2000. Authors should never be blamed for headlines.

[97] They are all periods of Labour government: 1998-99 (an average of 26), 1967-68 (25), 1976-77 and 1977-78 (both 19), 1975-76 (17), and 1968-69 (15). The average in 1946-47 was identical, at 14.

5. Not With a Bang But a Whimper

2000–01

The Conservative MP and diarist 'Chips' Channon once noted what he called the 'odour of dissolution'.[1] An approaching general election can make even the most unhappy of MPs hold their tongues in the final session of a Parliament and there is usually less serious legislation to cause trouble anyway.[2] That was certainly true of the Queen's Speech of December 2000, in which the odour of dissolution was particularly strong. The Speech was late coming as a result of the legislative logjam of the previous session and it did not say very much when it did arrive.[3] Robert Shrimsley of the *Financial Times* likened it to a leopard – 'unencumbered by heavy baggage and aerodynamically designed for a quick sprint to the polls'.[4] Unlike the heavy legislative load of the previous year, it outlined just 15 bills and four draft measures. And, with the forthcoming election assumed to be taking place in May, there was little likelihood that even these measures would make it to the statute book.[5] As one Labour MP admitted: 'There's nothing there. Even if there's something you're not happy with, there's no way it'll see the light of day because of the election'.[6] Many MPs, especially those in marginal seats, were already campaigning practically full-time in their constituencies by the beginning of the session, with their participation in Commons votes dropping accordingly.[7] Things were then made even worse by the effective postponement of the election as a result of the foot-and-mouth crisis, creating a month-long Parliamentary vacuum. As one MP put it, by March, MPs 'just want to get it over with'.[8] There was little appetite for rebellion, and even less to rebel over anyway. The forthcoming general election helped resolve the only issue to cause significant unease on the Labour benches during the session: the proposed abolition of Community Health Councils (CHCs), the patients' watchdog bodies in the NHS.[9] The measure, contained in the Health and Social Care Bill, was criticised by backbench Labour

MPs during the Bill's Second Reading. John Austin, a former chairman of the Association of CHCs for England and Wales, called for CHCs to be retained and to be given more resources and statutory powers.[10] David Hinchliffe, Chairman of the House of Commons Health Select Committee, described the replacement complaints procedure as 'clumsy and confusing'.[11] He claimed that backbench Labour MPs, many of them 'not the usual suspects', were 'deeply worried' by the Government's plans.[12] Hinchliffe had written to Alan Milburn, the Secretary of State for Health before Christmas, suggesting a possible compromise, involving beefing up the membership and powers of the existing CHCs, and there were signs that the Government was listening to backbench concerns. Hinchliffe had met with John Denham, the Minister of State, earlier in the week and believed that Denham had listened to his concerns.[13] In the end, it did not matter. Two weeks later the Lords voted to retain the main independent functions of regional patients' councils and in order to save the rest of the measures ministers backed down and dropped that section of the Bill.

In total the final session saw 13 backbench Labour rebellions. Although this figure is low in absolute terms, it is fairly high in relative terms: just four post-war Parliaments had more rebellions in their final sessions (those of October 1974, 1983, 1945 and 1992).[14] But there was little here to cause concern to the party managers. More than half of these 13 revolts (8) consisted of just one MP. Only one issue – the afterbirth of the previous year's Terrorism Act – saw a rebellion of ten or more MPs. The explanation for the (relatively) high number of revolts lies partly in the new system of voting employed during the session.[15] The majority of the session's revolts took place during what were called 'deferred divisions', a procedure introduced as part of the process of 'modernisation' of the Commons.[16] 'Deferred divisions' did exactly what it said on the tin, with some divisions being deferred until the following week. Motions (but not divisions on government bills) normally taken after 10pm continued to be debated as normal but if a vote was required the division stood over until the following Wednesday afternoon, when a list of the deferred divisions was printed and circulated with the Order Paper. Instead of walking through the division lobbies to record their votes, MPs handed in a ballot sheet between 3.30pm and 5pm, recording their votes on each division. A 'helpful whip' was usually on hand to advise MPs how to vote; any Labour MP who had not voted was paged and reminded.[17]

Some saw this method of voting as evidence of the executive's desire to restrict the potential for trouble. With the debate and the vote separated out, critics argued that it was easier for MPs to be pressurised by the party whips into sticking to the party line.[18] But in other respects deferred divisions make it easier for MPs to rebel almost unnoticed because, as one rebel MP explained, 'the whips have no way of knowing what you are doing until it's too late'.[19] Based on their first session in operation, the latter view appears to be more persuasive: 11 of the 13 rebellions in the final session took place on deferred divisions. The remainder of this chapter details and explains these 13 rebellions.

The rebellions

Deferred divisions were first employed on 13 December 2000, with one Labour MP, Denzil Davies, voting against a motion approving the EU Budget. A week later there were a further six small Labour rebellions during deferred divisions. Three Labour MPs voted against a statutory instrument extending funds to the Millennium Dome, and Frank Field voted against another motion on the Dome.[20] Denzil Davies was the only Labour MP to vote against the deregulation of Sunday dancing (an issue that was whipped for Labour MPs but free on the Conservative side of the House) and Davies was also the only Labour MP to oppose a motion on tax simplification. In a later vote, Davies was again the only Labour MP to object to a 'take note' motion on a European Budget report. Finally, two Labour MPs, Gwyneth Dunwoody and Llin Golding, voted against a statutory instrument that banned mink keeping in Britain. On the same day Llin Golding was the sole Labour MP to vote with the Conservatives on an amendment to a programming motion on the Hunting Bill. (The substance of the Bill was subject to a free vote, but the programming motions were whipped).

On 7 February Denzil Davies, who had obviously taken a marked dislike to both deferred divisions and the European Union, voted against an order granting a political exemption to EU companies. On 14 March 12 Labour Members voted against the draft Terrorism Act (Proscribed Organisations) (Amendment) Order, again in the form of a deferred division, implementing sections of the Terrorism Act passed in the previous session. Perhaps surprisingly, this group of rebels was not identical to the 13 MPs who had objected to the Terrorism Bill a year before: seven of the 12 who voted against the Order had not voted against the Bill.[21] On the same day three Labour MPs objected to a motion curtailing debate on the election of the new Speaker.[22] On 25 April, two Labour MPs, Dennis Skinner and Alan Williams, voted in favour of an Opposition prayer that sought to revoke the Road Vehicles (Display of Registration Marks) regulations, which allowed for the display of the EU flag on British car licence plates and which was a *bête noire* of the tabloid press.

It was perhaps fitting that the final Labour rebellion of the Parliament occurred over the issue that had been the most divisive within the party: welfare reform. During the Report stage of the Social Security Fraud Bill, Frank Field, the former minister for welfare reform, introduced a clause that would have compelled benefit claimants to reveal their benefit details, if the claimant had a conviction for fraud or there were grounds for believing the claim was fraudulent.[23] There was no reason for the Government to panic. Field was the only Labour MP to support his clause in the division lobby.

Conclusion

Field's was the 96th, and final, revolt by government MPs during the Parliament. Despite the small increase in the number of revolts in the third and fourth sessions a total of 96 rebellions for the entire Parliament was a relatively low figure by comparison to many other post-war British parliaments. As Figure 5.1 shows, just four of the 12 full-length post-war parliaments saw fewer revolts. All four date from the 1940s and 1950s. Since party cohesion began to weaken in the 1960s and 1970s, every full-length parliament bar none saw more rebellions than that of 1997. Excluding the short parliaments of 1964 and February 1974, therefore, we have to go back to 1955 to find a parliament with fewer rebellions by government backbenchers than the one elected in May 1997.[24] We are then back in the era in which an American observer, Sam Beer, wrote that British MPs behaved with a 'Prussian discipline'.[25]

Figure 5.1 Number of rebellions by government MPs, full parliament, 1945–2001

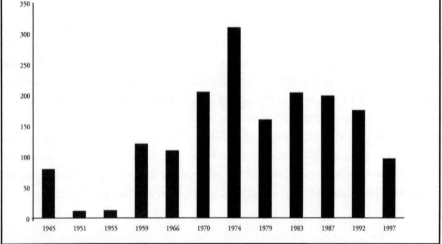

Even this, though, allows us to dismiss some of the wilder claims about the PLP's behaviour. Compared to the behaviour of Conservative MPs in the 1950s, for example, the PLP elected in 1997 was wild indeed. There were two sessions in the 1950s when not a single Conservative MP rebelled at any point. Labour MPs between 1997 and 2001 rebelled roughly *nine* times more often than did Conservative MPs in the 1950s. There were also more rebellions by Blair's MPs than there were by Attlee's backbenchers between 1945 and 1950. The 1997 Parliament, therefore, did not see the least rebellious governing Parliamentary party since the war. Nor was the PLP of 1997 even the least rebellious PLP since the war. But even so, in terms of the number of revolts, it was the least rebellious governing Parliamentary party for a generation.

Table 5.1 Size of Labour rebellions, 1997–2001

Size	N
1 only	22
2–5	25
6–9	8
10–19	13
20–29	9
30–39	6
40–49	10
50–59	2
60–69	1
Total	96

But if we look instead at the size of the revolts we get a very different picture. As has been clear throughout the last four chapters, Blair's MPs may not have rebelled often, but when they did they were likely to do so in numbers. As Table 5.1 shows, although about half the Labour rebellions during the Parliament consisted of five MPs or fewer, over a quarter saw 20 or more MPs rebel and there were 13 rebellions consisting of 40 or more Labour backbenchers. The average (mean) size of the revolts between 1997 and 2001 was 15. As Figure 5.2 demonstrates, this is a greater figure than in all but three post-war Parliaments (and greater than in all but two full-length Parliaments). The rebellions seen between 1997 and 2001 were on average larger than in every Parliament between 1945 and 1966; they were larger than those seen under Heath between 1970 and 1974; and they were larger than those seen during the four consecutive Conservative governments between 1979 and 1997. There was nothing very Prussian about this. For poodles, another phrase frequently used to describe Labour MPs, they could bark loudly when provoked – and a lot louder than Conservative MPs ever did.

Figure 5.2 Average size of rebellion by government MPs, full parliament, 1945–2001

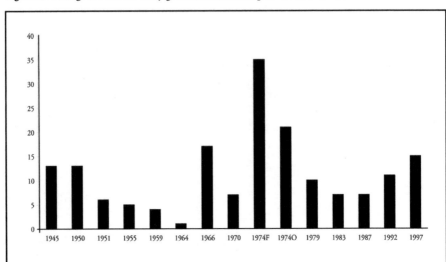

Nor were opponents of government policy always the same people. The final session itself saw just 18 MPs rebel, the majority (12) doing so just once. They are listed in Appendix 6. (The most rebellious was Denzil Davies, who voted against the Government seven times). But it brought the number of MPs who had been prepared to vote against the Government at some point in the Parliament to 133, around half Labour's backbenchers.

MPs who vote against their party soon get used to charges of disloyalty. 'Good to see you voting with us tonight' one whip snidely said to one of the more rebellious Labour MPs, the night after a rebellion.[26] Yet voting against their party is not something that British MPs do lightly and even the most rebellious of Labour MPs regularly voted the party line. As Table 5.2 shows, most rebels did not defy their whips often.

More than half of the rebels voted against the party line on fewer than 10 occasions. The most rebellious Labour MPs – those who voted against the party line 20 or more times – are listed in Table 5.3. Their names will not be much of a surprise, either to those who have read Chapters 2 to 5 or to anyone who is a regular Westminster-watcher. Jeremy Corbyn heads the list (64 dissenting votes), followed by John McDonnell (59) and Dennis Skinner (41). There are then another five MPs who rebelled on more than 30 occasions (Tony Benn, Dr Lynne Jones, Alan Simpson, Kelvin Hopkins and Bob Marshall-Andrews) with another 17 who did so between 20 and 29 times. But when these rebellions are seen as a proportion of all votes, the frequency of rebellion becomes slight. Even Jeremy Corbyn voted against the Labour whip in just five per cent of votes. So, half of the backbenchers did not vote against the party line at all; of those who did, more than half did so on fewer than ten occasions; and even the most rebellious cast a dissenting vote only once every 20 votes. Even the rebels, therefore, were overwhelmingly loyal.[27]

Table 5.2 Rebellious votes cast by Labour MPs, 1997-2001

Number of votes	N	%
1 only	22	17
2-5	40	30
6-9	18	14
10-19	28	21
20-29	17	13
30-39	5	4
40+	3	2
Total	133	100

Table 5.3 The 25 most rebellious Labour MPs, 1997-2001

Name	Number of dissenting votes
Jeremy Corbyn	64
John McDonnell	59
Dennis Skinner	41
Tony Benn	38
Dr Lynne Jones	38
Alan Simpson	38
Kelvin Hopkins	32
Robert Marshall-Andrews	32
Tam Dalyell	29
Gwyneth Dunwoody	27
Diane Abbott	26
Llewellyn Smith	26
Harry Barnes	25
Denzil Davies	25
Alice Mahon	25

cont'd

Name	Number of dissenting votes
Gordon Prentice	25
Audrey Wise	25
Ann Clwyd	24
Neil Gerrard	24
Bill Michie	22
Robert Wareing	22
John Cryer	21
Frank Field	21
Norman Godman	21
Michael Wood	20

But they were prepared to get their teeth into different issues. Between 1997 and 2001, Labour's party managers faced discontent on a number of different fronts, often at the same time. Table 5.4 lists (in descending order of size) the 19 issues to see rebellions of at least ten MPs during the Parliament. The topics range widely, including legal affairs, pensions, competition policy, civil liberties, defence and foreign affairs, terrorism, freedom of information, immigration, education, and, most explosively of all, welfare reform.

Table 5.4 Large Labour rebellions, 1997-2001

Issue	Total number of MPs to vote against the whip
Welfare Reform and Pensions Bill (10)	74
Transport Bill (8)	65
Social Security Bill (3)	47
Child Support, Pensions & Social Security Bill (3)	41
Freedom of Information Bill (6)	41
Criminal Justice (Terrorism and Conspiracy) Bill (4)	37
Criminal Justice (Mode of Trial) (No 2) Bill (5)	37
House of Lords Bill (2)	35
Teaching and Higher Education Bill (2)	34
Competition Bill	25
Iraq	22
Access to Justice Bill	21
Immigration and Asylum Bill (4)	17
Immigration appeals	17
Terrorism Bill (6)	14
Kosovo	13
Draft Terrorism Bill	12
Football (Disorder) Bill (6)	11
Defence White Paper	10

Note: The table shows the total number of Labour MPs to have voted against the Government. In cases where there were multiple revolts on an issue, the total number of rebels may be larger than the largest single revolt on that issue. The number of rebellions on each issue is given in parentheses if greater than one.

The picture we are left with, therefore, is not one of an acquiescent or timid PLP. It is not the PLP portrayed in the media, stuffed full of clones, Daleks, or sheep, all bereft of spine or independent thought, loyally trooping through the division lobbies. Nor, to be sure, do we have a picture of a Parliamentary party that was rebelling both frequently and in quantity – as the PLP did between 1974 and 1979 (and, to a lesser extent, as it did between 1966 and 1970). Rather, we have MPs who were prepared to rebel, and rebel in sizable numbers, but who did so infrequently. It was behaviour not seen in any other post-war Parliament. It was unique to the Blair Government. The next part of the book attempts to explain that behaviour.

[1] Robert Rhodes James (ed), *Chips: The Diaries of Sir Henry Channon*, London, Weidenfeld, 1993, p. 401.

[2] As one MP admitted, the prospect of a forthcoming election 'concentrates minds'. Interview, 6 February 2001.

[3] Philip Cowley and Mark Stuart, 'Parliament: A Few Headaches and a Dose of Modernisation', *Parliamentary Affairs*, 54 (2001).

[4] *Financial Times*, 7 December 2000.

[5] In all, seven government bills were lost due to the dissolution of Parliament.

[6] Interview, 13 February 2001.

[7] See Ron Johnston, Philip Cowley, Charles Pattie and Mark Stuart, 'Voting in the House or Wooing the Voters at Home: Labour MPs and the 2001 General Election Campaign', *Journal of Legislative Studies*, forthcoming.

[8] Interview, 13 March 2001.

[9] See also 'Health Councils Shake-up Under Fire', *The House Magazine*, 4 December 2001.

[10] HC Debs, 10 January 2001, cc. 1114-1119.

[11] HC Debs, 10 January 2001, c. 1106.

[12] HC Debs, 10 January 2001, c. 1107. Hinchliffe was probably right in his assessment that the 'usual suspects' were not enthused by the issue. Of eight of the more rebellious MPs interviewed at the time, none showed any real interest in CHCs, whilst one said he was happy with the Government's proposal.

[13] HC Debs, 10 January 2001, cc. 1106-1107.

[14] As with much of the earlier analysis, this excludes the three short Parliaments. The most rebellious final session was that of the October 1974 Parliament (40 rebellions), followed by 1983 (19), 1945 (17) and 1992 (14).

[15] Not least because the process led to an increase in the number of votes, up to 209, a high number given that it was just a runt of a session.

[16] See, for example, Philip Cowley, 'The Commons: Mr Blair's Lapdog?', in P. Norris (ed), *Britain Votes 2001*, Oxford, Oxford University Press, 2001, pp. 252-253; and Philip Norton, 'Parliament', in A. Seldon (ed), *The Blair Effect*, London, Little Brown, 2001.

[17] Usually but not always. As a result, the procedure does appear to have lead to a slightly higher number of mistaken votes on the part of MPs.

[18] See, for example, George Jones, 'Week in Westminster', *The House Magazine*, 17 July 2000.

[19] Interview, 21 March 2001.

[20] Frank Field, Mark Fisher and Tony Lloyd.

[21] Diane Abbott, Michael Clapham, Denzil Davies, Neil Gerrard, Jenny Jones, Dennis Skinner and

Robert Wareing.

22 Tony Benn, Jeremy Corbyn and Denzil Davies.

23 For Frank Field's speech, see HC Debs, 1 May 2001, cc. 760-762.

24 Even taking into account the fact that the Parliament of 1997 had only four sessions, whilst some others had five, the conclusion remains the same. The average number of rebellions per session between 1997 and 2001 was 24. Every full-length Parliament between 1966 and 1997 had a higher average; and the Parliament of 1959 had an identical average. You still need, therefore, to go back to the Parliament of 1955 before you find a full-length Parliament that saw fewer revolts.

25 Samuel Beer, *Modern British Politics*, London, Faber, 1969, pp. 350-351.

26 Interview, 27 June 2000.

27 Moreover, because some of the more rebellious MPs enjoy a higher-than-average voting record, not least because they are sometimes refused leave of absence from the Commons as a punishment for their actions (see Chapter 6), many of the rebels argue that they cast more loyal votes in favour of the Government than do some of the less rebellious MPs.

Part II

Explaining the Absence of War

Introduction

The relative cohesion of the PLP did not attract praise. Instead, streams of condemnation rained down upon the heads of Labour MPs. They were timid, acquiescent, gutless, sycophantic, cowardly, and lacking in backbone. They were like poodles, or sheep, or – bizarrely – Daleks.[1] Nor did such complaints come just from those outside the Commons. There were plenty of the more rebellious Labour MPs ready to put the boot into their colleagues. There were, said one, 'too many clones'.[2] Another said that most Labour MPs tended to see the Prime Minister as 'like the Pope, infallible'.[3] One long-serving MP described many of the new MPs as 'almost missionary' without them ever being able to define what they were being missionary about. They were 'natural loyalists to a machine… like the Communist Party of old'.[4]

This section explains the relative cohesion of the PLP between 1997 and 2001. Why was there this absence of war? Why did Labour MPs – traditionally a rebellious and fractious group – rebel so infrequently? Was it – as these complaints suggest – because of the type of people now sitting on the Labour benches ('clones', 'natural loyalists')? Or were the reasons more complicated, and possibly more positive, than this suggests?

The propensity of MPs, of whatever party, to vote with their party line should not be surprising. There are far more factors contributing to unity amongst British parliamentarians than there are contributing to disunity. With rare exceptions, in Britain voters vote for parties, not candidates, and nearly all MPs know that they were elected because of their party label not because of who they are.[5] As one MP admitted 'I'm only here because the Labour party got me here'.[6] Nearly all MPs' default position is therefore to vote with their party (especially if the measure under discussion was in its election manifesto) and decisions to deviate from that default position are not taken lightly.[7] One rebel confessed that before rebellions she would feel sick and have sleepless nights. 'I hate it'.[8] Another described dissenting as 'the hardest thing we do'.[9] For an MP to deviate from that default position and rebel over an issue there are three initial conditions that need to be met. First, an issue has to be on the legislative agenda. Second, MPs need to have a position on that issue that is different from their party's. And then, third, they need to have a conception of their role in Parliament that includes voting against the party line. If an MP meets all three of these conditions then there is at least the *potential* for a rebellion, and even these three initial conditions are fairly difficult to fulfil.

For example, issues with the potential to divide Parliamentary parties can wittingly or unwittingly be kept off the legislative agenda. We know, for example, that during the 1997 Parliament the PLP was divided over the issue of proportional representation for elections to Westminster.[10] But because the Government did not introduce legislation on the subject, these divisions never manifested themselves in the division lobbies of the Commons. To a lesser extent, the PLP was also split over British entry to the Euro.[11] But again: no legislation equalled no row. Producing disagreement within the party can also be more difficult than one might think. Of course, all MPs have opinions on matters of high policy but they are much less likely to have them on the more detailed aspects of legislation, and, as Hugh Berrington once noted, it is 'the steady conformity which Members display on obscure clauses and complex amendments which is the more important for the day-to-day working of government'.[12] Or as one new MP put it rather more bluntly: 'I go through the lobby a great number of times not knowing a fuck about what I'm voting for'.[13]

Moreover, because a British MP's default position is to vote with their party, they are usually unwilling to defy their whip unless they are certain that they are right and the government is wrong. As one rebel put it, 'a gut feeling that something's wrong isn't good enough'.[14] To move beyond that gut feeling, to the point where an MP is prepared to challenge what one described as the 'collective wisdom of the government', usually requires an in-depth knowledge of a topic, something which MPs only possess on one or two areas of policy.[15] Cohesion can therefore result as much from a lack of disagreement as from positive agreement. And even if they do take a distinctive stance on the issue, they may see their role in Parliament as largely or solely to do their party's bidding. Some MPs take the party-centred realities of British politics to what they see as their logical conclusion, seeing themselves as the delegate of the party. Between 1966 and 1970, there were Labour backbenchers who 'held a role conception that did not entail open rebellion under any circumstances'. These included some backbenchers 'who saw themselves as no more than passive instruments of the party leadership'.[16] Between 1997 and 2001, there were Labour backbenchers with a similar role conception.

But even if these three initial conditions have all been met – that is, an MP who sees his or her role as including rebellion disagrees with the government over an issue that is on the legislative agenda – there are still plenty of factors that can inhibit revolt, preventing potential rebellions being realised. Some – certainly the factors that are stressed by critics of MPs – are *egocentric*. An MP may, for example, decide not to rebel because they think that rebellion will harm their career prospects or otherwise work to their detriment, such as by causing them difficulties with their constituency party or with their electorate. But other pressures may be more *collective* (MPs may decide not to rebel because they believe that rebellion will harm their party) or *tactical* (because they feel that they will achieve more by remaining loyal than they will by rebelling). And at any stage in the process, potentially rebellious MPs may be convinced by the government, either by it explaining its reasoning in more detail, or – as we saw frequently in Chapters 2 to 5 – by offering concessions in some form. If any or all of the above happens, then latent rebellions may fail to develop.

Of course, few MPs ever sit down and think these stages through in a nice logical ordered manner. (It is for precisely this reason that there is no flowchart diagram here neatly delineating the stages of a rebellion; life, especially political life, is not like a flowchart). But as will become clear, most MPs have considered these issues in some form or at some point. This part of the book uses the broad framework outlined above to analyse the rebellions that took place in the 1997 Parliament.

Chapter 6 looks at the differences between those MPs who dissented from the party line and those who did not. Out of the massed ranks of Labour MPs elected in 1997, why was it those 133 MPs who decided to vote against their party whips? And why did some of them do so more often than others? Chapter 7 (co-authored with Sarah Childs) looks in more detail at the behaviour of the newly elected women MPs, a group that was said to be especially cohesive. Chapter 8 examines the mechanisms by which the PLP tried to mediate discontent within its ranks, attempting to ensure that internal disagreements did not spill over into public splits and divisions. And Chapter 9 brings the analysis together, and tries to explain why there were so few revolts in the Parliament.

But first, two boring methodological digressions. Because MPs who are in government cannot vote against their whips without first resigning their position, the inclusion of government MPs in any statistical analysis has the potential to skew the results. So for the purposes of the following analysis the PLP is split into three groups. First, there are those MPs – 87 in number – who were in government for the entire period. They have to be excluded from any analysis of rebellions. Second, there are those (191) MPs who were in government for some, but not all, of the period, either because they were promoted to, and/or ejected from, government during the course of the Parliament. And, third, there are those (151) MPs who were on the backbenches for the entire Parliament. Any analysis of the characteristics of the PLP as a whole – looking at, say, how many women there were in the PLP – utilises all three groups (that is, an N of 429). But, except where stated to the contrary, any analysis of the characteristics of rebels and loyalists is conducted with just the second and third groups; that is, it excludes those MPs who were in government for the entire period and uses all MPs who would have been able to vote against the Government at some point in the Parliament (so N=342). Lest it be thought that the results are being distorted by including those MPs who were on the backbenches for only some of the period, all the analysis was re-run using just the 151 permanent backbenchers; all differences – and there are very few – are reported in endnotes.

The analysis also draws repeatedly on two surveys of British MPs. The first, the British Representation Survey (BRS), was a national survey of prospective Parliamentary candidates and MPs from all major parties standing in the 1997 British general election. The survey was conducted in mid-1996, and garnered a total of 999 positive responses (a response rate of 61 per cent). Of these, the dataset records 277 respondents as having been elected in May 1997, of which 179 were Labour. It is these 179 that are analysed in this chapter.[17] The chapter also draws on a survey conducted by members of the Study of Parliament Group (SPG) into the socialisation of British MPs. Surveys were sent in February 1999 to all newly elected MPs and to a sample of longer-serving MPs, producing an overall positive response rate of 44 per cent, of which 129 respondents were Labour MPs.[18]

[1]   The Dalek comparison is correct in only one sense: just like Labour, the Daleks usually lost.
[2]   Interview, 7 March 2000.
[3]   Interview, 28 March 2000.
[4]   Interview, 25 May 1999.
[5]   Although the question was not asked in the 1997 BRS, in 1992 over 90 per cent of MPs agreed with the statement that 'Most people vote for the party not the individual candidate'. Pippa Norris, 'The Puzzle of Constituency Service', *The Journal of Legislative Studies*, 3 (1997), p. 40. Quite where the other ten per cent of MPs think their votes come from is a mystery.
[6]   Interview, 11 April 2000.
[7]   Interviews, 11 April 2000, 6 May 2000, 11 July 2000.
[8]   Interview, 15 February 2000.
[9]   Interview, 13 February 2001.

[10] The BRS found that 49 per cent of Labour MPs were in favour of introducing PR, but 39 per cent were opposed. Another 13 per cent said that it did not matter.

[11] See David Baker, Andrew Gamble, and David Seawright with Katarina Bull, 'MPs and Europe', *British Elections and Parties Review*, 9 (1999), p. 175.

[12] Hugh Berrington, 'Partisanship and Dissidence in the Nineteenth Century House of Commons', *Parliamentary Affairs*, 21 (1967-8), p. 339.

[13] Interview, 6 March 2001.

[14] Interview, 14 March 2000.

[15] Interview, 21 March 2001.

[16] J. Richard Piper, 'Backbench Rebellion, Party Government, and Consensus Politics: The Case of the Parliamentary Labour Party 1966-70', *Parliamentary Affairs*, 27 (1974), p. 392.

[17] The BRS 1997 was directed by Pippa Norris in collaboration with Joni Lovenduski, Anthony Heath, Roger Jowell and John Curtice. The results reported in this chapter are marginally different from those derived from the full dataset since the process of merging the survey data with data on dissent helped uncover some small errors in the original data.

[18] The SPG survey was directed by Michael Rush and Philip Giddings.

6. Who Were the Rebels?

Why them? Why out of the massed ranks of Labour MPs elected in 1997 was it those 133 who decided to vote against their party whips? And why did some of them do so more often than others? For example, why did Jeremy Corbyn vote against his party whips 64 times, but Andrew Miller did so not once, despite being of a similar age and even having a similar beard? Likewise, why was John McDonnell the most rebellious member of the 1997 intake, rebelling 59 times, whilst other male MPs of the same intake, and of a similar age, such as Peter Bradley or Stephen Ladyman, did not vote against the whips at all? These questions are interesting in themselves, because they tell us who the rebels were, but they also provide some important insights into the wider question of why there were so few backbench rebellions between 1997 and 2001.

Based on the model outlined in the introduction to this part of the book, this chapter focuses on four different types of explanations for MPs' behaviour. First, those that explain rebellion in terms of the MP's *ideology* or *beliefs*: the extent to which they may disagree with the Government. Second, there are explanations that focus on the MP's *legislative roles*: the extent to which they see their role in Parliament as including rebellion. Third, there are explanations that test *egocentric behaviour*: the extent to which the MP may be acting in his or her own best interest. And finally, fourth, there are explanations that focus on *other characteristics of the MP*: specific individual characteristics that may perhaps explain the MP's ability to withstand, or succumb to, the pressures placed upon them.

Ideology and beliefs

Labour MPs were often keen to stress that they were quite prepared to rebel against the Government, but that they did not feel the need to do so, because they agreed with the policies that it was putting forward. As a frustrated Michael Foster said at one point: 'When new Labour MPs vote with the Government, it may just be that we . . . are happy to be voting for the policies on which we were elected and with which we agree'.[1] Indeed it may. One of the key issues in studies of legislative voting is the extent to which legislative cohesion is artificial (the result of disciplinary pressures) or natural (resulting from agreement).[2] For if MPs agree, why should they rebel?

As part of the 1997 BRS, MPs were asked a series of questions about their ideological positions, including some basic scalar questions designed to tap their underlying political values. The scales measure their left-right self-placement, as well as the trade-offs between inflation and unemployment, taxation and public spending, nationalisation and privatisation, integration within the EU, and the issue of sex equality. For example, the question on inflation and unemployment was:

> Some people feel that getting people back to work should be the Government's top priority. These people would put themselves in Box 1. Other people feel that keeping prices down should be the Government's top priority. These people would put themselves in Box 11. Other people have views in between. Using the following scale . . . Where would you place your view?

The graphs in Figure 6.1 show the percentage of MPs in each ideological category that rebelled at least once in the 1997 Parliament. For example, of those Labour MPs who placed themselves on the most left-wing position on the left/right scale (graph a), 60 per cent voted against their party line, and of those who placed themselves on the next position to the right, 67 per cent rebelled. The N below the X axis shows the number of respondents who placed themselves in that position. So, five MPs placed themselves at position 1 of the left/right scale (graph a), of whom three (60 per cent) rebelled.

In general terms, there was a clear link between an MP's ideological position and his or her propensity to rebel. As we move to the right, so rebellion becomes less likely: 35 per cent of those in position 3 rebelled, down to 27 per cent in position 4, to 11 per cent by position 5, with not one of the handful of Labour MPs who placed themselves to the right of position 5 voting against their party line. Broadly similar trends occur with all of the first four scales: as we move to the right of the scale, so the likelihood that an MP has rebelled diminishes. This is especially clear with the taxation/spending scale (graph c), where *every* shift to the right produces a diminution in the percentage of MPs who voted against the party.

Figure 6.1 Linkage between ideology and rebellion, Labour MPs, 1997–2001

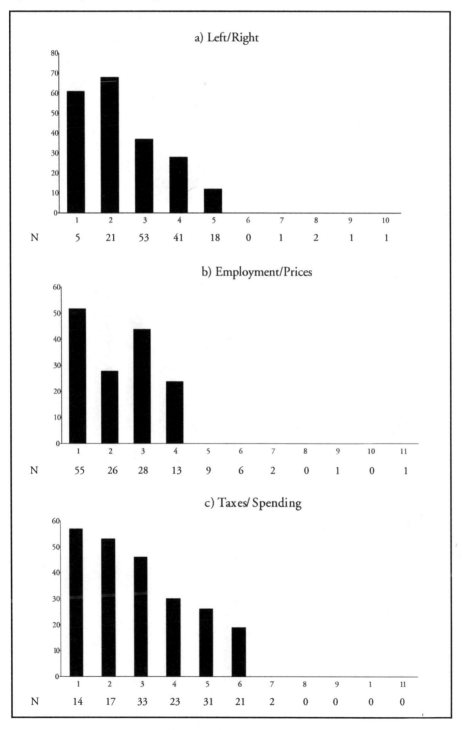

Figure 6.1 Linkage between ideology and rebellion, Labour MPs, 1997-2001 *cont'd*

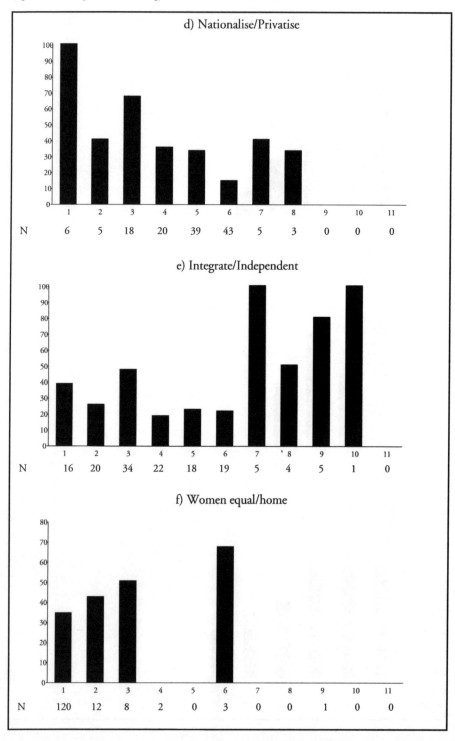

By contrast, an MP's position on the EU scale (graph e) produced almost no relationship with his or her propensity to rebel, perhaps not surprising given the lack of EU-related issues on the agenda during the Parliament.[3] The same applies to the scale asking about views on women's rights (graph f), which also suffers from a severe clustering – almost all Labour MPs place themselves at position 1 – which anyway renders it near useless as a predictor of behaviour within the PLP (although as an indicator of the difference between the PLP and the other parties it is still useful).[4]

We see something similar if we analyse MPs' responses to two batteries of questions tapping into basic socialist/laissez-faire and authoritarian/libertarian views, a standard way of measuring political attitudes.[5] Each battery consisted of six questions, such as 'Private enterprise is the best way to solve Britain's economic problems' (one of the socialist/laissez-faire questions) or 'People in Britain should be more tolerant of those who lead unconventional lives' (one of the authoritarian/libertarian questions). MPs were given five different possible responses, ranging from 'Agree Strongly' to 'Disagree Strongly'. Constructing a single score from each battery of six questions produces a range from 6 to 30, with a low score indicating a socialist or libertarian viewpoint, and a high score indicating a laissez-faire or authoritarian viewpoint. An MP's socialism/laissez-faire score correlates very well with their behaviour. The rebels were, on average, more socialist than the loyalists: the differences were fairly small – rebels averaged 11.2, loyalists 12.8 – but clearly significant.[6] By contrast, the libertarian/authoritarian scale was a very poor predictor of behaviour. There were almost no differences between rebels and loyalists on the scale: rebels scored 13.8, almost identical to the loyalists who scored 13.5.

Of course, these are all fairly crude measures of ideology. MPs rarely, if ever, vote on general political questions; instead they vote on very specific legislative proposals. In reality, MPs may have different views on different issues. But even this crude analysis makes two points clearly enough. The first is to reinforce the point made earlier: that the issues on the legislative agenda have the potential to influence the nature of rebellion. For example, had the 1997 Parliament contained lots of votes on European policy, then we might have seen MPs' views on the EU affect their propensity to rebel. But because it did not, so we do not. Instead (the second point) what appears to be driving rebellion is the basic left/right division within the PLP. The more 'left-wing' or 'socialist' an MP, the more likely he or she was to rebel.

Roles

The idea that MPs' roles influence behaviour is a long-standing one, best exemplified in Donald Searing's magisterial work on Parliament in the 1970s, *Westminster's World*.[7] How MPs behave can be influenced by how they see their role in Parliament. Between 1997 and 2001, there were certainly some Labour MPs who had a similar role conception to those MPs identified by Piper between 1964 and 1970, one which did not entail open rebellion under almost any circumstances. One newly elected Labour MP argued that he saw the role of the backbench MP as being 'to provide the executive with a permissive environment in which they can do their work', adding 'I didn't get elected to cause trouble'.[8] Another said that his role as a backbencher was to support the party and help it implement the manifesto.[9] These MPs saw their role as supporters of the executive, providing it with the ammunition it needed to do its job. MPs with this sort of party delegate role conception should be unlikely to be found in the division lobbies voting against the Government. That said, there were relatively few such party delegates on the Labour benches. The BRS asked MPs whether they would be willing to rebel against the party line, regardless of either their own consciences or the national interest. The results are shown in Table 6.1. The majority of MPs of all parties had a role conception that included rebellion. For sure, the PLP contained more delegates than either of the other two parties, but even amongst the PLP only 19 per cent at most ruled out rebellion. The SPG survey also found that the PLP was the most party-orientated group of legislators. Fourteen per cent of Labour MPs ranked 'representing the party' as their most important function, compared to not a single Conservative MP; and 47 per cent of Labour MPs said that they 'nearly always' relied on the whips when voting, compared to 34 per cent of Conservative MPs and 13 per cent of Liberal Democrats.

Table 6.1 Views on rebellion, 1997

| | Percentage agreeing | | |
	Cons	Lab	LibDem
MPs should vote the party line, irrespective of their consciences	10	19	4
MPs should vote the party line, even if against the national interest	8	10	4

Source: BRS, 1997.

As we might expect, there was a clear relationship between an MP's role conception and their behaviour. Thirty-nine per cent of those Labour MPs who said that they thought MPs should follow their conscience rather than the party line rebelled, compared to 21 per cent of the delegates. And 36 per cent of those who thought MPs should follow the national interest rather than the party line broke ranks, compared to none of the delegates. Similar findings came from the SPG survey: 60 per cent of Labour MPs who said that they saw their main role as representing the nation rebelled, as did 44 per cent of those who saw their main role as representing the constituency – but the figure for those who saw their role as representing the party was just 13 per cent. And 36 per cent of those who said that they relied on their personal opinions when deciding how to vote rebelled, as did 33 per cent of those who relied on their constituency's opinions. For those who relied on the party whip the figure was 25 per cent. However we measure it, therefore, those MPs who saw their role as being a delegate of the party were significantly less likely to vote against the party line than those with a different role conception.

Self-interest

So far we have looked at what could be termed creditable (or in Parliamentary terms, honourable) reasons for the cohesion of MPs. If MPs agree with the party, or see their role at Westminster as to be a delegate of the party, then why should they rebel? But the most commonly discussed reason for MPs sticking to the party line – implicit in all the comments about MPs suffering from a lack of 'backbone' – is less creditable or honourable: it is that MPs are somehow pressurised into voting with their party.

The most commonly cited source of this pressure is the party whips ('[i]n the study of party cohesion and the factors that encourage it . . . party whips are often viewed as of central importance') but MPs also face pressures from other quarters, such as their local party and their electorate, both of which can also have a potentially powerful effect on an MP.[10] Similarly, the most commonly cited reason for MPs giving in to this pressure is that they are acting in their own self-interest. This is implicit in much of the criticism of MPs being 'careerist', as well as being explicit in an enormous literature on political behaviour, Parliamentary and otherwise, known as rational choice theory.[11] This section examines both the internal and external pressures that might be applied to the self-interested MP.

Internal

The source of the power of the whips is clear: the Whips Office controls access to positions in Government – effectively acting as gatekeepers for promotion –

as well as being responsible for the distribution of other forms of patronage, such as places on select committees, offices, overseas trips, in addition to releasing MPs from the need to be around the precincts of the Commons.

Previous studies tended to debunk one important aspect of the whips' power, finding only a fairly weak correlation between an MPs' rebelliousness and damage to their future career prospects.[12] Governments, it was claimed, found it hard to ignore talented MPs, even if they were rebellious (at least so long as they were not *too* rebellious). 'If a Prime Minister was consistently to exclude dissenting backbenchers from office . . . it would fuel resentment on the back-benches and affect adversely the morale and effectiveness of the Parliamentary party'.[13] Indeed, it has even been argued that it was better for an MP's career prospects to rebel, both because that showed some fighting spirit and because party managers might offer posts to rebellious MPs to keep them quiet.[14]

The Blair Government did appoint some rebellious MPs to its ranks. Tony Banks, who just before the 1997 election had written that 'the chances of Tony Blair asking me to do anything other than shut up and vote are extremely remote', was made Minister of Sport at the beginning of the Parliament.[15] And Chris Mullin, the prime mover of several of the rebellions in the first half of the Parliament (see Chapters 2 and 3) was promoted to the post of Parliamentary Under-Secretary in the DETR in 1999. But these two high-profile promotions helped mask the extent to which the Blair Government excluded those who rebelled against it. Of the 56 newly elected MPs promoted to Government between 1997 and 2001, just one – Jim Fitzpatrick – had voted against the Government.[16] Staying loyal to the party line was not of itself a sufficient condition for promotion – of the 128 loyal new MPs, 78 remained on the back-benches throughout the Parliament – but it came extremely close to being a necessary one. The chances of promotion for those who did not rebel were significantly greater than for those who did: some 39 per cent of the loyal new MPs were promoted compared to just two per cent of the rebellious new MPs. Whilst there may have been other factors at work – as we have seen, the MPs who rebelled were on average more left-wing, and may therefore have been less likely to be promoted for their ideology as much as their rebellion – such nuances are much less likely to have been noticed than the simple fact that rebel-lious MPs did not prosper.[17] Ambitious MPs may have tempered their behaviour accordingly.

And even when they were not distributing Government jobs, the whips had other tools at their disposal. Although most of the writing on the Whips Office (see Chapter 8) now stresses the whips' consultative and communicative functions, some could still resort to old-fashioned macho bullying when they felt it was needed. One new Labour MP described the whips as 'very unpleasant'. 'When I say they bully you, I really mean physically bully you'.[18] Another back-bencher argued that if he had been a 'normal' employee working in a 'normal' company, he would now be 'waiting for the cheque from the tribunal'.[19] As one longer-serving MP said: 'If they [the whips] behaved like that outside of here, they'd be certified . . . they're ravers'.[20]

MPs who defied the whips would complain of being deliberately chosen to stay late, sometimes when the whips knew full well that there would be no votes that evening, denied better office facilities, refused service on select or standing committees, and not allowed to go on foreign trips.[21] The whips, claimed one persistent rebel, could be 'petty and bloody-minded'.[22] Any MP who wanted an easy life, therefore, had plenty of reasons to stick to the party line.

Of course, one of the problems investigating this in any detail is that MPs rarely admit to doing something out of rational self-interest. Survey questions do not ask 'Do you capitulate to the whips in order to further your career?', and for obvious reasons they would not be much use even if they did.[23] And perhaps not surprisingly, MPs rarely admit that these sorts of things explain their voting (although some do, such as the MP who summed his voting up with the short phrase: 'I'm a coward, really').[24] But such pressures are often implicit in the comments of longer-serving MPs, who argue that the whips have no hold on them. If an MP is uninterested in patronage, then, as one long-serving MP said, 'I want nothing that they can give me'.[25] The implication is that there are things that can be given to other MPs. So instead of looking directly at 'self-interest' we have to look at surrogate variables. Here, we can investigate the effect of three explanatory variables: self-declared ambition, of being newly elected, and of age.

Ambition. MPs who harbour little or no ambition for ministerial office and who have less to fear from the removal of patronage, might be hypothesised to be more likely to be willing to rebel. The BRS asked respondents where they would most like to be in ten years' time. The majority of Labour respondents said that they wanted to be a member of the Government; the second largest group said that they wanted to be an MP, but not in the Government; and the third largest group said that they hoped to have retired from public life. There were then clear relation-ships between these differing levels of ambition and the MP's voting. Of those who hoped to have left public life – and over whom the whips had least leverage – 53 per cent had rebelled. Of those who wished to remain a backbench MP – and over whom the whips had some, but not much, leverage – 47 per cent had rebelled. But of those who wanted to be in Government – and over whom the whips had most leverage – just 26 per cent had rebelled. As the extent of patronage increased, therefore, so the likelihood that the MP had rebelled decreased.

There were some even more striking findings from the SPG survey, which asked the question just of newly elected MPs. Of those who said they did not have ministerial ambitions, 66 per cent rebelled during the Parliament. But of those ambitious for ministerial office, the figure was just 13 per cent. Those not ambitious for ministerial office were therefore five times more likely to vote against their party whips than those who hoped to get their hands on a ministerial red box.

The new intake. Faced with the uncertainties of a new job, and with the potential for future promotion up the ministerial ladder, new MPs might also be less likely to rebel than their peers. As one long-serving male MP argued:

> For the first term, they are really fighting the next election, gaining a wide circle of friends. After that, [once] they realise that there's no point in being here, they'll want to make a mark, [and then] they'll start behaving like a real human being.[26]

This effect was felt by some MPs to be particularly strong in the 1997 intake, because the newer MPs had a different perception of the route to power. As one MP put it:

> The younger ones are the product of the party and they were, they think, elected because of the party. The older ones know that they survived despite the party.[27]

Whatever the cause, the diagnosis of the effect was spot on. Of the MPs elected for the first time in 1997, 28 per cent rebelled. The comparable figure for the long-serving MPs was 54 per cent, a difference that was highly statistically significant. Longer-serving MPs were therefore almost twice as likely to rebel as newly elected MPs.

Age. The potential for an MP's age to affect their propensity to rebel is clear. Before reaching the Cabinet, MPs normally have to serve a lengthy Parliamentary apprenticeship.[28] Older MPs have less time (and hence less chance) to do so and as a result may not face the same pressures to conform to the party line. (Older MPs might, perhaps, also be better at standing up to the sort of physical bullying described above). As Andrew Rawnsley claimed: 'Also fairly immune to carrot or stick is Grey Labour . . . . The past-it and the passed-over know that if they are not ministers by now, they almost certainly never will be'.[29]

The effect is striking: the average age of the Labour rebels was 52; the average age of the loyalists was 46, a difference that was highly statistically significant. Of course, in part, this could be the consequence of the newer MPs, who were on average younger than the longer-serving MPs. But there were also clear differences even within the new intake. The average age of the newly elected rebels was 47; the average age of the newly elected loyalists was 42, differences that were again highly statistically significant. So even when we control for intake, the older MPs – those with less chance of climbing high up the ministerial ladder – were noticeably more likely to have rebelled than their younger colleagues.

External

MPs also face two important forces external to the Commons: their local constituency party (which has the power to deselect them) and their electorate (which enjoys the ultimate power to eject them from Parliament altogether). Whilst the whips can make an MP's life uncomfortable, by denying them political creature comforts, both these external forces have the potential to snuff the MP's Parliamentary life out altogether.

The local party. Because candidate selection in the UK is decentralised, being made by local party members in individual constituencies, local party members wield a considerable power.[30] Those who select can deselect. Although in practice many deselection conflicts (real or threatened) often have little or nothing to do with the ideology of the MP concerned, such conflicts can also be ideological in nature.[31] In the 1950s, for example, Conservative rebels over Suez came under concerted pressure from their local constituency associations.[32] In the 1960s the Monday Club attempted to unseat Conservative MPs it considered too liberal, and in the 1970s similar pressure was brought to bear over the EEC, Northern Ireland and local Government reorganisation.[33] Similarly, the introduction of mandatory reselection within the Labour Party in the 1980s was an attempt by the left both to replace right-wing MPs with left-wingers, and to put pressure on other MPs to vote in a more left-wing direction.[34]

In theory, therefore, the local party is one of the most potent pressures on an MP, and one that some have claimed exerts a powerful influence. Writing in the 1960s, Austin Ranney argued that 'national leaders do not need to control local candidate selection in order to maintain party cohesion in Parliament; the local activists do the job for them'.[35] This influence certainly lay behind the Labour Party leadership's decision to circulate Constituency Labour Parties (CLPs) with the voting records of their MPs.[36] The aim was that local activists – horrified at the rebellious nature of their MPs – would vigorously urge them to toe the party line.

Did it work? Answer: absolutely not. Some Labour MPs complained that their local activists were putting pressure on them to toe the party line, often also complaining that the original source of this pressure was Millbank.[37] But the majority reported quite the opposite. Rather than local parties urging their MPs to stay loyal to the Government, CLPs were more likely to be urging revolt. Several loyal Labour MPs complained that their activists still had the 'mindset of Opposition', always seeing issues in terms of betrayal by the Government.[38] 'It's like a virus,' said one senior MP. 'I got my first betrayal letters two months after the election'.[39] One MP recalled a party member who came up to her after a large rebellion and said, 'If she's not prepared to vote against the Government, what good is she?'[40] Others reported similar pressures.[41] One MP got so fed up with pressure from his constituency party, he decided to rebel over student grants just to keep them quiet.[42] And as a result those MPs who rebelled received bouquets rather than brickbats from their activists. Distributing records of MPs' rebellions to local parties proved entirely counterproductive. In several cases, reading out the occasions when the MP had voted against the party line produced cheers of approval from CLP meetings.[43] One MP – who had previously not enjoyed entirely harmonious relations with his CLP – said that once his rebellious voting record was revealed to his activists he enjoyed his easiest reselection ever.[44]

Table 6.2 Labour MPs' views of their ideological position and that of their CLPs (mean scores)

Issue	Local party	MP	Difference
Left/Right	3.42	3.50	+0.08
Employment/Prices	2.35	2.43	+0.08
Taxes/Spending	3.28	3.82	+0.54
Nationalise/Privatise	4.01	4.94	+0.93
Integrate with EU/remain independent	4.92	3.95	-0.97
Women equal/in home	2.02	1.38	-0.64

Note: A positive difference indicates that MPs were to the right of their local parties; a negative difference indicates that they were to the left. Source: BRS, 1997.

The reason for this becomes clear from the BRS. Table 6.2 shows the responses given by Labour MPs to the BRS scalar questions used above. It shows the (mean) average scores Labour MPs gave to their perceptions of their own ideological position, as well as the score they gave to the position of their local parties. Low scores indicate a left-wing position. As the Table shows, in most cases there was very little difference between the MPs and their CLP, but if anything the CLPs were on average marginally to the left of the MPs on most of the questions. For example, on the general left/right scale, the vast majority of Labour MPs either ranked their constituency party as identical to them, or put them one place to the left or the right. When asking about the EU and the role of women, the constituency parties were on average to the right of their MPs (or more accurately, more opposed to integration or more traditionalist) but again the differences were very slight. It should not be a surprise, therefore, that constituency parties did not act as a huge constraint on Labour MPs nor that there is no evidence that MPs who diverged from their CLPs were any more or less likely to vote against the Government.[45]

Marginality. Re-election is the *sine qua non* of an MP's career, and it is one that much American literature on Congress draws on when helping to explain the behaviour of legislators.[46] In Britain, as pointed out in the introduction, the possibility that individual votes by MPs might boost their electoral prospects is at best slight, and at worst nonexistent.[47] But a desire to avoid the appearance of division – discussed in more detail in Chapter 9 – might be thought to apply most starkly to MPs with small majorities. As one MP, elected in a marginal constituency, said: 'you don't hold onto those sort of seats by bringing your party into disrepute'.[48] At the same time, MPs with small majorities who were elected for the first time in 1997 might also be hypothesised to be more loyal to the Blair leadership as the one that got it elected. As another new Labour MP from a marginal seat pointed out: 'The size of the swing means that many of us wouldn't be here without the Blair effect'.[49] And in general, this appears to be right: those Labour MPs who rebelled sat for seats with an average majority of 32 per cent; those who stayed loyal sat for seats with an average majority of 26 per cent.[50]

But this figure is slightly misleading. The scale of Labour's victory complicates examining the effect of marginality, because as we saw in Chapter 1, the size of Labour's landslide brought in many MPs who were not expected to win their seats. The party did not vet these MPs as carefully in advance nor did they have such close relations with the central party in the run-up to the election (many winning their seats with no assistance from the central party organisation), and their election brought fears within the party hierarchy that they might cause trouble within Parliament. So we should expect the most unlikely of MPs – those with the smallest majorities of all – to be slightly *more* rebellious than other MPs who were elected in 1997. And this is exactly what we do find. A total of 34 per cent of the 'unlikely lads' rebelled, compared to 25 per cent of the new MPs who expected (or realistically hoped) to win their seats, although this difference is not statistically significant.

Table 6.3 Marginality and rebellion, 1997–2001

| | Mean percentage majority | |
	Rebels	Loyalists
Long-serving	42	39
New MPs (expected winners)	22	23
New MPs (unexpected winners)	6	7

To take this into account, Table 6.3 shows the average majority of rebels and loyalists, splitting the PLP into three: those elected before 1997; those elected in 1997 from key seats or who inherited safe Labour seats; and those who came in unexpectedly in 1997. The table shows that the effect of marginality is actually far less dramatic than it at first seems. There is a difference in the marginality of longer-serving rebels and loyalists: long-serving MPs who rebelled had an average majority of 42 per cent, compared to the loyalists, who had a majority of 39 per cent, but this difference fails to achieve statistical significance.[51] Moreover, the differences between the two types of new MPs were much smaller, and both were in the opposite direction to that which we might expect. The average marginality of new MPs who rebelled was actually slightly lower than those who stayed loyal, whether they are expected or unexpected victors. So, much of the apparent difference in the marginality of rebels and loyalists actually appears to be caused by the fact that new MPs – who themselves sit for more marginal seats – were less likely to rebel, rather than being driven by the marginality of the seat itself.

Other characteristics

The variables examined above looked at whether MPs responded to their perceived self-interest. The results were mixed. Internal factors appeared to have some impact: MPs were less likely to rebel if they were ambitious, newly elected or young. External factors, by contrast, were much less powerful: pressures from the selectorate or the electorate appear to have had little impact. Yet different MPs may respond to these various pressures in different ways. Moreover, they may respond to them in different ways because of their different personal characteristics. Whilst we cannot test all aspects of MPs' personalities or characters, we are able to examine four variables with the clear potential to affect the way that MPs behave: their education, group membership, sex and previous council experience.

Education. The influx of university-educated MPs in the 1960s was said to have been one of the fundamental reasons behind a rise in the assertiveness of British MPs.[52] Given this, we might expect an MP's education to affect their propensity to rebel. In an ideal world, of course, what we would actually want to test is the relationship between an MP's intellectual ability (and self-confidence) and his or her rebelliousness. Given that we have no data on this, the best we can do is to use their level of formal education as a (pretty poor) surrogate. We would expect those with higher levels of formal education to be more likely to rebel against the party line, both because being more able to think for themselves they might be more likely to have their own opinions on an issue, opinions that might differ from those of the Government, but also because they might have the intellectual self-confidence to resist any plausible arguments to the contrary being advocated by their whips and others.

In fact, the initial results are slightly surprising. Of those Labour MPs educated at university, just over a third voted against the party (36 per cent). But of those without a university education, the figure was exactly half. So those without a university background – whom we might have expected to be less rebellious – turn out to be more rebellious, and by a degree that is statistically significant.[53] In part, this result may be caused by the extent to which the PLP – even more so than the rest of society – contains increasing numbers of those with a university education: by 1997, more than 70 per cent of Labour MPs, and nearly all of the more recent intakes, had been to university.[54] But we find that differences remain even when we try to control for this. For example, of those aged under 50 who went to university, 25 per cent had rebelled. Of those without university education, 36 per cent had rebelled. Of those aged 50 or over, the figures were 50 per cent and 63 per cent. Even when we control for differences in age, therefore, those without a university education were more likely to have rebelled than those with. However, neither difference now remains statistically significant. We can at least be clear that a university education does not produce a higher level of rebelliousness. If anything, the opposite is true.

Group membership. One of the striking features of the 1997 Parliament was the lack of any sizeable organised factional grouping with the PLP. The exception was the left-wing Campaign Group. A full 94 per cent of the Campaign Group rebelled at some point in the Parliament, compared to 33 per cent of other MPs (a difference that no one will be surprised to find was extremely statistically significant). Of course, membership of the Group cannot necessarily be assumed to be the cause of this difference. By definition, the Group's membership was disproportionately left-wing, and thus more likely to have rebelled anyway.[55] That said, membership of a group like the Campaign Group was a very public signal that an MP was opposed to much of the Government's programme and was not interested in promotion. As Alan Simpson, secretary of the Group at the beginning of the Parliament, said at one point: 'Let's face it, membership of the Campaign Group is hardly a career-enhancing move . . . Most people at Millbank think we're politically off the planet'.[56] And membership of an organised group also provides MPs with an alternative source of information to the Government and the whips office, as well as providing a sense of collective security to MPs about to defy their party line, making it easier to resist blandishments or bullying designed to persuade them otherwise. Membership of a group such as the Campaign Group might therefore be assumed to make one more likely to rebel, over and above the impact of ideology.

The numbers involved make testing this slightly difficult. The Group itself was fairly small (under 40 MPs); and they were (unfortunately) disproportionately unlikely to have responded to the BRS. We are therefore left with just ten cases where we have both behavioural data (that is, on rebellions) and attitudinal data (that is, from a survey). Given this, it would be unwise to carry out anything more than the most rudimentary of tests. But in the absence of anything better, rudimentary will just have to do. Of those who placed themselves in the most pro-spending category on the tax/spend scale (that is, at position 1 on the scale), and who were not in the Campaign Group, 33 per cent rebelled; of those with an identical ideological position but who were also in the Group, the figure was 100 per cent. Something similar happens for those in ideological categories 2 and 3. (No member of the Group placed themselves further to the right than position 3). Even holding ideology constant, therefore, members of the Campaign Group appear to be roughly two to three times more likely to have rebelled than those outside the Group.[57]

Sex. Throughout the Parliament Labour's women MPs – especially the newly elected women – came in for criticism for remaining loyal to the party's line. As we have seen (Chapter 2), these criticisms began with the lone parent revolt in December 1997, when just one of the newly elected women voted against the Government, and continued throughout the Parliament. At its most negative (and sexist), sex might be considered an significant variable because women might be said to be too frail to stand up to the pressures of Parliament, too delicate for the rough-and-tumble of Westminster politics. At its most positive (but probably still sexist), sex could affect behaviour because women are said to have a different approach to, or style of, politics – to 'do' politics differently – and this style might be one that eschews open rebellion in the division lobbies, seeing such acts as macho posturing. As one male MP said, conflating both arguments into one, 'If you are new, particularly if you are a woman, and culturally you prefer working things out consensually, [the whips] must be terrifying'.[58]

The problem with both of these arguments is that in the past there was little difference between the voting behaviour of women and male politicians. If anything, in previous Parliaments women MPs were more rebellious than their male counterparts. In every Parliament between 1979 and 1997, women MPs were (slightly) more likely to have rebelled than male MPs.[59] Yet in 1997 that pattern appeared to have reversed, with male MPs being noticeably more likely to have rebelled than women MPs. Twenty-six per cent of Labour women MPs voted against the party, compared to 43 per cent of Labour men.[60]

Table 6.4 Propensity to rebel, by sex and intake (per cent)

	Women	Men
Elected before 1997	63	53
Elected in 1997	17	34

The cause of this differential was not hard to find. Table 6.4 shows the percentage of men and women rebelling, broken down by year of entry. The new women were exactly half as likely as the new men to have rebelled and almost four times less likely than the more established women. Just as in previous Parliaments, the more established women MPs – admittedly a small group – were actually more likely to vote against the party line than the men (although the difference was not statistically significant).[61] So it was not that women MPs in general were any more cohesive than the men. Rather, it was just that the newly elected women were significantly less likely to have rebelled than other Labour MPs, and because there were more newly elected women MPs than longer serving ones, the overall figures were therefore skewed.

Because this was such a noticeable trend throughout the Parliament – and one that was so commented on – it is discussed in more detail in the next chapter. Here it is just sufficient to note that biological sex itself does not appear to be the crucial variable. Being a woman *per se* did not appear to make one any more or less likely to rebel; but being one of the 65 new women elected in 1997 – those that were rather bizarrely described as 'Blair's Babes' in the media – appears to have had a significant impact on their propensity to rebel.

Council experience. It is becoming increasingly common for MPs to have experience in local Government before arriving at Westminster. Over two-thirds of the new Labour MPs elected in 1997 had prior experience in local Government.[62] Several of the newly elected MPs thought that this was a cause of the small number of rebellions by Labour MPs: 'my view is that if you have been on a local Labour group in a council your loyalty to the party whip is installed'.[63] Robert Waller and Byron Criddle came to a similar conclusion: experience on local councils meant that Labour MPs 'had learnt the habits of group discipline and knew something of tight budgetary constraints'.[64] Whilst this is plausible, it is easy to construct an equally plausible argument that previous council experience will lead to less cohesive Parliamentary parties. As Tim Bale pointed out: 'These people [those with council experience] may, of course, be attuned to the new managerialism and the need for discipline, but they are also more used to having a say in the running of things – and used to putting over their views on the media – than ever before'.[65]

The latter appears to be the case. Experience in local Government is positively associated with voting against the party line. Of those Labour MPs with a council background, 43 per cent rebelled at least once. Of those without, the figure is 32 per cent.[66] Having a background in local Government, therefore, appears to make MPs less willing to stick to the party line.

Multivariate analysis

We have gone some way towards answering the question posed at the beginning of the chapter: why them? Why out of over 400 Labour MPs was it those 133 who rebelled? Rebellion is clearly not a random act. There is clear evidence linking it to *ideology* (with left-wing MPs more likely to rebel than right wing ones), to *roles* (with delegates less likely to rebel than trustees), to *self-interest* (with the young, the newly elected, and the ambitious being less likely to rebel), and to the *other individual characteristics* of the MPs (the less educated, those with council experience, those who are in the Campaign Group, and men, all appear more likely to rebel). Rebellious MPs are on average more left-wing, less party-orientated, older, longer serving, less ambitious, less educated, male, in the Campaign Group and/or with a background in local Government.

But many of these variables are not independent of one another. In the analysis above we have taken into account some of the most obvious interrelationships (such as that of age and experience, sex and intake, or Campaign Group membership and ideology), but it is likely that there are many other relationships. Some may be exaggerating the effect of individual variables upon an MP's propensity to rebel. Others may be masking interrelationships. In order to find out which variables are exerting an independent influence on an MP's propensity to rebel, we therefore need some multivariate analysis.

The dependent variable utilised here is simply rebelled (coded as 1)/not rebelled (0). The independent variables are analysed in two stages. First, data on the backgrounds or characteristics of MPs, where we have data on all MPs, is used. Then, second, data from the BRS, where we have data for a minority of MPs, is added. Our second model is thus more fully developed, but suffers from a lower number of cases. The first set of independent variables includes new MP (coded 1 for yes, 0 for no), age (at time of 1997 election), percentage constituency marginality, unexpected victor (coded 1 for yes, 0 for no), university educated (coded 1 for yes, 0 for no), Campaign Group membership (coded 1 for yes, 0 for no), sex (coded 1 for women, 0 for men), and council experience (coded 1 for yes, 0 for no). The second model then adds in data from the BRS: ideology (using the tax and spend scale, since of all the ideological variables that best measured propensity to rebel), delegate role (coded 1 for yes, 0 for no), ambition for Government office (coded 1 for yes, 0 for no), and, lastly, a variable measuring the difference between the MP's ideological position and their constituency party (where positive scores indicate that the party was to the right of the MP).

Table 6.5 shows the results. In the first model all of the independent variables point in the direction expected from the earlier analysis. New MPs, those that were university educated, and women, were all less likely to rebel, whilst older MPs, those in safer seats, those who won unexpectedly, Campaign Group members, or those who had a council background were all more likely to rebel. So none of the findings reported above appears to have been spurious. That said, once we control for other variables we find that only two variables – age and membership of the Campaign Group – remain statistically significant, although even this simple model – lacking as it does any attitudinal variables – can explain a full third of the variance in MPs' behaviour.

Table 6.5 Logistic regression, Labour rebellions, 1997–2001

	Model 1 B	Model 2 B
Ideology		
Tax/Spend	–	-0.79**
Roles		
Delegate	–	-12.86
Self-interest		
Ambition	–	-0.37
New	-0.14	-0.53
Age	0.06**	0.20***
Constituency party	–	-0.07
% Majority	0.01	-0.05
Unexpected victor	0.34	0.31
Other characteristics		
University educated	-0.53	-1.18
Campaign Group	3.44***	14.02
Sex	-0.56	-1.63
Council background	0.54	2.33**
Constant	–3.77***	–6.35*
% correctly predicted	69.4	86.2
Nagelkerke R^2	0.33	0.66
N	333	123

Note: * indicates p<0.05; ** p<0.01; *** p<0.001

When we add in the additional variables into model 2, nearly all of the variables used in model 1 continue to show the expected effects. So too do the variables just added: even once we control for other variables (and remember: this model is examining the impact of each variable, controlling for another 11) we find that being right wing, a delegate, or ambitious makes MPs less likely to rebel, as does having a constituency party which is more right-wing than the MP (although the size of this last effect is very small). The one exception is percentage marginality, which changes from having a small and insignificant positive relationship with propensity to rebel, to having a small and insignificant negative relationship.

As with model 1, many of the variables – although exerting the effect we would expect – do not do so in a statistically significant manner, but there are three exceptions. Even once we control for all other variables, an MP's ideological position – as measured on the BRS's tax and spending scale – exerts a significant relationship on his or her propensity to rebel. The more the MP is in favour of lowering taxes and spending (in crude terms, the more right wing) the less likely they are to have rebelled. And conversely, the more they are in favour of raising taxes and spending (more left-wing) the more likely they are to have rebelled. Similarly, age remains clearly significant: even once we control for everything else, the older an MP the more likely he or she was to have voted against the party line. We find that membership of the Campaign Group, significant in model 1, ceases to be significant in model 2 (perhaps not surprisingly: in model 1 it was the only variable measuring ideological position; but as soon as the tax/spend variable was introduced, it ceased to be significant), but that council experience becomes significant. The pattern noted in the earlier analysis – that having prior experience of representative Government makes an MP more likely to have rebelled – is confirmed, even once we control for everything else.

The most striking feature about this model, however, is that it performs extremely well in predicting MPs' behaviour. Adding in the survey-based data doubles the explanatory power of the models. Model 2 has an R^2 of 0.66, which means that these 11 variables are collectively able to explain some two-thirds of the variance between those who do or do not rebel. Given the limitations of survey data, and the (of necessity) crude nature of some of the variables, this is a very impressive figure.

Of course, all of the foregoing analysis has made no distinction between the extent to which an MP was rebellious. MPs like Iain Coleman or Oona King who vote against the party just once were classed as rebellious as Jeremy Corbyn or John McDonnell. Yet we might expect the more frequent rebels to be motivated by different factors to those that motivate the less rebellious. So Table 6.6 shows the results of a linear regression where, instead of rebelled/not rebelled, our dependent variable is the number of times that an MP has rebelled.

The first model – with no attitudinal data – finds the variables performing as would be expected. Some (such as percentage majority or sex) have almost microscopic effects but others are more important. Exactly the same two variables are statistically significant here as they were when using the dichotomous dependent variable (rebelled/not rebelled): age, and Campaign Group membership.

Table 6.6 Linear regression, Labour rebellions, 1997–2001

	Model 1 Beta	Model 2 Beta
Ideology		
Tax/Spend	–	-0.26**
Roles		
Delegate	–	-0.19**
Self-interest		
Ambition	–	-0.02
New	-0.05	-0.16
Age	0.16**	0.20*
Constituency party	–	-0.04
% Majority	0.00	-0.06
Unexpected victor	0.02	0.01
Other characteristics		
University educated	-0.03	0.00
Campaign Group	0.53***	0.48***
Sex	-0.00	0.00
Council background	0.06	0.14
R^2	0.37	0.54

Note: * indicates $p<0.05$; ** $p<0.01$; *** $p<0.001$

When we add in the attitudinal data, nearly all of the variables continue to exert an effect in the direction expected, with four doing so in a statistically significant way. That ideology, age and Campaign Group membership all affect rebellion will not be a surprise. But so too does the delegate variable, which it did not do in the earlier analysis. MPs who saw their role as not being to vote against the party line were (once we controlled for everything else) not especially less likely to have rebelled than other MPs. But when we examine the frequency of rebellion, their role conception does have an impact. In other words, once we control for everything else, having a delegate view of their role as an MP may not stop them rebelling once or twice, but it does appear to be a significant barrier on frequent rebellion.

There is one other noticeable difference from the earlier analysis: council membership does not exert a statistically significant influence on the number of rebellions (although its effect is still in the same direction: those with a council background cast more dissenting votes). So, once we control for everything else, having been a councillor may make an MP more likely to have rebelled once or twice, but it does not necessarily mean they will be especially frequent rebels. By contrast, ideology, age and Campaign Group membership affected both the propensity to rebel and the frequency of rebellion. MPs on the left, who are old, or in the Campaign Group are both more likely to have rebelled at all *and* more likely to have rebelled frequently.

Conclusion

We can therefore identify the characteristics and motivations that make MPs more or less rebellious. Rebellion results from a combination of ideology, roles, self-interest (age) and other characteristics (of which group membership is easily the most important). Of course, these variables alone do not explain all of the behaviour we see. At their best, these models explain around two-thirds of the variation in behaviour. There will be all sorts of other factors influencing behaviour, the sort of unmeasurable random noise that bedevils all empirical social science. The social and political characteristics of British MPs therefore do not explain everything. But they do explain an awful lot.

[1]   *Observer*, 27 September 1998.

[2]   See, for example, Keith Krehbiel, 'Where's the Party?', *British Journal of Political Science*, 23 (1993); or Keith Krehbiel, 'Paradoxes of Parties in Congress', *Legislative Studies Quarterly*, 14 (1999).

[3]   'Some people feel that Britain should do all it can to unite fully with the European Union. These people would put themselves in Box 1. Other people feel that Britain should do all it can to protect its independence from the European Union. These people . . . .'. At first glance, it appears that the more eurosceptic MPs (those who placed themselves at positions 7 to 10 on the scale) were more rebellious: but as the N shows, there were relatively few such MPs among the PLP, and so the percentages are somewhat misleading.

[4]   'Recently there has been discussion about women's rights. Some people feel that women should have an equal role with men in running business, industry and Government. These people would put themselves in Box 1. Other people feel that a women's role is in the home. These people . . . .'.

[5]   Anthony Heath, Geoffrey Evans and Jean Martin, 'The Measurement of Core Beliefs and Values: the Development of Balanced Socialist/Laissez-faire and Libertarian/Authoritarian scales', *British Journal of Political Science*, 24 (1994).

[6]   Restricting the analysis to just the permanent backbenchers produced both a larger difference (rebels: 10.7; loyalists: 13.2) and one that was even more significant.

[7]   D. D. Searing, *Westminster's World*, Cambridge, MA, Harvard, 1994. See also the special issue of the *Journal of Legislative Studies* on 'Members of Parliament in Western Europe: Roles and Behaviour', 3 (1997). No-one can hope to replicate Searing's study, with its 521 interviews, constituting 83 per cent of the Commons. Mind you, since it took him 20 years to publish his findings, that might not be a bad thing.

[8]   Interview, 7 March 2000.

[9]   Interview, 21 March 2000.

[10] Philip Norton, *Conservative Dissidents*, London, Temple Smith, 1978, p. 163.

[11] For just one example, see Thomas Saalfeld, 'Rational Choice Theory in Legislative Studies: Models of Politics Without Romanticism', *Journal of Legislative Studies*, 1 (1995).

[12] See J. Richard Piper, 'British Backbench Rebellion and Government Appointments, 1945–87', *Legislative Studies Quarterly*, 16 (1991).

[13] Philip Norton, *Dissension in the House of Commons, 1974–1979*, Oxford, Oxford University Press, 1980, p. 465.

[14] See Anthony King, 'The Chief Whip's Clothes', in D. Leonard and V. Herman (eds), *The Backbencher and Parliament*, London, Macmillan, 1972.

[15] 'Foreword', to Paul Flynn's *Commons Knowledge*, Bridgend, Seren, 1997, p. 9.

[16] He had rebelled just once, over the issue of student grants.

[17] That said, some simple multivariate analysis taking this into account found that whether an MP had rebelled or not remained highly statistically significant in explaining promotion, even once we controlled for age, sex, and self-defined ideological position.

[18] Interview, 30 March 2001.

[19] Interview, 14 March 2000.

[20] Interview, 21 March 2001.

[21] Interviews, 14 March 2000, 21 March 2000, 11 July 2000.

[22] Interview, 11 July 2000.

[23] As George Orwell once remarked: 'A pickpocket does not go to the races wearing a label 'pickpocket' on his coat lapel'. *The Collected Essays, Journalism and Letters of George Orwell*, Volume 4, Harmondsworth, Penguin, 1970, p. 227. However, for an attempt, see Edward Crowe, 'The Web of Authority: Party Loyalty and Social Control in the British House of Commons', *Legislative Studies Quarterly*, 11 (1986).

[24] Interview, 21 March 2001. Or, as Stephen Pound said at one point: 'I'm a cringing coward. I always vote the way they tell me to vote. I'm a balls-achingly, tooth-grindingly, butt-clenchingly loyal appa-ratchik' (*Observer*, 7 May 2000).

[25] Interview, 7 December 1999.

[26] Interview, 6 February 2001.

[27] Interview, 11 December 1998.

[28] Michael Rush. 'Career Patterns in British Politics', *Parliamentary Affairs*, 47 (1994), pp. 579–580.

[29] Andrew Rawnsley, 'First stirrings of Blair's rebels-in-waiting', *Observer*, 25 May 1997.

[30] See Pippa Norris and Joni Lovenduski, *Political Recruitment*, Cambridge, Cambridge University Press, 1988, chs. 2–5.

[31] See A. Dickson, 'MP's Re-adoption Conflicts: their Causes and Consequences', *Political Studies*, 23 (1975). For a fictional account of an MP's difficulties, see Wilfred Fienburgh, *No Love For Johnnie*, London, Hutchinson, 1959.

[32] Leon Epstein, 'British MPs and their Local Parties: the Suez Case', *American Political Science Review*, 54 (1960).

[33] See Stephen Ingle, *The British Party System*, Oxford, Basil Blackwell, 1987, p. 71; and Norton, *Conservative Dissidents*, ch. 7.

[34] Hugh Berrington, 'The Labour Left in Parliament, in D. Kavanagh (ed), *The Politics of the Labour Party*, London, Allen and Unwin, 1982; and Philip Williams, 'The Labour Party: the rise of the left', *West European Politics*, 6 (1983).

[35] Austin Ranney, *Pathways to Parliament*, New York, Macmillan, 1965, p. 281.

[36] 'Labour moves to rein in rebels', *The Times*, 27 May 1998.

[37] Interviews, 27 June 2000, 30 March 2001.

[38] Interviews, 21 March 2000, 27 June 2000.

[39] Interview, 28 March 2000.

[40] Interview, 27 June 2000.

[41] Interviews, 21 March 2000, 23 May 2000, 21 March 2001.

42 Interview, 13 February 2000.

43 After the lone parent revolt, for example, one Northern MP was clapped into her local party meeting and given a standing ovation (interview, 21 March 2000). At a London MP's reselection meeting, every time one of his revolts was read out, a cheer went up (interview, 27 June 2000). Nor was this a new phenomenon. Hugh Berrington's research discovered that this was also true in the 19th century, where Liberal radicals who dissented were more likely to be applauded by their caucuses than disciplined ('Partisanship and Dissidence in the Nineteenth Century House of Commons', *Parliamentary Affairs*, 21 (1967–8), p. 363).

44 'My local party was thrilled'; 'I've never got through reselection so easily'. Interview, 21 March 2001.

45 The crude results show that MPs whose constituency parties were to the right of them were more likely to rebel (and rebel more often), whilst those with CLPs to the left were less likely to rebel (and less often). But this counterintuitive finding – constituency parties to the right should reduce rebelliousness, those to the left should encourage it – is simply a result of the MPs' own ideological position, since MPs on the left of the ideological spectrum are more likely to have constituency parties to their right, and *vice versa*. Once we control for the MP's own ideological position, the effect of constituency parties disappears.

46 For the classic exposition of this argument, see D. R. Mayhew, *Congress: The Electoral Connection*, New Haven, CT, Yale University Press, 1974.

47 See, for example, Ivor Crewe, 'MPs and their Constituents in Britain: How Strong Are the Links?', in V. Bogdanor (ed), *Representatives of the People*, Aldershot, Gower, 1985, pp. 44–65, and the comments of MPs reported in Philip Cowley, 'Parliament and the Poll Tax: A Case Study in Parliamentary Pressure', *The Journal of Legislative Studies*, 1 (1995). For some slightly contradictory evidence, see C. Pattie, E. Fieldhouse, and R. J. Johnston, 'The Price of Conscience: The Electoral Correlates and Consequences of Free Votes and Rebellions in the British House of Commons 1987–1992', *British Journal of Political Science*, 24 (1994). MPs do, however, spend a considerable amount of time responding to their constituents in other ways. There is a mass of literature on the MP-constituent relationship. For just one example, see Philip Norton and David M. Wood, *Back From Westminster*, Lexington, KY, The University Press of Kentucky, 1993.

48 Interview, 6 February 2001.

49 Interview, 27 June 2000. Also, interview, 6 February 2001

50 This is one of the rare occasions when the data selected makes a difference to the findings. Using all Labour MPs produces no statistically significant differences (although even here the rebels sit for slightly safer seats than the loyalists). But once we exclude those Labour MPs who were in Government for either the entire Parliament or any part of it, the differences become larger and statistically significant.

51 If we exclude all MPs who were in Government at any point in the Parliament, then the difference becomes significant.

52 See, for example, David Marsh, 'Dr Norton's Parliament', *Public Administration Bulletin*, 41 (1983).

53 The difference becomes just slightly smaller and ceases to be statistically significant if we examine just those permanent backbenchers. But the effect remains the same: those without a university background were noticeably more likely to have rebelled.

54 Philip Cowley, Darren Darcy and Colin Mellors, 'New Labour's Parliamentarians', in S. Ludlam and M. J. Smith (eds), *New Labour in Government*, London, Macmillan, 2001, p. 98.

55 On the taxation/spending scale discussed above, members of the Campaign Group averaged 1.7, whilst the rest of the PLP averaged 4.0.

56 'Hard-left group attracts new MPs', *Sunday Times*, 21 September 1997. Similarly Waller and Criddle described the Group's members as 'the non-office seeking scorched-earthers of the Campaign Group'. Robert Waller and Byron Criddle, *The Almanac of British Politics*, Sixth Edition, London, Routledge, 1999, p. 471.

57 The same is true on all the other scales used in Figure 6.1 (with one small exception: all those who

placed themselves at position 1 on the nationalisation scale rebelled, whether they were in the Group or not).

58 Interview, 21 March 2001.

59 See Philip Cowley, 'The Absence of War? New Labour in Parliament', *British Elections and Parties Review*, 9 (1999).

60 The difference narrows, and ceases to be significant, if we exclude all MPs in Government at any point in the Parliament. But even here the difference is still 11 percentage points: 39 per cent of the women rebelled, compared to 50 per cent of the men.

61 When we excluded all MPs who were in Government at any time, it became significant.

62 Philip Cowley, Darren Darcy, Colin Mellors, Jon Neal and Mark Stuart, 'Mr Blair's Loyal Opposition? The Liberal Democrats in Parliament', *British Elections and Parties Review*, 10 (2000), p. 104.

63 Philip Cowley and Sarah Childs, 'Critical but not Rebellious? New Labour Women in the House of Commons', unpublished paper presented to the APSA Special Session on Women and Politics, San Francisco, CA, 29 August 2001. The quote is taken from interviews with Labour women MPs conducted by Sarah Childs, and used in Chapter 7. Also interviews, 13 June 2000, 23 May 2000.

64 Waller and Criddle, *The Almanac of British Politics*, xxi. Andrew Rawnsley came to a similar conclusion ('First stirrings of Blair's rebels-in-waiting').

65 Tim Bale, 'Managing the Party and the Trade Unions', in B. Brivati and T. Bale (eds), *New Labour in Power*, London, Routledge, 1997, p. 171.

66 The finding differs slightly depending on what dataset is used. The difference between the two groups remains the same size – 11 percentage points – whatever set is used, but when we exclude all those MPs who were in Government at any point during the Parliament the difference ceases to be statistically significant.

7. An Uncritical Critical Mass?

New Labour's Women MPs

(with Sarah Childs)[1]

If the most striking feature of the 1997 Labour intake was the presence of so many women, then the most striking feature of the rebellions in that Parliament appeared to be the lack of these women from amongst the ranks of the rebels. The media, which criticised all Labour MPs for their cohesion, reserved special venom for the newly elected women. As Anne Perkins wrote, the women suffered 'derision as centrally-programmed automatons . . . being reviled for failing to rebel, condemned as careerists – in short, one great fuschia-suited failure'. She continued:

> [I]t was their failure to fight collectively, in particular to unite against the lone parent benefit cuts that caused such rumpus in late 97, that earned them the reputation of betraying women who needed them for the sake of their own political futures. Most damaging, it was a view shared by more experienced women colleagues.[2]

One long-serving Labour women MP found the new intake 'very depressing' – 'I don't know what they believe in' – and saw their behaviour as a 'betrayal' of all-women shortlists (AWS), the system of sex quotas used by Labour in order to raise the number of women candidates selected in winnable seats.[3] A second thought that the new women MPs included 'a lot of clones'.[4] A third said that she did not know why the women had come to Parliament.[5] One male Labour MP, Brian Sedgemore, famously compared them to the Stepford Wives, 'those female new Labour MPs who've had the chip inserted into their brain to keep them on-message and who collectively put down women and children in the vote on lone parent benefits'.[6] In a twist on the concept of a 'critical mass' (the idea that once the number of women in a Parliament reached a certain point the institution will be changed) another male Labour MP described the newly elected women as an 'uncritical mass'.[7]

Yet many of the women MPs themselves – and many of their male colleagues – pointed to other, often less critical, explanations for the differential rates of cohesion. Several even doubted it was true that the newly elected women were less likely to rebel. They argued that the media only picked up on those occasions when this was true and ignored those when it was not, in an attempt to denigrate the women MPs ('there are some rebellions they haven't even spotted 'cause I think they are so locked into this Blair's babes thing [that] some of them can't even think straight if they tried now').[8] Moreover, several argued that even if there were fewer women in any rebellion that was merely because there were fewer women in general ('I'm not sure that's true statistically'; 'there are just as many nodding . . . male dogs on Government benches . . . in fact, actually, percentage-wise more, because there are more of them than women').[9]

This chapter therefore attempts to answer two questions. First, were the newly elected women MPs in fact less rebellious than their colleagues? And second, if it was true, how can we explain it?

New Labour women and the propensity to rebel

In total, as was shown in Chapter 5, there were 96 separate rebellions by Labour MPs in the 1997 Parliament, with 19 issues (broadly defined) seeing individual rebellions consisting of at least ten MPs. These 19 rebellions are listed in Table 7.1, together with the total number of MPs to have voted against the Government. The two right-hand columns of the table show the number of newly elected women who rebelled on each issue, together with that figure as a percentage of the total number of rebels.

Table 7.1 New Labour women's participation in large Labour rebellions, 1997–2001

Issue	Total number of rebels	New women rebels	As % of total number of rebels
Access to Justice Bill	21	0	0
Child Support, Pensions & Social Security Bill	41	2	5
Competition Bill	25	0	0

cont'd

Issue	Total number of rebels	New women rebels	As % of total number of rebels
Criminal Justice (Mode of Trial) Bill	37	2	5
Criminal Justice (Terrorism and Conspiracy) Bill	37	2	5
Defence White Paper	10	0	0
Draft Terrorism Bill	12	1	8
Football (Disorder) Bill	11	0	0
Freedom of Information Bill	41	3	7
House of Lords Bill	35	2	6
Immigration and Asylum Bill	17	0	0
Immigration appeals	17	2	12
Iraq	22	0	0
Kosovo	13	0	0
Social Security Bill	47	1	2
Teaching and Higher Education Bill	34	1	3
Terrorism Bill	14	1	7
Transport Bill	65	7	11
Welfare Reform and Pensions Bill	74	6	8

Note: In cases where there were multiple revolts on an issue, the total number to have rebelled may be larger than the largest single revolt on that issue.

This last figure varies from the seven issues that saw no newly elected women rebel to the revolt over the immigration appeals process on 20 November 2000, when 12 per cent of the rebels were newly elected women. Yet even at its peak, this percentage is below what might be expected. Newly elected women constituted 16 per cent of the PLP. Not one of the rebellions consisted of 16 per cent newly elected women.[10]

In total, taking all 96 revolts together, just 11 newly elected women Labour MPs voted against their party whip. That constitutes 17 per cent of the 65 newly elected Labour women and compares to a figure of 44 per cent for the rest of the PLP, a difference that is statistically significant.

Moreover, even when they did rebel, the newly elected women did not rebel frequently. Table 7.2 lists the 11 newly elected women who voted against their whips. The most rebellious were Ann Cryer and Betty Williams, both of whom voted against their whips on 16 occasions. Whilst considerable when compared to other newly elected women, 16 dissenting votes makes Cryer and Williams only the (joint) 30th most rebellious Labour MPs. In total, the new women who voted against the party line did so on an average of six occasions. The comparable figure for the rest of the PLP is 11.

Table 7.2 The 11 'rebellious' new Labour women, 1997–2001

Name	Number of dissenting votes
Ann Cryer	16
Betty Williams	16
Julie Morgan	14
Jenny Jones	6
Eileen Gordon	5
Christine McCafferty	4
Janet Dean	3
Christine Butler	2
Tess Kingham	2
Oona King	1
Geraldine Smith	1

This difference became noticed after the first major rebellion of the Parliament, during the Social Security Bill, when 47 Labour MPs voted against the reduction in lone parent benefit (along with a considerable number of deliberate abstentions). Of the 47 rebels, just one (Ann Cryer) was a newly elected woman. Indeed, in the whole of the first session of the Parliament just two of the newly elected women MPs (three per cent) voted against their whips (the other being Christine Butler), compared to 27 per cent of the rest of the PLP.[11] Other Labour MPs were, then, *nine* times more likely to have rebelled than were the newly elected women. As the number of rebellions increased, the difference between the newly elected women and the rest of the PLP did narrow – from nine times after the first session, to a three-fold difference after the second – but the differences did not disappear over time. Similarly, as the Parliament progressed, the percentage of new women in any rebellion increased – rising from a high of five per cent in the first session, to eight per cent in the second, to 12 per cent in the third – but even this new high remained lower than the proportion in the PLP as a whole.

The newly elected women were, then, less than half as likely to rebel against the party whip as the rest of the PLP; and even those who did rebel did so around half as often. There was therefore a genuine difference in legislative behaviour between the newly elected women and the rest of the PLP, rather than one born of partial data or (deliberately?) crude arithmetic.

Explaining away the difference

The general assessment of the newly elected Labour women appeared to be that they were too spineless to rebel, and simply not up to the job; if they couldn't stand the heat, they should 'get out of the kitchen', a jibe to which one replied: 'New Labour, New Kitchen'.[12] But there are a wide range of other explanations for this differential cohesion. Broadly speaking, these consist of two different types. The first group of explanations argue that any apparent differences between the new women and the rest of the PLP are spurious, that any differences are in fact caused by the type of MPs under examination, rather than being genuine differences between the new women and the rest of the PLP. And that once we control for other characteristics or factors then any apparent differences will disappear. As we saw in Chapter 6, rebellion was not a random act: certain characteristics made MPs more or less likely to rebel. If the women first elected in 1997 had more (or less) of the characteristics, then we should not be surprised if they were more (or less) rebellious. By contrast, the second group of explanations do not deny that a difference existed, but explain it – if not celebrate it – by highlighting the way that women MPs behave. We start by examining the attempts to explain away the difference, beginning with the three most obvious explanations: sex, newness, and the role of AWS.

Sex. The most obvious explanation for the cohesion of the newly elected women MPs was that it resulted from nothing more than the fact that they were women. Many Labour women MPs – along with many of their male colleagues – argued that the apparent differences in the behaviour of the newly elected women were in effect sex differences. Women, they argued, have a different political style to men – they 'do' politics differently – and this manifests itself in different political behaviour.[13]

But as was clear from Chapter 6, there are some obvious empirical problems with this argument. It is not the case that women MPs have been more cohesive than male MPs in previous Parliaments. If anything, in the past, women Members have been slightly more rebellious than their male counterparts. And as Chapter 6 also demonstrated, the longer-serving Labour women in the 1997 Parliament were in fact *more* rebellious than their longer-serving male colleagues. Some 63 per cent of the longer-serving women rebelled compared to just 17 per cent of those elected in 1997.[14]

This suggests that biological sex can be rejected as an explanation for the differential rate of cohesion. Any explanation must look at the newly elected women MPs in particular rather than at women *qua* women. This may be an occasion when the distinction between sex and gender is important, a point to which we return below.

New intake. We can also quickly reject the other obvious explanation for the difference: that the new women are behaving differently simply because they are new MPs. This explanation trips over almost identical empirical hurdles to the argument (made above) about biological sex. If it was valid, then we would expect the new male MPs to be similarly less likely to rebel.

Whilst it is true (as we saw in Chapter 6) that new MPs are less likely to have rebelled than other MPs (although once we controlled for all other variables, any differences ceased to be significant), there was still a clear difference between the newly elected women and their male peers. As Table 6.4 showed, some 17 per cent of the newly elected women had rebelled, compared to 34 per cent of the new men. So once we control for the cohort of entry the difference narrows somewhat, but it does not go away. The new women were still half as likely to have rebelled as the new men, a statistically significant difference in behaviour.[15]

All-women shortlists. One of the reasons – perhaps *the* reason – for the high number of Labour women elected in 1997 was the use by the Labour Party of AWS.[16] It has been argued by some that this process brought into Parliament MPs who, because they had not been subject to the full rigours of an open competition, were somehow not up to the job.[17] For example, Ann Widdecombe complained of the 'docility and absence of ability' displayed by many of the new women MPs. She linked this directly to the use of AWS, arguing that:

> Serious politicians arrive in the House already battle-hardened . . . Blair's Babes have arrived with starry eyes and a pager, shielded by positive discrimination from any real competition. They nod in unison behind the front bench . . . Some of the dear little souls have even whinged that Madam Speaker is too hard on them and indeed has caused more than one to burst into tears. Can anyone imagine Bessie Braddock, Barbara Castle or Margaret Thatcher dissolving at a ticking off from the Speaker?[18]

There is, however, an obvious empirical problem with this argument: there was no difference in behaviour between those women selected on AWS and those selected on 'open' shortlists. Of those selected on open lists, five (17 per cent) broke ranks; the figure for those selected on AWS is six (also 17 per cent).

Moreover, the three most rebellious of the new women – Ann Cryer, Betty Williams and Julie Morgan – were all selected on AWS.

Whatever the advantages or disadvantages of AWS, then, there is little evidence that it brought into Parliament less rebellious MPs. With a few exceptions, the newly elected women MPs were not rebelling, no matter how they were selected.

Other explanations. As well as these three obvious (if ultimately unconvincing) explanations for the differences, many of the new Labour women attempted to explain away the differences in their behaviour by reference to other socio-economic or political characteristics. For example, one argued that the reason they were not rebelling was *ideological*: it 'may be because we happen to agree with the policies and understand the policies'.[19] (It was for this reason that one male Labour MP described the new women MPs as 'true believers').[20] Others explained it with reference to their *ambition*: 'Ambitious' politicians have to vote with the Government. As one said: 'younger women who want to make a career out of this . . . know . . . [that] in the long term they will not make their voice heard at the level which is needed unless they do incorporate'.[21] She added that she thought they had 'been quite sensible really'.[22] Another put it in terms of their age:

> Some of the men who were selected to fight safe seats are people who are in their late fifties who, you know, hold some pretty traditional views, and . . . [it's those] men who tend to vote against the Government, whereas the newly elected women in many cases are, you know, going to be here for a much longer period of time.[23]

Several others thought the differences resulted from the differing *electoral situations* of the women MPs ('it may be because we are in more marginal seats'; 'most of us come from key seats, they are marginal seats and to be frank we are not stupid').[24] As another put it: 'I think if you compared the men in target marginal seats who are newly elected with the women in target marginal seats who are newly elected I think you'd find a . . . real similarity in their voting experiences'.[25] Another MP thought the difference lay in the *previous political history* of the MPs. 'It would be interesting to see how many of us came from local council backgrounds because my view is that if you have been on a local Labour group in a council your loyalty to the party whip is instilled'.[26]

There are two potential empirical problems with many of these suggestions and with other attempts to explain away the differences between the new women and other MPs. The first is that we know from earlier analysis that not all of these variables exert a strong or necessarily significant effect on the propensity to rebel; and, even if they do, they may do so in a different direction to that suggested by the MPs. For example, as was shown in Chapter 6, the effect of marginality on an MP's propensity to rebel is limited once we control for the MPs' intake cohort. And experience on a local council does not help to instil loyalty to the party whip. Quite the reverse: experience on a local council appears to make MPs more likely to rebel.

The second potential problem is that for any one of these factors to explain the differential behaviour we also need to show that the newly elected women have more (or less) of this factor than other MPs. For example, if the age of the women MPs is a valid explanation, it is not enough for an MP's age to influence their behaviour (as it does), we also need to show that the newly elected women are younger than some comparison group. Since we showed (above) that the differences between the new men and new women are less dramatic (though still clear) than between the new women and the rest of the PLP, in what follows we compare the new women with the new men.

We examine whether each of the remaining variables analysed in Chapter 6 helps explain the differential loyalty displayed by the new women. Just as in the last chapter, we start with their ideological attitudes.

Ideology and beliefs. It could be, for example, that the new women were noticeably more 'Blairite' than their colleagues. If they were, then it should not be surprising that they did not rebel. If they agree, why should they rebel? Table 7.3 shows the responses to the basic scalar questions in the BRS, split between the new women and the new men.

Table 7.3 New Labour MPs' political attitudes (mean scores), by sex

	New women	New men	Difference
Left/Right	3.97	3.65	+0.32
Employment/Prices	2.23	2.97	-0.74
Taxes/Spending	4.19	3.98	+0.21
Nationalise/Privatise	5.26	4.97	+0.29
Integrate with EU/remain independent	3.87	3.97	-0.10
Women equal/in Home	1.00	1.23	-0.23

Note: The significance of the difference is tested by ANOVA: * 0.05; **0.01. The difference is the per cent of new women minus per cent new men.

As Table 7.3 shows, there were few noticeable differences between the newly elected women and their male colleagues. On three of the scales, the women were more to the right (although not by much). On the other three they were more to the left (although again not by much).[27] But none of these differences was of a scale sufficient to be statistically significant. The only difference that approached statistical significance was the question on the Government's economic priorities (jobs/prices), where the new women were slightly more to the left than their male peers.[28]

Similarly, if we look at their scores on the socialist/laissez faire scale, or the libertarian/authoritarian scale, we find few significant differences. On the two overall scale scores there are no significant differences between the new men and the new women.[29] Of the 12 questions that make up the scales, there were differences on just two. The new women were somewhat less tolerant of homosexuality than the new men and (more broadly) less tolerant of those with unconventional life styles (with in both cases the difference being statistically significant).[30] But Chapter 6 found the libertarian/authoritarian scale a very poor predictor of voting behaviour. On the variables that better explained voting – such as the tax/spend scale or the socialist/laissez-faire scale – there are no noticeable differences.

There is thus little evidence that the new women constituted a Blairite praetorian guard within the PLP. It is difficult to argue that the new Labour women constitute an ideologically distinct grouping within the PLP, yet alone 'true believers' for Blairism.

Roles. We find more mixed evidence when we look at political roles. Table 7.4 shows the responses to the questions about party discipline contained in the BRS.

Table 7.4 Views on party discipline, by sex

	New women	New men	Difference
MPs should vote with their party, regardless of their conscience	14	20	–6
MPs should vote with their party, regardless of the national interest	7	9	–2

Note: The figures show the proportion that agree, or agree strongly, with each of the statements. The difference is the percentage of new women minus the percentage of new men.

If anything, the new women claim to be more willing to vote against the party line than the new men (although the differences are not statistically significant). The SPG survey produced slightly different results. While there was almost no difference in the proportion of new men and new women who thought that representing the party was their most important task (16 per cent of women, compared to 14 per cent of men), there was a slightly larger difference in the proportions who said that they relied on the party whips when voting. A majority of the new women (57 per cent) said that they relied on the party whips 'nearly always' when voting, compared to 46 per cent of the new men.

Ambition. The BRS also revealed almost no difference between the future ambitions of the new women and those of the new men. Some 61 per cent of the new women wanted to be a Government minister in ten years' times, compared to 64 per cent of the new men, a difference that was not statistically significant. Differing levels of ambition in themselves do not, therefore, appear to be behind the differing levels of cohesion.

Age. We saw clearly in Chapter 6 how age was an excellent indicator of an MP's propensity to rebel. This relationship is strikingly clear from Table 7.5, which shows the ages (when elected) of the 11 rebellious new Labour women, along with the number of times they rebelled.

Table 7.5 'Rebellious' new Labour women and age

Name	Number of dissenting votes	Age when elected
Ann Cryer	16	57
Betty Williams	16	52
Julie Morgan	14	52
Jenny Jones	6	49
Eileen Gordon	5	50
Christine McCafferty	4	51
Janet Dean	3	48
Christine Butler	2	53
Tess Kingham	2	33
Oona King	1	29
Geraldine Smith	1	35

All but three of the 11 rebels are older than the average age of women of the 1997 intake (43) – and these three are near the bottom of the league table of rebels (having cast just four dissenting votes between them). Of the top six rebels, all but one is aged 50 or more (with the one who is not, Jenny Jones, aged 49 when elected).

Yet although this is interesting as an explanation for rebellion, it appears to do little to explain the differential rates of rebellion between new women and the new men because there is no evidence that the new women are especially young. The average age of a woman MP elected for the first time in 1997 was 43.2 years, almost identical to the average for a new male MP (43.5).[31] So, although age is important when explaining the propensity to rebel in general, it does not appear to be a plausible explanation of why the new women are not rebelling when compared to the new men.

Local party. Given that we saw in the last chapter that local parties exerted almost no influence on an MP's propensity to rebel, we would be surprised if we found sizeable differences between the new men and the new women. And there is no surprise. On average new male MPs and new women MPs faced almost identical constituency parties. The new men had constituency parties that were, on average, 0.2 points to the left of them on the ideological scale. The new women also average a difference of 0.2, also on the left.

Type of contest and marginality. The scale of Labour's victory brought in many MPs who were not expected to win their seats. Importantly, these people were disproportionately likely to be unlikely lads rather than lasses, because AWS applied only to key (winnable) and inheritor seats (where the incumbent MP was standing down). Thus most of the newly elected women came from these seats, and just 15 per cent of the MPs elected in the unexpected gains were women. In Chapter 6 we saw that these unlikely victors were slightly more likely to have rebelled – although the differences were neither huge nor statistically significant. This therefore might be a plausible explanation for a slightly lower level of rebellion amongst the new women.

Less plausible, however, is the effect of marginality *per se*, cited above by several of the new women as an explanation for their cohesion. For a start, we saw in the last chapter that once we controlled for the intake cohort the marginality of MPs has very little impact on propensity to rebel. Moreover, because of the effect of the unexpected gains the new women did not sit in the most marginal seats. The average marginality of a newly elected woman MP in 1997 was 19 per cent. That of a newly elected man was 17 per cent. So while the newly elected women MPs did sit for more marginal seats than the rest of the PLP that was because they were newly elected, rather than because they were women, and compared to the male MPs of the new intake – who were twice as likely to rebel – they actually sat for slightly safer seats. It seems difficult therefore to attribute much significance to the marginality of their constituencies as a cause of their cohesion.

Education. There is also little evidence that the answer lies in their educational backgrounds. Some 71 per cent of the new women had been educated at university, compared to 72 per cent of the new men.

Group membership. We can also swiftly reject membership of the Campaign Group. Three women from the 1997 intake joined the Campaign Group (five per cent of the women elected in 1997), compared to six men (also five per cent).[32]

Previous political history. A rare piece of evidence demonstrating some difference comes with the final variable, when we examine the previous political history of the MPs. The new women MPs were disproportionately likely *not* to have been local councillors. Almost three-quarters of the newly elected men (74 per cent) had been councillors, compared to exactly two-thirds of the new women (although this difference is not statistically significant). And since, as we saw in Chapter 6, experience in local Government appears to make MPs more rebellious, this is at least a plausible explanation for the different rates of cohesion.

Multivariate analysis

There appears therefore to be little evidence to support most of the attempts to explain away the difference between the new women and the new men. Only two of the variables examined point in a consistent direction. The unexpected victors (who were more likely to rebel) were disproportionately men. And MPs with a background in local Government (who are more likely to rebel) were also disproportionately men. Other evidence is more mixed – such as with political roles – or appears to show no effect at all.

But just as in the last chapter, it is possible that some of the variables discussed above may have an additive impact, or may be masking other effects, and so we again need to perform some multivariate analysis. Our dependent variable is rebelled (1)/not rebelled (0). The independent variables are identical to those used in Chapter 6, except that because the analysis is limited to just new MPs, there is no variable indicating newness. And, as before, we enter data in two stages: first data where we have information on all MPs, and then, second, attitudinal data from the BRS, where we have data from just a minority of MPs. The second model is more fully developed, but suffers from a lower number of cases.

The results are shown in Table 7.6. The first model – using data on all MPs – finds three variables exerting a statistically significant impact on the propensity to rebel: age, university education, and sex. Of these, the third is the most important for our purposes here, because it means that even once we control for everything else, and when examining just the new MPs, sex remains a significant variable. By contrast, a similar logistic regression (not reported here in full for reasons of space) concentrating on just the longer-serving MPs does not find sex to be significant. The presence of sex as a significant independent variable amongst the new MPs, and its absence from the older MPs, confirms that what we have with the new women is not a sex effect, but something specific to that group of women MPs.

Table 7.6 Logistic regression, Labour rebellions, new MPs, 1997–2001

	Model 1 B	Model 2 B
Ideology		
Tax/Spend	-	-0.90*
Roles		
Delegate	-	-10.84
Self-interest		
Ambition	-	-0.54
Age	0.12***	0.21**
Constituency party	-	0.31
% majority	-0.01	-0.10
Unexpected victor	-0.16	-0.10
Other characteristics		
University educated	-0.96*	-1.37
Campaign Group	10.26	16.85
Sex	−1.29**	-2.33
Council background	0.83	3.99
Constant	−5.96***	-7.73
% correctly predicted	78.0	86.4
Nagelkerke R^2	0.40	0.66
N	182	81

Note: * indicates p<0.05; ** p<0.01; *** p<0.001

When we introduce the attitudinal data (Model 2), however, only two variables appear to remain statistically significant: ideology and age. Sex continues to exert an influence on the propensity to rebel, with women MPs being less likely to have rebelled, but the difference is no longer large enough (or consistent enough) to be statistically significant. Yet this model, because it is examining only the new MPs, and of the new MPs only those where there is attitudinal data from the BRS, is based on just 81 cases in total. The smaller the number of cases, *ceteris paribus*, the larger any differences need to be before they are significant. And even here, sex only just fails to be statistically significant.[33] What appears to be happening is that, once we control for everything else that might be explaining the differences, sex still appears to exert an influence on the propensity to rebel; even controlling for everything else, the women from the 1997 intake were less likely to rebel than their male peers. The difference is not large enough (or consistent enough) to be statistically significant (that is, large enough for there not to be the possibility that it was created by chance) but it still exists.

This finding does, though, help put some of the claims about the behaviour of the newly elected women MPs into perspective. The initial large difference in behaviour between the newly elected women and the rest of the PLP becomes smaller (but still statistically significant) once we compare the new women with the new men. It becomes smaller still (and no longer statistically significant) once we control for the women's other characteristics. There *is* still a difference between the newly elected women and the newly elected men, but it is a difference of degree, not direction. But attempts to explain that difference away completely remain unconvincing.

Women's style of politics

However, the majority of the women MPs themselves do not seek to explain this difference away. Rather, they claim it is part of a different, women's, style of political behaviour.

The contention that women practice politics in a different, feminized, way to men is a long-standing one. Women are said to 'introduce a kinder, gentler politics', one that is 'characterized by cooperation rather than conflict, collaboration rather than hierarchy, honesty rather than sleaze'.[34] The one explanation for the new women's loyalty that receives the greatest support from the women MPs – being mentioned by more than half – is precisely this: that women MPs employ a different style of politics.[35]

Importantly, this style of politics was perceived by many of the women to be both distinct from, and more effective than, a style of politics involving overt rebellion, the latter being perceived as reflecting a masculine mode of politics more concerned with gesture politics than effecting change. (Several of the women also thought that loyalty itself was a female attribute).[36] Many of the newly elected women were also forthright in their questioning of the assumption that voting with the Government was a negative activity. As one said: 'I don't actually think that loyal women or loyal MP actually equals bad'.[37]

Yet we have already demonstrated that a simple sex difference as an explanation of the women's loyalty does not stand up to empirical analysis. However, some of the newly elected women believed that this style of politics was not shared by all women MPs, rather that some of the more established women MPs practised what they saw as a 'masculine' style of politics.[38] Before 1997, this argument goes, when the number of women MPs was significantly lower, women MPs had to 'outmacho the men' (they had had to be 'hard and tough [and] played the game like one of the boys') but with the increase in number comes a 'culture of confidence' that allows women MPs to behave in a feminized way.[39] One senior male MP put it in the following terms, in the past the women MPs who were elected were 'male women' or 'atypical women' but now they were 'conventional women'.[40] Another put it more bluntly: the previous women MPs were 'odd'.[41] The difference, therefore, is one of gender, not sex.[42]

Rather than rebelling, the new Labour women MPs claim to operate 'behind the scenes': 'we've probably tend[ed] to use the tools that are available to us behind the scenes as a first course of action . . . I have always found it possible to use the avenues that are open behind the scenes'.[43] They consider that criticism can be communicated to Government in many different ways through lobbying, private conversations and holding meetings with ministers and through the PLP's backbench groups.[44] One woman MP discussed her loyalty in analogous terms to the family: 'Sometimes I don't like one or two things my . . . [children] do . . . privately I will give them all sorts of grief about it . . . publicly I support them wholeheartedly'.[45] Whilst it is hard to document such behind the scenes activities, the women MPs themselves are convinced that it is important:

[A] lot of working behind the scenes goes on and I think [that] is not appreciated, anyone who thinks that . . . all the Labour women are too loyal, if I can put it that way, has not been at meetings with say the Home Secretary over hunting, with the Trade and Industry Secretary over employment rights'.[46]

Many of the women also rejected the idea that rebelling was an effective strategy to achieve reform.

> If you are a sort of macho 'oh I'm going to vote against the Government' . . . I don't [think] that your influence is even as much as the people that are saying 'look Jack, this is . . . not working . . . you don't really get anywhere [by] being a rebel . . . people [who] vote against the Government [are] . . . not really doing anything other than making a gesture.[47]

Or, as Fiona Mactaggart argued in a Fabian pamphlet:

> Public rebellion is not generally a reliable indicator of the ability of a Member of Parliament to achieve change, but you can count votes. Voting against your own party is one way to claim political virility and independence, but it doesn't get results unless the total number actually changes the legislation.[48]

Moreover, as Phyllis Starkey pointed out, much of the media criticism was based on the premise that 'only MPs who criticise the Government in public are influencing Labour's policies', and that 'constructive debate does not make for good copy'.[49]

Some of the women argued that supporting the Government in the lobby has the effect of ensuring that when they raise criticisms with ministers they are more likely to be listened and responded to: 'If those of us who genuinely vote with the Government come along and say 'this has got to stop' you know people listen . . . '.[50] She then added, discussing specifically the cut in lone parent benefit:

> I don't think that any Government would have reversed it [the lone parent cut] if there had been a mass rebellion . . . if they'd won it by a handful of votes, I don't think then a few months later they would have turned it around . . .

Another MP agreed:

> I think particularly on that [lone parent] Bill and on others there were women who have abstained or voted with the Government . . . [they felt] we have been loyal, so what are you going to do about it? . . . we didn't vote against you we voted for you [pause] . . . we should have something in return, what are you going to do?[51]

In themselves, the newly elected Labour women MPs' claims about their loyalty are revealing, for they show that many of the women MPs have thought through, and can defend, their decision to remain loyal to their party. Their loyalty, therefore appears to result not from being Stepford Wives or spineless, but – at least for more than half of them – from a different style of politics. It also reflects a calculating and instrumental approach to cohesion and rebellion, rather than the unthinking one portrayed in the media.

Plausible as this is, though, we are faced with a problem: for this to explain the behavioural difference between the newly elected women and the rest of the PLP, we need to show that the new women were *more likely* to practice this style of politics than other MPs. As will become clear in the next two chapters, interviews with male Labour MPs and with the longer-serving women often reveal almost identical explanations for their loyalty. They too work behind the scenes. They too take problems to ministers. They too often have a calculating and instrumental approach to cohesion and rebellion. The idea that the newly elected women are more likely to use, or are more effective at using, such behind-the-scenes avenues is anyway a disputed one. One of the more established women MPs, for example – once she had stopped laughing – described the idea that women were better at behind-the-scenes pressure as 'absolute nonsense' and 'an excuse'.[52] Even one of the newly elected women argued that such behind the scenes contacts were less useful than they might appear:

> I do feel sometimes [that] people . . . who have not been in what I call the hard edge of politics before think that because they say something and they appeared to be listened to [that] that's a very big deal and actually I think it makes them think they've been listened to but really [they] have minimal impact . . . I'm probably over cynical.[53]

Conclusion

The lack of rebellions by the newly elected women MPs was one of the most striking features of the 1997 Parliament and one that attracted much criticism. As this chapter has shown, the high levels of cohesion are not merely the product of biased, misogynistic or inaccurate media reporting (although there was undoubtedly more than a little of this). Rather there was a difference between the voting of the newly elected women and the rest of the PLP.

Moreover, many of the explanations that seek to explain away this difference do not stand up to empirical verification. Once we control for all of the variables, we find that the difference between the new men and the new women fails to remain statistically significant, but only just (at the conventional measurement of $p < 0.05$), even with a very small sample size. Some difference still remains.

We are left with three possible explanations. The first is that put forward by most of the women's critics: that there was, for some reason, something feeble or second rate about this particular batch of women MPs that was responsible for their differential rate of rebellion. It is not an argument that either of the authors of this chapter feel is convincing but there is almost no way of definitively disproving these sort of claims.

The second explanation is that it is possible to explain the difference away, but that this analysis has failed to do so, either (i) because it has failed to include variables that are responsible for the difference; or because (ii) the data employed are not sufficiently fine to spot the differences between the different groups. Both are possibilities.

For example, it could conceivably be that despite being similarly ambitious, the new women perceive the costs of rebelling to be greater than do the men. This argument was contained in Douglas Hurd's latest novel (of all places), in an argument between Roger Courtauld, a former Conservative Home Secretary, and Sarah Tunstall, another senior Conservative politician:

> 'You don't understand about women in politics.'
>
> 'Don't change the subject, Sarah.'
>
> 'It is the subject. Or part of it, as it concerns me.'
>
> 'What do you mean?'
>
> She tidied her hair with one hand. 'There are still too few of us. We still feel it's a world run by men, under the rules they made. Loyalty to the party is one of them.'
>
> 'Rules are there to be broken, when necessary.'
>
> 'That's a silly remark, as you know. Frivolous, masculine. Women feel they must hold on to the rules even more tightly because they did not make them. Men can fool about with rebellion and disloyalty. We women can't afford that.'[54]

Of course, as a general explanation for cohesion, this argument falls down because women MPs in general clearly have not felt so constrained, having been just as likely to 'fool about' with rebellion as much as, if not more than, the next man. But if for some reason this particular batch of women had a higher than normal perception of the cost of disloyalty, then this could be (part of) the explanation for their behaviour. Unfortunately we have no way of knowing if this is the case or if other variables not examined here could explain the difference. Given what data is available, some difference still remains.

The dominant explanation put forward by the new women themselves is that they 'do' politics differently. The problem is that it is extremely hard – if not impossible – ever to test this empirically. It is at best a plausible argument, one that awaits further research and one that is far more positive to the newly elected women than the standard media line that they are just too feeble to stand up to the nasty whips. Given that many of the other explanations appear to have little validity, it will continue to be used by many of the newly elected women and their supporters, whilst their detractors will dismiss it as wishful thinking.

[1] In addition to the data used for the rest of this book, this chapter also draws upon in-depth interviews with 23 of 65 newly elected Labour women MPs conducted in the summer of 2000 by Sarah Childs. As with the other interviews for this book, anonymity was guaranteed to all interviewees.

[2] Anne Perkins, 'Women: So far, so what?', *Guardian*, 29 April 1999.

[3] Interview, 21 March 2000.

[4] Interview, 4 July 2000.

[5] Interview, 28 March 2000.

[6] *The Times*, 7 February 1998, reporting a speech of Sedgemore's the previous day. The paper also reported Ann Widdecombe's claim that the comparison was an insult to the Stepford Wives.

[7] Interview, 11 December 1998. For the concept of critical mass see, for example, D. Dahlerup 'From a Small to a Large Minority: Women in Scandinavian Politics', *Scandinavian Political Studies*, 11 (1988); or D. T. Studlar, and I. McAllister 'Does a Critical Mass Exist? A Comparative Analysis of Women's Legislative Representation Since 1950', forthcoming.

[8] Interview, 12 July 2000.

[9] Interviews, 13 June 2000, 22 May 2000.

[10] The difference becomes even sharper when we consider that once we remove the MPs who were in Government (disproportionately male) the new women constituted 19 per cent of MPs on the backbenches at any point in the Parliament, and 17 per cent of the permanent backbenchers.

[11] Remember: this is the figure once we remove all MPs in Government for the entire Parliament. The raw figures – for the entire PLP – are three per cent and 21 per cent; the figures for those on the backbenches throughout the Parliament are five per cent and 35 per cent. These are a mere seven-fold difference, rather than a nine-fold difference.

[12] Interview, 12 July 2000.

[13] Sarah Childs, 'The New Labour Women MPs in the 1997 British Parliament: issues of recruitment and representation', *Women's History Review*, 9 (2000); 'The Week in Westminster', Radio 4, 22 October 1998.

[14] The rebellious longer-serving women MPs include Dr Lynne Jones (who rebelled on 38 occasions), Gwyneth Dunwoody (27), Diane Abbott (26), Alice Mahon (25), Audrey Wise (25) and Ann Clwyd (24).

[15] If we examine just the permanent backbenchers, we find that the difference reduces slightly – to 45 per cent of the new men and 26 per cent of the new women – but it remains both sizeable and statistically significant.

[16] Maria Eagle and Joni Lovenduski, *High Time or High Tide for Labour Women*, London, Fabian Society,

1998.

[17]   Indeed, one of the authors (Cowley) was (mis)quoted saying something similar when early findings from this research were first published (*Observer*, 20 September 1998).

[18]   *Sunday Times*, 4 October 1998. Elsewhere, Widdecombe argued that AWS had 'led to a very substandard intake of women MPs – they are not up to it' (*The Times*, 7 February 1998). One male Labour MPs also saw AWS as a cause of the high levels of cohesion, if for slightly different reasons. AWS was, he argued, 'without question, a device to get ultra loyalists in place . . . an easier route in for ultra-loyalists'. Interview, 6 February 2001.

[19]   Interview, 13 June 2000.

[20]   Interview, 21 March 2000.

[21]   Interview, 22 June 2000.

[22]   Two other women MPs were explicit in recognizing the costs associated with rebelling. Reflecting on her rebelliousness, one woman MP admitted that it 'does disadvantage you . . . [it] does stand against you, probably' (interview, 21 June 2000; also, interview, 20 June 2000).

[23]   Interview, 21 June 2000.

[24]   Interviews, 13 June 2000, 10 May 2000.

[25]   Interview, 21 June 2000.

[26]   Interview, 15 May 2000.

[27]   Every new Labour woman who responded to the survey scored 1 on the question about the role of women in society, the most 'pro-women' response possible.

[28] $P=0.076$

[29]   The new men averaged 12.7 on the socialism scale, compared to 12.6 for the new women. The scores on the libertarian/authoritarian scale were 13.2 and 14.2 respectively.

[30]   More precisely, in both cases, the new women were overwhelmingly tolerant, but they were less tolerant than were the men. The difference lay in the degree of tolerance. For example: **Homosexual relations are always wrong %**

	New women	New men	Difference
Agree strongly	3	0	+3
Agree	3	0	+3
Neither agree nor disagree	7	3	+4
Disagree	26	24	+2
Disagree strongly	61	73	–12

The question on 'unconventional lifestyles' yielded similar differences.

[31]   The median age of both new men and new women was 43. The new men and the new women also contain almost identical proportions of MPs aged over 50 (21.5 per cent and 21.0 per cent respectively).

[32]   Ann Cryer, Eileen Gordon and Tess Kingham. Gordon's membership of the Group was, however, the source of some controversy. She denied it ('I don't join groups') but was regularly listed in Socialist Campaign Group News as a member. 'Hard-left group attracts new MPs', *Sunday Times*, 21 September 1997.

[33]   Sex: p=0.086; council experience: p=0.054.

[34]   See, for example, C. Bochel and J. Briggs, 'Do Women Make a Difference', *Politics*, 20 (2000); Pippa Norris, 'Women Politicians: Transforming Westminster?', in J. Lovenduski and P. Norris (eds), *Women in Politics*, Oxford, Oxford University Press, 1996; P. Norris and J. Lovenduski, *Political Recruitment*, Cambridge, Cambridge University Press, 1995; K. Ross, 'Women in the Boyzone', *Parliamentary Affairs*, 2002, forthcoming.

[35]   Sarah Childs, 'A Women's Style of Politics' (unpublished paper) found that almost two-thirds of the

interviewed newly elected women MPs thought that women MPs had a different style of politics in general; just over half thought this was the cause of the differences in cohesion.

36   Interviews, 19 June 2000, 10 May 2000, 16 May 2000.

37   Interview, 22 May 2000.

38   For a fuller account, see Childs, 'A Women's Style of Politics'. Many of the newly elected women also claimed (i) that the newly elected men are more likely to reject the traditional masculinized style of politics; and (ii) that party differences are also important.

39   Childs, 'The New Labour Women MPs', p. 67; Ross, 'Women in the Boyzone'.

40   Interview, 6 January 2000.

41   Interview, 21 March 2000.

42   Gender is 'a culturally shaped group of attributes and behaviours given to the female or the male'. Sex is biological, but gender is a social construction. Maggie Humm, *The Dictionary of Feminist Theory*, Hemel Hempstead, Harvester Wheatsheaf, 1989.

43   Interview, 23 May 2000.

44   A point made repeatedly in interviews in 2000: 13 June, 22 June, 8 June, 23 May, 16 May, 12 July, 15 May, 20 June, 10 July.

45   Interview, 10 May 2000.

46   Interview, 15 May 2000.

47   Interview, 15 May 2000. Note the name of the minister used to illustrate the point: Jack.

48   Fiona Mactaggart, *Women in Parliament: Their Contribution to Labour's First 1000 Days*, London, Fabian Society, 2000.

49   Letter to *The Times*, 4 April 1998.

50   Interview, 12 July 2000.

51   Interview, 20 June 2000.

52   Interview, 4 July 2000.

53   Interview, 15 June 2000.

54   Douglas Hurd, *Image in the Water*, London, Little, Brown, 2001, p. 236.

8. Washing Dirty Laundry In Private:

The PLP and the Internalisation of Discontent

From its creation in 1906 the PLP has always been the British Parliamentary party with the most developed internal structures. It was established with whips, written rules, weekly meetings, and elected officers. In 1924, on entering Government for the first time, it established a Liaison Committee to keep the Government informed of the views of the PLP. It also acquired other ad hoc backbench groupings: by the 1920s there was *inter alia* a union group, a miners' group, an ILP group, and a temperance group; in 1945 these were superseded by a formal and elaborate structure of backbench subject groups.[1]

All of these mechanisms fulfilled two basic functions. The first was top-down: to enable the leadership to communicate its desires to the backbenchers (and, then, in the case of the whips, to ensure that these were carried out). The second, though, was bottom-up: to help communicate the thoughts and concerns of the backbenchers to the leadership. Not the least of the motivations for the latter was that by ensuring the leadership was aware of the views of the backbenches, it might be able to contain and mediate discontent within these private forums, preventing it ever becoming public. Yet if the aim of these channels of communication was to prevent (or at least lessen) public acts of dissent, then (as Chapter 1 showed) they were not entirely successful. One senior member of the PLP of 1997 claimed to be well aware of what he called 'the lessons of history': that is, the damage that had been done by the very public disagreements between the PLP and previous Labour governments.[2] The aim in the 1997 Parliament was not to let that happen. This chapter examines the channels of communication between front and backbenches during the Blair Government. How well did they work? And to what extent did they manage to facilitate communication between leaders and led? It begins with the oldest – and most maligned – part of Parliamentary life: the whips.

Whips

Whips have been an essential part of Parliamentary life since at least the eighteenth century. Confusingly, 'the whip' has two distinct meanings. In its written form, it is the document circulated weekly by party managers to their MPs to inform them of the coming business and the importance that the party attaches to it. In its human form, the whips are the party managers, with the written whip being just one of their tools.

Throughout the 1997 Parliament, the Labour Whips Office consisted of 16 MPs. The Chief Whips were Nick Brown (until 1998) and Ann Taylor, the first woman Government Chief Whip in the Commons (1998 to 2001).[3] Beneath them were the Deputy Chief Whip and another 14 whips of various descriptions, each covering both a regional and a subject area.[4]

Whips of all parties fulfil three main functions: those of management, communication and persuasion.[5] The task of management derives from the need of the Government to 'maintain a House', to secure a majority in divisions (and, on behalf of the Opposition to try to keep that majority as small as possible). It encompasses the need to organize the business of the House, to liaise with the Opposition parties through the 'usual channels', and to keep backbench MPs informed and organized. For this reason, the whips were once described as 'more of a shepherd than a sheep dog' and as doing little more than 'serving to achieve cohesion among those who wished to be cohesive'.[6] The issuing by the PLP of pagers to its MPs attracted widespread criticism (being seen as evidence of an excessive tendency to want to control its MPs); but completely overlooked was the fact that they were essentially just a very efficient means by which the Party could communicate with its backbenchers, and appreciated by most backbenchers for precisely that reason.[7]

The task of management is the longest-standing function of the party whips, and one long serving Labour MP claimed that it became their main role from 1997 onwards. Because of the size of Labour's majority, the role of the whips had, he said, become little more than 'a technical management job making sure people turn up on time and less about curbing dissent and feeding information to the leadership'.[8] But technical job or not, no Government would survive long without the effective management of its business and its Parliamentarians. The need for effective management, even when the Government has a majority of 179, became clear in February 1999. During the passage of the Rating (Valuation) Bill, the Tory whips ordered their MPs to leave the Commons en masse. Labour MPs followed. Then, five minutes before the vote, '140 or so well-refreshed Tory MPs appeared on the horizon, like something from the film *Zulu*. In the event the Government scraped through by a margin of 25, but only with the help of a few, ever-indecisive, Liberal Democrats'.[9]

The communication function is to constitute a channel of communication between the front and the back benches. As part of their management role, the whips need to inform backbench MPs of the leadership's plans. But whips also need to communicate the views of the backbenchers to the leadership, especially when discontent is brewing. They need to be the Government's eyes and ears, monitoring feelings on the backbenches. In 1997 the Whips Office aimed to be 'consultative and inclusive', hoping 'to prevent problems arising as early as possible'.[10] The aim was to allow a 'two-way relationship to mature so that back-benchers never feel alienated from the policy making process'.[11] As one whip put it: 'We beg for mercy and grace and petition that policy without widespread support should no longer be pursued'.[12] Blair was said by one Whips Office insider not to have appreciated the value of the Whips Office as a means of iden-tifying backbench discontent at the beginning of the Parliament. By the end he did.[13]

It is the third function – that of persuasion – that attracts the most attention and the most criticism from outsiders. If an MP looks likely to deviate from the party line, then it is the role of the whips to persuade him or her back into the fold. Tales of the tricks used by the whips to 'persuade' MPs are legion.[14] Yet the formal sanctions available to the whips are, and always have been, limited, espe-cially if MPs rebel in numbers. (And some of the formal sanctions, such as informing constituency parties of their MPs' rebellions are – as was shown in Chapter 6 – entirely counterproductive). One MP therefore famously described them not so much as 'whips as feather dusters', a description largely borne out by the experience of the 1997 Parliament.[15] As noted in Chapter 1, before the 1997 election, for example, there were claims that the Labour leadership would be heavy-handed with dissident MPs, and that rebellious Labour MPs would have the party whip removed.[16] But as was shown in Chapter 2, once its size became clear, all threats to discipline MPs after the lone parent rebellion in 1997 were abandoned. And throughout the Parliament no Labour MP lost the whip as a result of his or her rebelliousness. Dissenting MPs did sometimes get snotty letters from the whips reprimanding them (Austin Mitchell once auctioned off one of his at a Party conference) but most rebellious MPs can live with snotty letters.

The whips' main weapon is simply the power to persuade. One Labour whip therefore compared his job to parenting:

You can make children behave well by threatening them – this is one tactic – but it cannot be used all the time. They are, however, much more likely to behave well if you explain clearly why you want them to do things and why you don't want them to do things. The response you get is much better and certainly more positive.[17]

It is, said another, 'no good just threatening people, we are not going to get anywhere. There is no point employing a system of kneecapping at dawn. It should be a rewarding system rather than a threatening system'.[18]

Much of the academic literature on the whips office therefore tries to play down the role of the whip as arm-twister, bully and Machiavelli all rolled into one – as personified by Andrew Dobbs' fictitious Francis Urquhart – stressing instead the more prosaic functions of the whips. This is summed-up by the title of an article on the whips by Peter Dorey: 'Much Maligned, Much Misunderstood'.[19] Yet in turn, this runs the risk of going too far in the other direction, portraying the whips as entirely toothless, entirely feeble. The truth is somewhere in between. To be sure, the whips do far more than just force MPs into line; and even when it comes to trying to ensure cohesion, they achieve more by persuasion, diplomacy and appeals to loyalty than by threats or bullying. But it would be wrong to underestimate the extent to which whips are willing to attempt to coerce MPs. Most of the metaphorical sticks available to the whips may merely be the absence of equally metaphorical carrots, but the whips are not averse to withholding those carrots from MPs when they think it will be helpful.

The whips can (and did) make life less pleasant for the troublesome. They can (and did) deny places on the more prestigious select committees, deny time away from the House, deny time for overseas trips, deny promotion, deny better office space and so on. And as Chapter 6 showed, the whips could also revert to good old-fashioned physical bullying at times. Even these tactics, however, could backfire. Pushed too far by what they saw as small-minded punishments from the whips, including being kept late whilst other more loyal MPs were allowed home, several of the more rebellious MPs simply began to ignore the whips' instructions to remain in the Commons, thus (potentially at least) putting at risk the effective management of the Government's majority.[20]

Much depended on the nature of the individual whip concerned. Some whips, like Graham Allen or Gerry Sutcliffe tended to be praised by their MPs ('friend, mentor'); others were universally described as 'thugs'.[21] (One was described as 'a Catholic Stalinist thug', which presumably meant that he was a dictatorial bully who felt guilty about it afterwards).[22] Much depended also on the nature of the

MP concerned. One formidable rebel claimed not to get any hassle from the whips: 'They find me more intimidating!'[23] Many of the older persistent rebels tend to be ignored by the whips.[24] The whips could live with what they saw as 'the serial offenders'. What they had to do, one said, is to 'make sure that that group does not get any bigger'.[25] During one vote, as a previously loyal Labour MP went to vote against the Government, a whip was heard muttering, 'There goes another virgin'.[26] The whips knew that they could do little to influence the promiscuous; their task was to ensure the chaste remained unsullied.

From right across the political spectrum backbench views about the Labour whips were largely negative. A loyalist described them as 'dreadful'.[27] A long-time rebel thought they were 'grossly incompetent'.[28] As one long-serving woman MP put it: the whips were 'hopeless', 'incompetent beyond belief and idle to boot'.[29] Complaints were especially raised against Ann Taylor, Chief Whip for most of the Parliament. One rebel described her as 'useless'.[30] One soon-to-be-promoted Blairite loyalist described her as 'hopeless – if she's not sacked, I'll be gobs-macked'.[31] Complaints about Taylor came particularly from other women MPs, who felt that she had done little to change the 'laddish nature' of the Whips Office.[32] Although the increased numbers of women in the Whips Office in general from 1997 onwards was said to have modified their approach somewhat – 'they are,' wrote Michael White in the *Guardian*, 'lubricating the harsh message with small kindnesses unknown in more blokeish times when there were no women in the Whips' Office' – one Labour woman MP described Taylor as 'remote', claimed that she 'doesn't like women', and was 'surrounded by a coterie of young men' known on the backbenches as Ann Taylor's 'football team'.[33] Despite the increase in the number of women whips, the Labour whips were widely criticised for their macho behaviour and for being 'too bar-based', thus failing properly to listen to all sectors of the PLP.[34]

Criticisms were raised over all three aspects of the whips role, but the main criticism of the whips under Blair was neither of arm-twisting nor bullying, but just of poor and ineffective time-management.[35] A number of backbenchers felt that there was a 'psychological desire' on the part of the whips to have a majority of at least 100 in every vote.[36] As another put it: 'They [the whips] are like First World War generals. They don't need to think; they just throw numbers at the problem'.[37] To a certain extent, many of these comments are the inevitable conse-quences of the whips' job. One MP likened the whips to the 'military police, dragging people out of bars and beating them over the head'.[38] Another described them as 'NCO-like'.[39] Neither the Military Police nor NCOs are usually popular amongst the troops. As one experienced Labour MP put it:

many of the comments about whips are 'just the sort of "club-like" talk that you get when you cram hundreds of people into an institution for hours on end'.[40]

It was also an inherent problem resulting from the large majority. With a majority of one, Labour MPs would have understood the need to be permanently at the Commons. But with a majority of almost 200, many wondered why the whips could not be more relaxed.[41] Things were made worse by the activities of the Conservative awkward squad. As will become clear in Chapter 10, one of the aims of Eric Forth and his Conservative colleagues was to create unease amongst Labour's ranks, and to divide the troops from their officers. In this, they were successful, and at least some of Ann Taylor's apparent unpopularity with backbenchers can be attributed to the fact that she was Chief Whip when the activities of the Conservative awkward squad began in earnest.

Perhaps most importantly from the point of view of this book, however, was the fact that many Labour MPs also felt the whips failed to perform the communication or persuasion tasks well. It was striking how few MPs said that they would raise issues of concern with their whips.[42] 'I don't contact the whips over anything . . . they are useless', said one.[43] If the role of the whips was supposed to be both to communicate from the top-down and from the bottom-up, then most Labour MPs felt that the whips largely only fulfilled the former. One MP, summing up the views of many, described the Whips Office as 'the instrument of the Government, not the voice of MPs'.[44]

The PLP

Since its creation, the PLP has had a formalised internal structure. From its establishment in 1906, it has had weekly meetings and elected officers. From 1924, it also began to establish a Liaison Committee when in Government, designed to facilitate communication between Government and backbenches. All three continued between 1997 and 2001, and all three, to a greater or lesser extent, helped maintain contact between the leaders and the led, and prevent discontent spilling out into more public arenas.

The full PLP met weekly, on Wednesdays at 11.30am. Meetings began with a report from the Parliamentary Committee (see below), followed by the Chief Whip, who would report on the forthcoming business, followed in turn by reports from the PLP representatives on the NEC or National Policy Forum, if relevant. There would then usually be at least one main speaker, often a minister or a senior member of the party staff. Formal votes were rare, with the meetings being a chance for discussion rather than decision. PLP minutes are uniformly (and presumably deliberately) anodyne in the extreme. They note merely that 'a discussion took place', list those who contributed and then say that the speaker 'responded to the points raised'.

The very earliest Parliamentary party meetings – held in the eighteenth and nine-teenth centuries – were designed essentially for one-way communication: from party leaders to followers. 'The leaders, who summoned the meetings, attended to inform their supporters of decisions already taken, not to seek their advice or invite discussion'.[45] It would be an exaggeration to say that the main PLP meeting has now regained this role – but only just. 'It's now an information meeting,' said one MP, '[explaining] why we are doing this'.[46] Whilst some MPs thought this was a negative development (one described it as 'useless'), others found it more positive. One MP described the PLP meeting as a 'bonding exercise'.[47] Another found the various talks 'inspiring', a bit like a 'manager's team talk'.[48] One new MP said that he would make 'every effort to go if Tony was there'.[49]

Many MPs anyway doubted the wisdom of trying to discuss controversial policy at such a large meeting. There were also doubts about the motives of some of those who raised matters at the PLP, and therefore the meeting's utility as a means of influence. 'The sort of people who spout off at the PLP', said one MP, 'are the ones who have 200 people inwardly groaning'.[50] Or, as another put it, the PLP was only used by two types of MPs: 'dripping sycophants' and those who 'want to oppose', to 'show how tough they are'.[51]

The second problem – also militating against frank and open two-way discus-sion – was that the full meetings of the PLP had acquired a widespread reputation for leaking. 'Lobby journalists sit outside the PLP, waiting to hear what's said'.[52] And details of PLP meetings often leaked verbatim into the next day's newspapers.[53] As a result, some MPs chose not to raise controversial matters there – nor did they expect frank responses from ministers. Yet for all that, the full PLP meeting still had its moments: the PLP meeting at which Harriet Harman attempted to defend the changes to lone parent benefit was described by one MP as 'brutal'. 'The meeting was so bloody that we all assumed they would go back and change it'.[54]

A more private route was the Parliamentary Committee, a sub-committee of the PLP, established to facilitate contact between the front and backbenches. Some form of Liaison Committee has been a part of all previous Labour govern-ments, with the Committee established in 1997 being similar in composition to that formed when Labour was last elected to Government in 1974. It consisted of the Leader, Deputy Leader, Chair of the Parliamentary Party, the Chief Whip (all of whom sat *ex officio*), four ministers appointed by the PM, one elected Lords backbencher along with six MPs elected by backbenchers.[55] The last were variously seen by MPs as 'the trade union reps', there to 'represent the infantry'.[56] Whereas in 1974 the Committee had been weakened by being ideologically unrepresentative (by 1977 no backbench member of the Tribune Group was serving on it), the elected representatives from 1997 onwards represented a much wider range of backbench opinion, including several persistent rebels.[57] They would meet once a week, with their discussions reported back to the PLP and their minutes circulated to every Labour MP, along with the written whip.

Again, MPs had mixed views about how useful they found the Parliamentary Committee. One rebel described it as 'hopeless'.[58] Several MPs did not seem to know that it even existed, or (if they did) they did not understand how it worked: a puzzled look came over their faces in many cases. There was a great deal of confusion in the minds of some MPs between the Parliamentary Committee and the various backbench committees (see below). And, of those who did know about the Committee and did understand its function, several saw it as the place to raise 'housekeeping' matters, such as MPs' allowances, rather than policy matters.[59] In many ways this was a huge missed opportunity on the part of Labour backbenchers. The Prime Minister turned up to around half the meetings, with the Deputy Prime Minister standing in when Blair was away.[60] Those who attended the Committee found it an 'incredibly useful' way of raising backbench concerns.[61] Committee members found Blair 'very willing to get into dialogue' at these meetings, more so than in a public setting like the full meetings of the PLP, and very willing to listen to constructive suggestions for changes to policy.[62] 'The trick', said one, 'was to engage with him. The PM differentiates between those who just complain and those who are onside but with suggestions'.[63]

The Chair of the PLP throughout the 1997 Parliament was Clive Soley, MP for Ealing, Acton and Shepherd's Bush. Towards the end of the Parliament Soley was the subject of what Jackie Ashley in the *New Statesman* described as 'a vicious, passionate, largely subterranean campaign' to replace him.[64] The campaign was ultimately unsuccessful, with Soley remaining Chair until the election, but his victory was (like Waterloo) a damn close run thing, and one that (unlike Waterloo) was largely pyrrhic: he stood down soon after the election.

The campaign against him had three distinct origins. First, there was the general frustration with some of the Government's decisions, in particular the issue of pensions up-rating (Chapter 4), where Labour MPs felt the Government was not listening to them (or to anyone else, for that matter), and the lack of a Government Bill on fox hunting. Second, there was also a growing sense of frustration at the Government's failure to deliver on more radical 'modernisation' of the House of Commons, especially the failure to bring forward sizeable increases in Office Cost Allowances.[65] As one insider put it, many MPs had the attitude, 'They're not listening, Clive, so we're going to have to shoot the messenger'.[66] And once the press started to describe the issue as 'a chance to give Blair a bloody nose', some Labour MPs started to think, 'Well, we better give Blair a bloody nose then'.[67]

Then, third, there was Soley's style. From his election in 1997, he had always seen his job as representing both the troops to the generals and the generals to the troops. Aware of the damage that had been caused to past Labour governments by the separation of back and front benches, his aim was to be the buckle that joined. He would put backbenchers' views to the leadership but he would do so privately. Unfortunately, that was not how many of the backbenchers saw him. He was widely seen as too much the 'boss's boy' or 'effectively Tony's PPS', and as having a tendency to tell 'the PM what he wanted to hear'.[68] As one Labour backbencher put it, 'Soley was not seen as a shop steward for us, but there to keep us in order'.[69] Another put it more bluntly: Soley thought his role was to 'control the ranks', and he showed 'a lickspittle subservience to the leadership that was almost embarrassing'.[70] Others felt that Soley was too often making appearances on radio and television defending the Government's position.[71] In short, he had become 'too established and establishment'.[72] Many Labour MPs wanted a person who would defend the rights of Labour backbenchers more vociferously – and more openly.[73] On top of that, there was a story in the *Sunday Times* claiming Soley had described pensioners as racist – a story he denied – and some Labour MPs were dismayed by his vote in the election of the Speaker, where rather than supporting Michael Martin, the preferred choice of the bulk of the PLP, he had voted for Sir George Young – 'an educated Baronet rather than a Glasgow sheet metal worker'.[74] One, or perhaps two, of these factors he might have been able to survive without a challenge but the combination of all of them together proved too much.

A challenge had been rumoured to be coming in 1999, only to fail to materialise.[75] In an attempt to put off a challenge the following year too, in November 2000 Soley wrote to all Labour MPs, warning that any challenge would 'create uncertainty and negative publicity'. The Party should not risk a 'war with itself'.[76] He also hinted that he might not stand again for the job after the general election.[77] But it did not work: Andrew Mackinlay and Tony Lloyd both stood against him.

Andrew Mackinlay represented 'the classic protest candidate'.[78] Despite not being an (old-style) left-winger, as an outspoken critic of some aspects of New Labour he attracted support from the left of the PLP and from those MPs who wanted to 'put more of the willies up [the leadership], ruffle their feathers', safe in the knowledge that Mackinlay stood no chance of winning.[79] Tony Lloyd was the more serious of the two challengers. He had served in the Government, and benefited from some sympathy following his sacking as Minister of State at the Foreign Office after the Arms to Sierra Leone Affair.[80] He was more popular than Soley with 'the lads in the bar room' who wanted a more macho figure and appears to have done well with Northern MPs and, as chair of the Trade Union Group, amongst trade union MPs (although the downside of this was that some London MPs saw him as a 'Northern plotter').[81] Conversely, Soley did well with new Labour women MPs who, although frustrated by what they saw as slow progress over modernisation, reacted against Lloyd's macho image.[82]

Soley eventually won – but only just. In the first ballot, on 21 November 2000, he finished top of the poll with 169 votes but failed to win an outright majority. Lloyd polled a strong 121 votes, Mackinlay a highly respectable 77.[83] In the second round, held the following day, Soley scraped home by a majority of only six MPs. Given the proximity of the election, and the fact that he had said that he might anyway be standing down, it was far from a vote of confidence.

Ironically, although the contest came about because the Government was not seen as listening enough, it had a positive side. It relieved some of the tension and frustration that had been building up in the Parliamentary party. It allowed Labour backbenchers to deliver what one called 'a shot across the bows'.[84] After his re-election, Soley was more careful about the appearances he made on television, made sure he gave more regular feedback to MPs and went out of his way to be seen to be more on the side of the troops.[85] One Labour MP believes that Soley found it 'a salutary lesson', while a Labour rebel accepted that, in the months after his re-election, the PLP chairman became 'less deferential'.[86] Whether he became more effective as a conduit to the leadership is, of course, much more debatable. But that may not be the point: the contest allowed Labour MPs to take out their various frustrations on someone, without seriously damaging the Government. The process was not entirely private – the story was covered in the press – but it was very much the stuff of the inside pages, tucked safely away from general consumption. Prime Ministerial whipping boy may not be the standard job description for the Chair of the PLP but on this occasion it served a useful purpose none the less.

Back-bench groupings

The PLP first established backbench subject groups in 1945. During the 1997 Parliament, there were 16 such groups, each covering a specific policy area, such as Agriculture, Defence, Social Security or the Treasury. All Labour MPs are able to attend any group (although those who formally join a group at the beginning of the Parliament receive notice of meetings by letter, rather than just spotting notices in the weekly whip). In addition, there were 12 Regional Groups, each consisting – as their name rather implies – of MPs from particular regions of the country, as well as other specialist groupings, such as the Trade Union Group. The groups vary in their levels of activity, largely depending on the competence and activism of the chair, but most meet regularly – usually every fortnight – and are frequently addressed by ministers or other speakers on topics of concern.

In theory, such groups are an excellent way of ensuring private communication between ministers and the most informed and interested backbenchers. As one whip said, the groups mean that MPs and ministers do not have to 'wash dirty laundry in public'.[87] The Chair of one of the groups described the meetings as a good way of keeping backbench MPs 'off the streets', and presumably out of trouble.[88] That the practice does not quite live up to the theory has been noted every time the PLP has been in Government.[89] The groups have (at best) a patchy reputation for influence and are usually seen as less effective than their Conservative counterparts.[90]

A regular problem has been the level of participation. In 1976 a PLP committee set up to investigate communications between the PLP and the Government noted that the numbers attending subject committees 'are often small, sometimes embarrassingly so'.[91] Little appears to have changed in the intervening years. One of the officers of the International Development Committee in the 1997 Parliament was unwilling to volunteer an average figure for attendance at his committee, precisely because it was so low. Another group meeting addressed by the Indian High Commissioner saw just three MPs in attendance, much to everyone's embarrassment. That said, when an issue was of current import and the relevant minister was addressing the meeting then attendance could be substantial. The Home Affairs Committee had over 100 for a meeting on fox hunting.[92] The Trade Union Group had over 140 MPs attend a meeting to push for a national (as opposed to a regional) minimum wage.[93] Some 150 attended when it discussed trade union recognition.[94] So it was not that the groups suffered from a permanently low attendance; rather that they lacked a respectably large regular attendance.

Part of the problem was MPs' time. Busy with other things, attendance at party committees became (as one MP put it) 'the first thing to cross off the diary'.[95] Or, as another said, he would go only 'if I'm bored, or I've got a spare hour'.[96] And there was a discernible dropping off in attendance at the various backbench committees as the Parliament wore on. Towards the end of the Parliament, one backbencher claimed that the groups had 'gone into complete disuse', another that 'only New Labour people go now'.[97]

Yet noting that MPs are busy can only be half of the answer. If MPs felt that attendance at the group meetings was worthwhile, then they would (somehow) find the time to attend. That they do not implies that they did not find them especially useful or at least not useful enough.[98] One new Labour loyalist MP thought the groups were 'a very effective way of putting concerns to ministers'.[99] But his views were not typical.[100] One Labour rebel avoided the meetings claiming that they were nothing more than a 'rallying meeting for the Third Way'.[101] Another felt that they were chaired by people who could be relied upon to be loyal to the Government, while yet another felt that the idea behind the committees was 'to spread the message down' from the leadership to the backbenchers (although this in his view did not work 'if the message is crap anyway').[102]

For all their faults, the groups were, however, far from completely useless. Even though very few MPs turned up, the process gave the five or six who did up to a full hour with the minister responsible. Small in numbers they may be, but these MPs constitute an important 'public' for the minister, because the MPs who are interested enough in a subject to attend the relevant backbench group are precisely the ones who could cause trouble in more public arenas. Even if ministers just 'come and say what they want', the meetings remain a useful way for ministers to take the temperature of the party on an issue.[103] On his appointment as Social Security Secretary, Alastair Darling was advised by the whips to go to every backbench meeting he could fit into his diary for precisely that reason.[104] After the Home Affairs Committee meeting on fox hunting, at which members of the group pushed the Government to introduce legislation on the issue, the Home Secretary was heard to say that he could see there was 'no point in lying in front of a tank'.[105]

Access to ministers

The most direct route for an MP with a concern is to contact the relevant minister directly. Some MPs do this by letter; others speak to the minister in person. This contact may be an ad hoc meeting (grabbing the minister when he or she is nearby, especially when in the division lobby), or it may be more formal, often arranged through either a whip or the minister's Parliamentary Private Secretary (PPS). MPs' practices differed. Some of the more experienced backbenchers tended to go for the more informal meetings (as one of them put it: 'There's no one I don't know well enough just to grab'), whilst others deliberately eschewed casual meetings, because they wanted to impress upon the minister the importance of the issue and because it is easier for the minister to slip away, without having dealt with the issues at hand, which then makes it harder for the MP to raise the matter again.[106] Similarly, some MPs deliberately chose not to bother ministers too often. As one put it: 'If you were banging on the door every five minutes, then he's going to think, "Oh fuck off"'.[107] Instead, they will prefer to raise the issue with their whip or with the minister's PPS, who will then pass their concerns on to the minister. The minister may then choose to contact the MP to arrange a more formal meeting to discuss the issue.

There was a wide variance in the degree to which individual ministers were willing to see backbench MPs and the degree to which they were perceived as listening to backbenchers at these meetings. Sometimes the lack of consultation was down to the differing cultures of openness within Government departments. The Foreign Office and the Ministry of Defence traditionally have a culture of secrecy. The Treasury was also regarded as being less open with backbenchers than other Government departments. Another variable is the physical availability of the minister involved. In some cases, the problem for ministers such as Peter Mandelson and Robin Cook (although in both cases, only part of the problem) was that they were rarely in the Commons because their jobs – as Northern Ireland Secretary and Foreign Secretary respectively – meant that they were needed elsewhere. Personality was also crucially important. As was clear from Chapters 3 and 4, Jack Straw was by far the most assiduous of ministers, being described by one backbencher as 'the senior minister most often in the tea rooms'.[108]

But whilst there was a general feeling that it was relatively easy for MPs to contact ministers and that (most) ministers were (usually) accessible – especially after the lone parent revolt made the Government realise the importance of communication with its backbenchers – there was much less consensus on the value of these meetings. As one Labour rebel argued, 'They're not inaccessible – anyone can get access – but it won't make any difference'.[109] Another made a similar distinction between gaining access to ministers (which was relatively easy) and getting them to change policy (which was 'slightly harder').[110] As yet another put it: 'We might have a good discussion . . . with arguments flying about . . . but we'll never change their mind, because they cannot change the legislation without losing face. If one of them doesn't cave in, then none of them will'.[111] Accessibility is however important in itself. Meetings give the minister a chance to explain the policy; and allow MPs a chance to let off steam, explaining their concerns to the person at the top. That cannot be done with the aloof and distant.

The minister most accused of being aloof and distant was the Prime Minister himself, much criticized in the media and by the Opposition for his absence from the Commons. Blair's voting record was extremely poor – participating in around five per cent of divisions – and he was rarely seen in the tea room.[112] But he devoted considerable time to more formal meetings with MPs. Between the start of the Parliament and the end of May 1999, the Prime Minister had 364 meetings with MPs. In relative terms, this was more contact with his backbenchers than John Major had.[113]

In addition to *ad hoc* meetings (during the foot-and-mouth crisis, for example, Blair requested a meeting of Labour MPs with rural seats, although this lasted only 15 minutes), there were a series of regular meetings, with MPs seeing the Prime Minister in groups of around 20, organized alphabetically, with each MP getting to ask one question each.[114] The aim was that every backbench Labour MP would attend at least one meeting each year. At first the gatherings were rather sycophantic: 'people [were] just so amazed to be there'.[115] But as the Parliament progressed, MPs became slightly more assertive and less deferential, and in turn the Prime Minister appears to have become better at dealing with questioning. Initially, Blair was said to be quite hurt if anyone questioned him ('more hurt than anyone I've seen in public life'), but as the Parliament progressed, Blair grew better at responding to MPs' concerns, being described as 'appallingly frank' in one meeting.[116] Another meeting was described as 'very traumatic' by one of the MPs present.[117] One MP summed the meetings up well: 'fine as far as they go'.[118]

Conclusion

The discontented Labour backbencher had, therefore, plenty of channels through which he or she could communicate concerns to the executive. Individually, each of these channels suffered from significant drawbacks. The whips were not widely felt to be effective in communicating discontent upwards. The formal mechanisms of the PLP were not much better in the 1997

Parliament than they had been under previous Labour governments. Just before he stood down as PLP chair Clive Soley – himself the focus of much backbench criticism – wrote a damning report on the effectiveness of the PLP's structures, singling out the backbench groups as being ineffective. These formal mechanisms were augmented by relatively easy access to ministers, and sporadic formal (but very infrequent informal) contact with the Prime Minister. The problematic nature of each individual channel was, however, ameliorated by the sheer number of ways that a Government backbencher could communicate with the executive. Although *individually* the mechanisms for consultation may have been poor, *collectively* they were more effective.

Some of the more persistent rebels eschewed these internal pathways altogether, believing them to be 'completely impotent'.[119] Others attended the various meetings, but only to 'register their opposition'.[120] But these were minority viewpoints. The majority of Labour backbench MPs utilised various Parliamentary mechanisms to influence their leadership. MPs differed greatly in their choice of channels, how they used them, and how effective they believed them to be; the old cliché about there being 659 different ways to be an MP is not true but it is not far off.

How effective were they? As was clear in Part I (in particular in Chapters 3 and 4), there were plenty of occasions when the Labour leadership managed to negotiate with its backbenchers in order to lessen backbench revolt, most notably during the Criminal Justice (Terrorism and Conspiracy) Bill, over immigration and asylum, during the Terrorism Bill and over Freedom of Information. Where it did not effectively negotiate – as over lone parent benefit, incapacity benefit, or NATS – the rebellions were large and vocal (although even in the last two of these three, there were some small concessions to make the medicine slightly less bitter). There were other cases where there were no dissenting votes at all, precisely because the Government managed to negotiate itself out of trouble behind the scenes. These include such issues as trade union recognition, the minimum wage (both that it was national rather than regional, and that it be increased), access to the countryside and fox hunting. Where the Government was prepared to sugar the legislative pill, rebellions could be small or nonexistent.

One backbench MP explained the lack of rebellions during the 1997 Parliament precisely because 'the mechanisms exist for us to make our feelings known'.[121] On its own, this is not a convincing argument. Given the scale of the difference between the behaviour of the PLP between 1997 and 2001 and the behaviour of previous governments, the explanation cannot lie simply in the mechanisms of consulation, not least because – as this chapter has shown – these mechanisms were far from roaring successes. But, when taken together with other factors, the willingness of the Government to consult and negotiate with its backbenchers is most certainly part of the explanation. The next chapter considers these other factors.

1. Philip Norton 'The Organization of Parliamentary Parties', in S. A. Walkland (ed), *The House of Commons in the Twentieth Century*, Oxford, Clarendon Press, 1979.

2. Interview, 6 January 2000.

3. Though not in the Lords, where Baroness Llewelyn-Davies was Government Chief Whip between 1974 and 1979. See Philip Cowley and David Melhuish, 'Peers' Careers. Ministers in the House of Lords, 1964–95', *Political Studies*, 45 (1997).

4. As well as the Comptroller of HM Household, and the Vice-Chamberlain of HM Household, there were the Lord Commissioners of HM Treasury (Government Whips) and – the lowest in the food chain – the Assistant Whips. The precise numbers of the last two categories varied throughout the Parliament: at the beginning of the Parliament there were five Government Whips and seven Assistant Whips; as the Parliament progressed, so the number of the former went down whilst that of the latter went up. A total of 26 MPs served in the Whips Office during the Parliament; eight were there the whole time.

5. Norton 'The Organization of Parliamentary Parties'. Searing and Game identified the same three functions, although they called them management, liaison, and discipline. See Donald Searing and Chris Game, 'Horses for Courses: The Recruitment of Whips in the British House of Commons', *British Journal of Political Science*, 7 (1997). The whips have increasingly begun to acquire a fourth function, as a sort of Parliamentary personnel department. This includes educating MPs in Parliamentary procedure and tactics, and training MPs, such as by breaking them in on standing committees.

6. Ian Gilmour, *The Body Politic*, London, Hutchinson, 1969, p. 261; Norton, 'The Organization of Parliamentary Parties', p. 13. This can be seen most clearly by looking at how MPs behave when they do not have the whip, either because they have lost it (see Appendix 2) or because, like Martin Bell, they never had one in the first place (see Appendix 9).

7. As one whip explained pagers were introduced so that Members would not have to hang around at Westminster 'for a moment longer than necessary at night – they are simply there to remind them which way to vote and are not some sinister remote control'. From Christine Coates, 'Whipping the Government into Shape: The Changing Functions of the Whips Office Under New Labour', unpublished undergraduate dissertation, University of Hull, 1999, p. 40.

8. Coates, 'Whipping the Government into Shape'. One Conservative MP therefore described the role of the Labour whips under Blair as 'a piece of cake'.

9. *Telegraph*, 26 February 1999. Also see Jane Kennedy's 'Ambush Alert!', *The House Magazine*, March 1999. 'In the opposition lobby,' she said, 'there were Tories we hadn't seen in months'.

10. Coates, 'Whipping the Government into Shape', p. 24.

11. Coates, 'Whipping the Government into Shape', p. 26.

12. Coates, 'Whipping the Government into Shape', p. 26.

13. Coates, 'Whipping the Government into Shape', p. 62.

14. For a good example (though only one of many), see Michael Cockerell, 'Westminster's Secret Service', *Spectator*, 20 May 1995, and the accompanying TV programme.

15. Anthony King (ed), *British Members of Parliament: A Self-Portrait*, London, Macmillan, 1974, p. 59.

16. Steve Richards, 'What reasons are there for supposing a Blair Government will not be stricken by party dissenters as Major's has been? Plenty, actually', *New Statesman*, 13 December 1996.

[17] Coates, 'Whipping the Government into Shape', p. 34.

[18] Coates, 'Whipping the Government into Shape', p. 44.

[19] Peter Dorey, 'Much Maligned, Much Misunderstood: The Role of Party Whips', *Talking Politics*, 5 (1992).

[20] Interview, 13 March 2001.

[21] Interviews, 25 October 2001, 13 February 2001, 14 March 2001.

[22] Interviews, 15 February 2000, 21 March 2001.

[23] Interview, 11 July 2000.

[24] One of the more rebellious MPs described himself as 'beyond redemption'. Interview, 13 February 2001.

[25] Coates, 'Whipping the Government into Shape', p. 47.

[26] Interview, 27 June 2000.

[27] Interview, 13 June 2000.

[28] Interview, 28 March 2000.

[29] Interview, 30 March 2001. Similar views, 29 February 2000, 7 March 2000: the last used the term 'twats'.

[30] Interview, 21 March 2000. Nick Brown, by contrast, was reasonably popular, often being described as 'excellent'. Interviews, 29 February 2000, 21 March 2000. Also 25 May 1999.

[31] Interview, 13 June 2000.

[32] Interview, 13 June 2000.

[33] Michael White, 'Labour MPs get quality time off', *Guardian*, 24 June 1997. Interviews, 21 March 2000, 13 March 2001, 21 March 2001.

[34] Interview, 21 March 2001.

[35] Interview, 4 July 2000. What one described as 'pretty crap' (interview, 21 March 2000).

[36] Interviews, 14 March 2000, 21 March 2001, 30 January 2001.

[37] Interview, 14 March 2000. Also see the comments of Austin Mitchell in his Commons Diary (*The House Magazine*, 12 April 1999): 'The Whips are too nervous to let us go because they treat a majority of 178 as if it were five. So we're kept kicking our heels, pushing the Refreshment Department into profit, and wasting our youth – at least mine'.

[38] Interview, 13 February 2001.

[39] Interview, 6 March 2001. Another said that in order for the whips to do their job, they have to have had 'a charisma bypass' (interview, 30 January 2001).

[40] Interview, 21 March 2000.

[41] This was a particular problem at the beginning of the Parliament, when newer MPs would sometimes think 'well, if I miss the vote that is OK, my vote will be neither here nor there'. Coates, 'Whipping the Government into Shape', p. 46.

[42] A clear minority of those MPs interviewed said that they would contact their whips if they were concerned about an issue; moreover, only a minority of those that would utilise the whip trusted the whip to pass their concerns on, preferring instead to use the whip to arrange a meeting with a minister.

[43] Interview, 6 March 2001.

[44] Interview, 13 June 2000. Or as another put it in an interview the same day: the whips office was better at 'discipline and control than accommodation'.

[45] Norton, 'Organization of Parliamentary Parties', p. 21.

[46] Interview, 6 February 2001. Or as another put it: 'They're always having briefings to make sure we're saying the same thing' (interview, 13 February 2001).

[47] Interviews, 30 January 2001, 13 June 2000.

[48] Interview, 11 April 2000. One MP thought that Blair viewed the PLP meeting in the same light, addressing it when he felt it needed 'geeing up' (interview, 21 March 2001).

[49] Interview, 23 May 2000.

[50] Interview, 27 June 2000.

[51] Interview, 13 June 2000. Perhaps unwittingly, one of the more frequent rebels agreed, saying that he

found meetings of the full PLP useful for 'sounding off' (interview, 6 February 2001).

52 Interview, 29 February 2000.

53 Interview, 7 March 2000.

54 Interview, 25 October 2001.

55 In addition, the Chief Whip in the House of Lords and the General Secretary of the Party had a formal right of attendance. The former made full use of his right, attending frequently.

56 Interviews, 6 January 2000, 28 March 2000.

57 The initial six members were Jean Corston, Charlotte Atkins, Sylvia Heal, Ann Clwyd, Chris Mullin and Llin Golding. After a year, Andrew Mackinlay replaced Golding. Following Mullin's appointment to Government, he was replaced by Colin Pickthall. At the beginning of the final session, Atkins, Heal and Mackinlay were replaced by Tony Lloyd, John McFall and Angela Smith. The elected members were rightly described by one of their number as representing the 'whole spectrum' of the PLP (interview, 23 May 2000; similar views, 28 March 2000). For the 1970s, see Norton, 'The Organization of Parliamentary Parties', p. 25.

58 Interview, 21 March 2000.

59 Interviews, 15 February 2000, 7 March 2000. Another MP felt that the Parliamentary Committee was 'very good at bread and butter' issues (interview, 28 March 2000).

60 Although Prescott's role was mainly that of 'taking messages to pass on' (interviews, 6 January 2000, 28 March 2000).

61 Interview, 29 February 2000.

62 Interviews, 28 March 2000, 28 February 2000.

63 Interview, 28 March 2000; Chris Mullin and Ann Clwyd were said by one member of the Committee to be especially good at engaging Blair (interview, 6 January 2000).

64 *New Statesman*, 20 November 2000.

65 Interviews, 13 March 2001, 6 March 2001, 21 March 2001, 27 March 2001. One MP described the Office Costs issue as 'a running sore'.

66 Interview, 13 March 2001.

67 Interview, 21 March 2001.

68 Interviews, 30 January 2001, 13 March 2001.

69 Interviews, 21 March 2001, 13 February 2001.

70 Interview, 13 March 2001.

71 Interviews, 13 March 2001, 21 March 2001. To make matters worse, Soley only ever seemed to be on the TV or radio when there was bad news. If the Government had a good news story, then a minister would easily be found to put their case. But when someone was needed to defend the indefensible, ministers were more reluctant to appear and the task was given to the Chair of the PLP.

72 Interview, 6 February 2001.

73 Interviews, 30 January 2001, 6 March 2001, 13 March 2001, 30 March 2001.

74 Interview, 13 March 2001.

75 The candidate rumoured to be about to stand was appointed a PPS, a useful coincidence.

76 Rosemary Bennett, 'Blow for Blair in backbench ballot', *Financial Times*, 22 November 2000.

77 Roland Watson, 'Soley warns of party at war', *The Times*, 15 November 2000. He did not promise to stand down but pointed out that few people had done the job of PLP Chair for more than one Parliament.

78 Interview, 21 March 2001. One MP described him as 'an unguided missile'.

79 Interview, 27 March 2001.

80 Interviews, 30 January 2001, 6 March 2001.

81 Interviews, 30 January 2001, 13 March 2001, 21 March 2001. One Northern MP admitted, 'I was voting for the Northern candidate, and I make no bones about that'. Interview, 27 March 2001.

82 Interview, 13 March 2001.

83 Another 45 Labour MPs failed to vote. Roland Watson and Philip Webster, 'Labour rebels deny job to Downing Street choice', *The Times*, 22 November 2000; Andrew Grice, 'Backbenchers force Soley into

run-off for party chairman', *Independent*, 22 November 2000.

84 Interviews, 6 March 2001, 27 March 2001.

85 Interview, 13 March 2001.

86 Interviews, 30 March 2001, 13 March 2001.

87 A whip quoted in Coates, 'Whipping the Government into Shape', p. 27.

88 Interview, 21 March 2000.

89 See James Macgregor Burns, 'The Parliamentary Labor [sic] Party in Great Britain', *American Political Science Review*, 44 (1950); J. J. Lynksey, 'Backbench Tactics and Parliamentary Party Structure', *Parliamentary Affairs*, 27 (1973); and the comments in King, *British Members of Parliament*.

90 Jack Brand, *British Parliamentary Parties*, Oxford, Clarendon, 1992, pp. 50–54.

91 Norton, 'Organization of Parliamentary Parties', p. 44.

92 Interview, 7 March 2000. One source even put the attendance figure for the Home Affairs Committee meeting on fox hunting at over 200. Interview, 3 May 2000.

93 Interview, 29 February 2000. Another MP described that meeting as 'standing room only'. Interview, 9 May 2000.

94 Interview, 6 March 2001.

95 Interview, 27 March 2001.

96 Interview, 29 February 2000. Or, as another put it dismissively: 'I wouldn't bust a gut if it was Nick Brown or Peter Mandelson'. Interview, 27 June 2000.

97 Interviews, 21 March 2001, 13 February 2001.

98 Burns, 'The Parliamentary Labor [sic] Party', p. 859.

99 Interview, 11 April 2000.

100 Interviews, 6 February 2001, 27 March 2001, 7 March 2000.

101 Interview, 16 May 2000.

102 Interviews, 6 February 2001, 30 March 2001.

103 Interview, 13 June 2000. One MP used the phrase 'taking the pulse' (11 April 2000), while another spoke of the backbench committees as a 'sounding board' (28 March 2000).

104 Coates, 'Whipping the Government into Shape', p. 64.

105 Interview, 3 May 2000.

106 Interview, 6 February 2001.

107 Interview, 27 June 2000; also 6 February 2001.

108 Interview, 30 March 2001. Even the Conservatives noticed (and appreciated) this. Interview, 6 February 2001. See also Peter Riddell, 'The Forgotten Parliament?', *The House Magazine*, 8 February 1999.

109 Interview, 21 March 2000.

110 Interview, 6 March 2001. Even loyal backbenchers acknowledged this point: 'Ministers talk, not listen. All they are interested in is getting the measure through.' Interview, 13 June 2000

111 Interview, 30 March 2001.

112 See, for example, the two articles by Peter Riddell: 'President Blair Told: "You Have Lost Touch"' (*The Times*, 16 March 1998) and 'We're missing you, Mr Blair' (*The Times*, 10 June 1998).

113 Compare the tables in Dennis Kavanagh and Anthony Seldon, *The Powers Behind the Prime Minister*, London, HarperCollins, 2000, pp. 210 and 286.

114 See Kavanagh and Seldon, *The Powers Behind the Prime Minister*, p. 284. The Chancellor, Gordon Brown, also held similar meetings, although these tended to be more social.

115 Interview, 15 February 2000. It was, said another MP, just 'such a thrill to be around the Cabinet table'. Interview, 27 June 2000. Not all took it so seriously. One MP, realising that he was sitting at Robin Cook's seat, wrote a list of women's names on Cook's blotting pad. Private information.

116 Interview, 7 March 2000. At one, for example, Blair admitted he'd 'dropped a bollock' over the London Mayor. Interview, 14 March 2000.

117 Interview, 28 March 2000.

[118] Interview, 6 March 2001.
[119] Interviews, 3 June 2000, 11 July 2000.
[120] Interview, 3 June 2000.
[121] Interview, 29 February 2000.

9.   Explaining Cohesion

Why did Labour MPs rebel so infrequently between 1997 and 2001? The last three chapters have gone some way to providing an answer. They have examined the factors that explain why some MPs rebel (and why some do so frequently), whilst others stay largely or totally loyal to the party line. They have examined and analysed the behaviour of the newly elected women, disproportionately likely not to rebel. And they have described and analysed the (not altogether satisfactory) ways in which the PLP attempted to mediate and internalise back-bench discontent during the Parliament.

This chapter attempts to draw the strands of the last three chapters together, to explain the cohesion that predominated during the Parliament. It starts by looking at the issues that came before Parliament. To what extent does the answer lie in the absence of controversial issues from the Government's legislative programme? It then looks at the composition of the PLP. Chapter 6 showed the factors that made MPs more or less rebellious. To what extent could the relative absence of rebellions result from the sort of MP sitting on the Labour benches? It then turns to the more collective (but less systematic) explanations for loyalty amongst Labour MPs, especially the strong desire of Labour MPs not to appear disunited, before finally examining the tactical reasons that may make MPs choose not to rebel.

The issues

The issues that come before Parliament are clearly important in determining the level of rebellion. To put it at its most facile: had the Blair Government attempted to enact the Murder of the First Born (No. 2) Bill there would have been an enormous backbench revolt.[1] At a slightly more sensible level it is clear from Part I (see especially Table 5.4) that the larger rebellions between 1997 and 2001 occurred over aspects of social security reform (especially lone parent benefit and incapacity benefit) or over measures involving the private finance of public services (such as NATS). Smaller rebellions took place over foreign affairs (such as the Defence White Paper, Iraq, Kosovo) or matters involving civil liberties (such as the Football (Disorder) Bill or the Terrorism Bill). So a Parliament that saw lots of measures reforming the social security system or other aspects of public services would have produced higher levels of backbench Labour rebellion than one predominantly dealing with, say, terrorism or civil liberties. (The rather obvious implications of this statement for the 2001 Parliament are discussed in Chapter 12). And as was noted in the introduction to Part II, there were issues known to divide the PLP – such as British entry into the Euro or PR for Westminster elections – which did not feature on the legislative agenda of the 1997 Parliament. Had they done so, there might have been more division.

Moreover, although not quantifiable, it was striking how interviews with Labour MPs – even with many of those on the left of the PLP – revealed a reasonable level of satisfaction with the majority of what the Government was doing. As one rebel MP put it: 'What we [the current Government] did in three months, it took them [previous Labour governments] three years not to do'.[2] As another said 'we can argue about how good the New Deal is in practice but it's a hundred times better than anything that's come before'.[3] Even a member of the Campaign Group was able to say that the Government was 'doing most of the things that we want it to do. It might not be doing them quite at the speed some of us want but lots of good things are happening none-the-less'.[4]

This widespread generalised support was often qualified by an equally widespread awareness that this was partly a reflection of the positive economic situation – especially when comparing 1997 with the Labour Government of the 1970s – and the backdrop of a benign set of economic indicators. Low inflation, falling unemployment, sound public finances and steady economic growth all helped make the 1997 Parliament what one MP called an 'unreal Parliament'. 'It's easy [to govern] when there's an economic success, harder if there's a downturn'.[5] In short, this was not the 1970s. Labour MPs were not watching their Government cut expenditure on the health service. The Blair Government may not have been going quite as fast, or as far, as some of its backbenchers would have liked – and occasionally it took a wrong turn – but for the most part its backbenchers thought it was at least going in the right direction.

Yet as a general explanation for the relative lack of rebellions seen between

1997 and 2001, the composition of the legislative agenda (and, concomitantly, the Government's actions) still remains unconvincing. The Government introduced a total of 154 bills, covering almost every area of policy. Much of this legislation was far from anodyne. To take just four examples: it scrapped student grants and introduced tuition fees; it introduced a controversial asylum policy, hugely unpopular on the Labour left; it implemented some draconian changes to laws on civil liberties, including restricting the right of freedom of movement and the right to trial by jury; and it was involved in military action in two countries. There was plenty here to cause unease on the backbenches. Moreover, much of the Government's programme – such as devolution or reform of the Lords – had caused serious headaches for previous Labour leaderships. What was noticeable repeatedly in Part I of this book was not that some Labour MPs revolted but how few did so. And although it was possible to criticise the Labour leadership for being too cautious (as, for example, did the Liberal Democrats with monotonous regularity), that very caution in initially refusing to depart from Conservative spending limits should if anything have fuelled discontent on the Labour benches.

Had the Blair Government introduced different legislation then it may have seen more (or fewer) rebellions, depending on the nature of the legislation. But it cannot seriously be argued that the only (or even the most serious) difference between the Blair Government of 1997 and all other modern governments, both Conservative and Labour, was the nature of the legislation brought forward.

The people

But whilst the issues may not have been all that different, the people certainly were. In some ways, this was a PLP like none before. And many of the ways in which it was different from its predecessors were exactly those that were conducive to a more cohesive Parliamentary party.

Chapter 6 identified five variables that exerted a statistically significant independent influence on the likelihood that an MP would rebel (at all and/or frequently): ideology, role conception, age, Campaign Group membership and council experience. Being precise about the extent to which any of these variables have changed over time is difficult, if not impossible: we unfortunately lack complete information about the state of earlier Parliamentary parties. Even surveys from just five years previous often did not ask the same questions, preventing comparability. For example, the scalar questions used to explain rebellion in Chapters 6 and 7 were only introduced in the BRS of 1997 and did not feature in its predecessor, the British Candidate Survey of 1992. These difficulties aside, there is still sufficient data to allow us to make some general points about the composition of the PLP.

Ideology. The ideological centre of the PLP has clearly moved rightwards in recent years, making rebellion less likely. Table 9.1 shows the responses given by Labour MPs in both 1992 and 1997 to the six questions that formed the socialist/laissez-faire scale used in Chapter 6.

Table 9.1 Labour MPs' support for socialist/laissez-faire values, 1992–97

% giving 'socialist' response in different Parliaments

Statement	1992	1997	Change
Ordinary working people get their fair share of the nation's wealth	91	94	+3
There is one law for the rich and one for the poor	91	93	+2
There's no need for strong trade unions to protect employees working conditions and wages	92	90	–2
Private enterprise is the best way to solve Britain's economic problems	75	48	–27**
Major public services should be in state ownership	70	48	–22**
It's the Government's responsibility to provide jobs for everyone who wants one	65	50	15*

Note: * $p<0.05$; ** $p<0.01$, using ANOVA.
Source: BCS, 1992; BRS, 1997. Adapted from Table 2.1 in Pippa Norris, 'New Politicians? Changes in Party Competition at Westminster', in P. Norris and G. Evans (eds), *Critical Elections*, London, Sage, 1999.

There was a 'falling endorsement for classic 'Old Politics' articles of faith on three out of six indicators'.[6] In 1992 three-quarters of Labour MPs disagreed with the statement that 'private enterprise is the best way to solve Britain's economic problems'; by 1997 that figure had fallen to less than half, 48 per cent. In 1992, 70 per cent of Labour MPs thought that 'Britain's public services should be in state ownership'; by 1997 that figure too had fallen to 48 per cent. And in 1992 almost two-thirds of Labour MPs (65 per cent) thought that it was the state's responsibility to provide jobs. By 1997, that figure had fallen to 50 per cent. None of the other three questions saw statistically significant changes between 1992 and 1997, but the overall shift in direction was clear enough.

There were similarly dramatic shifts in the responses Labour MPs gave to the questions that formed the libertarian/authoritarian scale, with the PLP becoming more authoritarian between 1992 and 1997. 'From 1992 to 1997 significantly more Labour MPs endorsed censorship to uphold moral standards while fewer expressed tolerance of political rights for anti-democratic parties'.[7] And the percentage of Labour MPs who agreed that 'Young people today don't have enough respect for traditional values' rose from eight per cent in 1992 to 23 per cent just five years later.

Of course, in not all cases did the beliefs of the PLP move so dramatically. Some of the changes in response to other questions were slightly more nuanced. For example, between 1992 and 1997 there was very little change in the percentage of Labour MPs who thought that the Government should put more money into the NHS, but the percentage who said that they 'definitely should' fell from 96 to 65, whilst those who thought they 'probably should' rose from four to 33 per cent. But the overall direction of the PLP was clear: it was to the right, and – confirmed by another survey into MPs' attitudes towards European policy – in an increasingly pro-European direction.[8]

Much of this shift was due to the new cohort of MPs elected for the first time in 1997. Pippa Norris found that the 1997 entrants were significantly more 'Blairite' than their colleagues; in other words, that new Labour MPs were also New Labour MPs.[9] Tony Blair's belief, expressed before the 1997 election, that the new MPs would be supporters of what he termed 'the need to modernise' appeared to have been confirmed.[10] Yet the ideological movement of the PLP was not caused solely by the new cohort of MPs. There was also evidence of a (slight) shift in the attitudes of incumbents, as they too became converted to Blairite positions.[11]

It is, though, important not to overstate the degree to which the PLP changed its attitudes. As well as showing a noticeable alteration in attitudes, the survey data also revealed considerable division within the Parliamentary party on a number of issues. And whilst the overall shift in attitudes was to the right, the PLP remained a clearly left-of-centre body. For example, in 1992, just 12 per cent of the PLP did not believe it was the Government's responsibility to provide jobs. By 1997, the figure had risen to 22 per cent.[12] The Blairite grouping therefore still constituted a minority, albeit a minority that was considerably larger than one would have thought possible just a few years before. The PLP of 1997, therefore, was far from being a Blairite love-in.

Roles. Unfortunately we lack comparable data on MPs' perceptions of their roles from before the 1997 Parliament. There is, though, some evidence that the newer

Labour MPs in 1997 were more likely to see their role as being a party delegate than other MPs, although even this evidence is slightly mixed. The BRS, for example, found no sizeable difference between the new MPs and the longer-serving ones.[13] The SPG survey, on the other hand, found the new Labour MPs somewhat more party orientated. The respondents to the SPG survey who said that they thought representing the party was their most important function were all newly elected. And 47 per cent of the new MPs said they 'nearly always' relied on the party whip, compared to 41 per cent of the older MPs. The figures for personal opinion were the opposite: 57 per cent of the newly elected MPs said that they 'nearly always' relied on their personal opinion, compared to 43 per cent of the longer serving MPs. So, according to the SPG survey, the newer MPs were more likely to rely on the whips than their own views; the more established MPs were more likely to rely on their own views than the whips.

In itself, however, this is not necessarily proof of a shift in the PLP's attitudes. It could be that newly elected MPs are always more likely to adopt a delegate role, and to rely on the whips; but that with time, MPs become more independent.[14] Moreover, even if we assume that there were more delegates in the PLP of 1997 than before – and it is worth stressing that we cannot be sure that there were – the overall number of delegates within the PLP remained small. Their numbers may have been swelled by some in the 1997 intake who saw themselves as mainly fulfilling a delegate view of the MP's role, but they still remained a clear minority in the PLP.

Age. The 418 Labour MPs elected on 1 May 1997 constituted the youngest PLP ever elected to Government. Table 9.2 shows the age structure of the PLP in 1997, February 1974 and 1964, the last three occasions Labour won power.[15]

Table 9.2 Age composition of the PLP when first elected to Government, 1964–1997 (column %)

Age	1964	Feb 1974	1997
20–29	–	1	2
30–39	14	16	13
40–49	25	33	43
50–59	33	31	33
60–69	22	18	8
70–79	5	2	1
80+	–	0	0

Note: a dash (-) indicates a sum greater than 0 but less than 1
Source: adapted from Nuffield election studies

In the immediate aftermath of the 1997 election much media attention focused on the very young Labour MPs, especially the ten – five men, five women – aged under 30. But some 15 per cent of the PLP in 1997 was aged under 40, almost identical to the situation in 1964 (14 per cent) and lower than in February 1974 (17 per cent). The most important difference came not in the numbers of very young MPs – the babies of the House – but in the slight shift in the ranks of the middle-aged. The difference comes with those MPs in their 40s: 43 per cent of the PLP elected in 1997 was aged between 40 and 49, noticeably larger than the proportion in 1964 or 1974. This meant that a total of 58 per cent of the PLP of 1997 was aged under 50, compared to 39 per cent in 1964 or 50 per cent in February 1974.

Chapter 6 showed how age was an important variable in explaining the rebelliousness of MPs. As MPs become older, so the chances of MPs rebelling become greater. Crudely speaking, in the 1997 Parliament a majority of Labour MPs over 50 rebelled, compared to a minority of those aged under 50.[16] And for the first time ever when in Government, the PLP elected in 1997 had a minority of MPs aged over 50. So, although the differences in age composition between the PLP of 1997 and that of previous Labour governments were not huge, they were still important.

The Campaign Group. Another key difference between many previous Labour governments and the one elected in 1997 was the absence of any large-scale organised opposition. In the 1920s, the MacDonald Government had faced concerted opposition from a minority within the Independent Labour Party.[17] In the 1940s, there had been the Keep Left Group. And in the 1960s and 1970s, the Party leadership had had to contend with the activities of the Tribune Group.[18] But by 1997 Tribune, though still in existence, was effectively moribund, and the only coordinated opposition to the Blair leadership within the PLP came from the Socialist Campaign Group.

Luckily for the Labour leadership, the Campaign Group was not the A Team of Parliamentary opposition. It suffered from three significant drawbacks. The first was its size. Its numbers varied across the Parliament, but it never contained more than 40 MPs; it frequently contained just over 30. In part this was a result of the decreasing size and influence of the left within the PLP, but the Group was far from pervasive even in terms of covering the whole of the left of the Party. As a rough measure of its inability to reach out to what should have been its natural constituency, consider the fact that some 44 per cent of Labour respondents to the BRS placed themselves at points one to three on the BRS's tax/spend scale, the same range of responses given by members of the Group. As a proportion of the PLP, that represents 184 MPs, more than five times the number of people in the Group. Even if we restrict our analysis just to those who placed themselves on points one or two then the numbers are 84, more than double the number of members of the Group.

The second problem was its image. The Campaign Group was seen as a group on the fringes of the party, marginalized and ignored. Indeed, one of the reasons some left-wing MPs did not join was precisely because they felt it would lead to them being marginalized within the PLP.[19] In turn, members of the Campaign Group realised, for example, that it was important for them not to be seen as leading rebellions. If the Campaign Group led on an issue, then 'there's some that'll not come along'.[20] So instead of leading rebellions as an organisation – as Tribune had in the 1960s and 1970s – the Group was forced to take a back seat. As a result, it punched below its (already slight) weight.

The third problem was its organisation. One Campaign Group member went so far as to claim that there was 'no organised opposition', describing the Group as just a 'group of individuals who have seen it [all] before'.[21] Meetings of the Group were somewhat chaotic – described by one of its members as a 'total shambles' – although they were said to have become somewhat better organised after John McDonnell took over the chair from Alan Simpson midway through the Parliament.[22] Indeed, to talk of the Campaign Group as a bloc 'deciding' or 'rebelling' may be misleading, as the group deliberately did not issue a whip, a sign of its desire not to be seen as a party within the party.[23] As a result, the Campaign Group could not always deliver its own MPs.

As Chapter 6 showed, membership of an organised group makes MPs more likely to rebel, over and above their ideological leanings. And facing Blair was one of the smallest, most marginalized and least organised factional groupings ever to face a Labour Prime Minister.

Council experience. There were more local councillors on Labour's benches than ever before. Over two-thirds of Labour's 1997 intake had experience in local Government. That included 23 former leaders of councils. In part this was because of the professionalisation of politics but it was also due to the changes in Labour's selection procedures, to One Member One Vote, which tended to produce – just like in 'The League of Gentlemen' – local candidates for local people.[24] The effect of this – as shown in Chapter 6 – should have been to produce more rebellious MPs.

Other variables. That, though, was the only exception to a generalised rule. The other four variables found to correlate significantly with rebellion all saw changes to the benefit of the Government: there were fewer left-wingers; there were (probably) more delegates; there were more young MPs; and there was little organised opposition to the Government. Even when we move onto the variables that appeared to exert a less significant impact on the propensity to rebel, we find pretty much the same story. Again, there is rarely perfect data to enable comparisons. We do not, for example, have data on previous MPs' levels of ambition. But there were certainly more new MPs in 1997 than since 1945; there were also more university educated MPs than ever before; and there was a large cohort of newly elected women. All three factors also contribute to a lower level of rebellion. Overall, then, the changes in the composition of the PLP appear to have acted in the interests of the party leadership. On almost every measurable criteria the changes to the PLP in recent years – and certainly since the last time Labour were in power – all made rebellion less, rather than more, likely.

Yet just as with the composition of the legislative agenda, these changes on their own do not make a convincing case for the differences in the behaviour of the PLP between 1997 and 2001 when compared to earlier periods. For one thing – just like with the behaviour of the newly elected women – most of these are differences of degree, not direction. For example, the PLP may have got younger, but it did not get that much younger. If we assume that everything else remained constant, but that the PLP of 1997 had the same age composition as that of February 1974, then we would have expected to see around 170 rebellious MPs, rather than 133. The same applies to the other variables. There are differences, to be sure, but they are not sizeable enough to explain the difference in behaviour on their own. Moreover, if the composition of the PLP was the explanation for the lower levels of rebellion, then we would have expected to see a less rebellious PLP across the board: that is, both fewer, and smaller, rebellions. Instead, we saw a small number of large rebellions.

We now need to turn, therefore, to two less measurable factors: the extent to which Labour MPs wanted to preserve the appearance of a united party and the extent to which the Government was able to negotiate with its backbenchers.

The desire for unity

When Labour MPs were asked directly why they were not rebelling, they tended to stress more collective explanations. The most common was the concern of MPs for the unity of their party. Chapter 6 demonstrated that this did not (as some thought) apply more starkly to MPs in marginal seats; but just because something does not apply to individuals *qua* individuals, it can still apply to them collectively. MPs in both marginal and safe seats wanted their party to appear united.

This was precisely the message contained in Blair's Church House speech, which began this book. Three year's after that speech, one MP summed it up simply: 'if you rock the boat, we all go in'.[25] It was a message that the party hierarchy constantly repeated. In an article in the *Independent* in November 1998, Blair (or Blair's ghost writer) argued that 'ill discipline allowed us to be painted as extremist, out of touch and divided'. Labour, he said, 'won't return to the factionalism, navel-gazing or feuding of the Seventies and Eighties, no matter how much a few people long for those heady days of electoral disaster'.[26] Yet in one sense Blair's speech and the message's constant repetition were largely unnecessary. Even before the election many Labour MPs were already placing a high premium on the appearance of unity and on the need to be self-disciplined.

That self-discipline derived from two different sources. The first was the effect of spending 18 years in opposition, opposition which some blamed on splits within the party. Being out of power for so long undoubtedly increased the desire for discipline: it 'concentrates the mind wonderfully' as one MP put it.[27] As one Cabinet minister said:

> 1992 was a watershed. We'd blown it. It got to the soul of the party. If you're in politics, you're in politics to get power. They'd got the message that a divided party is a losing party.[28]

One of the 1997 intake claimed that 18 years spent in the wilderness was 'funda-mental' to what she termed her 'abiding party loyalty'.[29] Many Labour MPs had fought long and hard to get back into power – 'some of them have worked a third of their working life for that'.[30] 'We know', said one MP, 'quite how damaging splits can be'.[31] One new MP described himself as 'scarred' by the party's divisions in the 1970s and 1980s.[32] Another spoke of making a 'funda-mental pledge: never again'.[33] One former rebel from the 1970s claimed that he could not bring himself to rebel no matter how unhappy he was with the new Government, because of those 'dark days'.[34] One of the new woman MPs put it forcefully:

> I will not bring this party into disrepute because I happen to remember how bloody awful it was living under a Tory administration . . . and if they have forgotten, [or] it was never particularly bad for them, it was very bad for me.[35]

The second source was the widespread belief that Conservative divisions in the 1992 Parliament had damaged the Party. As Ivan Lewis put it:

> [D]isunity made a massive contribution to the 18 years that we spent in opposition and ultimately rendered the Conservative party unfit to govern. Disunited parties not only do themselves a disservice, but become paralysed and unable to pursue the public interest.[36]

As one long-serving MP put it: 'The Tories were undermined by their own troops. Are we going to do the same? That's the message Blair was hammering out – and it sunk in'.[37] This led to a desire amongst some new Labour MPs to avoid the appearance of disunity at almost any cost. As one MP said: 'If it's a choice between being seen as clones or being seen as disunited . . . then I'd choose the clones any day'.[38] After 18 years in opposition, Labour MPs had no desire to do anything that might help send the party back to the wilderness.

This message was taken on board by most Labour MPs, including many of those on the left. As was shown in Chapter 2, the Campaign Group deliberately did not rebel on some issues where it believed that the public would not understand the reasons for any rebellion, such as the Bank of England Bill at the beginning of the Parliament. And on those occasions when it did rebel, the Group tended not to do so on Second Reading but instead rebelled on specific issues at later stages in a Bill's passage, because it believed that this appeared less obstructionist. There was a clear feeling even amongst those on the left that they should justify their actions when choosing to rebel, and that they could not do so 'willy-nilly'. Rebellions were engaged in to change policy, not for rebellion's sake.[39] Even many of the more rebellious worked on the basis that it was sensible to rebel only when there were sufficient numbers of MPs to make their collective voice heard – 'Don't bark unless you can bite'.[40] Other MPs often abstained rather than vote against, in order not to draw attention to their disquiet. Sometimes these quiet abstentions were the result of collusion with the whips. After one MP told his whip of his concerns over an issue, the whip replied that he had heard that the MP's constituency 'was very nice at this time of the year'. 'Why didn't he spend a night there?'[41]

Although the desire to appear united applied to most, though not all, Labour MPs, it appears to have been strongest amongst those MPs elected for the first time in 1997. The impact of these factors on the voting behaviour of newer MPs, said one long-serving MP, was that they had this idea that 'you never dissent', and therefore built dissent into an 'enormous bogey'. The new intake 'came in with two delusions. First, that rebellion was disloyal and undermining. And second, that complete discipline was helpful'. She argued that this was not so: 'It's like a marriage. The woman who says she never argues with her husband ends up divorced or dug into the concrete'.[42]

No Labour MP ended up dug into the concrete. Instead, the ability to remain so self-disciplined began to wear off as the Parliament progressed. This was clear both quantitatively and qualitatively. Quantitatively, as was shown in Chapter 4, the third session saw more rebellions than the first two put together. And qualitatively, it also saw a clear increase in low intensity conflicts, as MPs began to break ranks in small numbers. If at the beginning of the Parliament, MPs were only rebelling to try to change policy, by the end some (and it was still only a minority) were also rebelling for symbolic reasons. Some increasingly began to bark even when they knew they could not bite.

In part, this was because it was asking a lot for MPs to remain that self-disciplined for that long. But it was also because the imperatives for cohesion appeared to have become less important. As the Parliament progressed and it became increasingly clear that the Conservatives were not recovering in the polls, so rebellion became less damaging, less risky, and thus far easier.

Tactical concerns

It was the Conservative MP, Sir Ian (now Lord) Gilmour who wrote that 'concord and peace may signify backbench influence, not dull obedience'.[43] Studies have repeatedly shown the influence that backbenchers can have on Government policy without resorting to dissent.[44] Backbench MPs may be exercising all sorts of control behind the scenes, without the need to rebel in the division lobbies. As one rebel put it: 'When you're voting against, you're saying "You haven't listened"'.[45] Another described rebellion as 'an admission of failure'.[46] A lack of rebellions, on the other hand, may indicate backbench success.

The Government elected in 1997 attracted a widespread reputation for being autocratic 'control freaks', who ignored and marginalized Parliament. Yet as was clear from Chapter 8, the Government utilized contacts with its backbench MPs extensively, particularly after the scale of the lone parent benefit rebellion in December 1997 made them realize that they could not rely solely on coercion to retain cohesion. And as the chapters in Part I showed, the Government would frequently give concessions to its backbenchers in order to ease the passage of a Bill through

Parliament. 'The usual Government tactic', wrote the *Guardian*, 'is to publish details of a proposed Bill . . . test the reactions and, if necessary, make concessions'.[47]

These concessions were often small. The accusation about certain ministers was that although they may give ground, in policy terms, it was always 'the minimum they can get away with'.[48] Even those who admired Jack Straw's willingness to negotiate with backbenchers believed that his desire to conciliate was based more on 'low political cunning' than any genuine desire to change policy.[49] The Home Secretary would only make 'cosmetic' changes.[50] Negotiation with ministers rarely yielded everything that discontented backbenchers wanted. But the mere fact that the Government was willing to discuss and/or negotiate with its backbenchers can have a dramatic effect on rebellions for three reasons.

First, any negotiation or concession – 'it doesn't matter what it is', said one MP – can give any MPs who were not fully committed to the cause an excuse to back down, feeling that they have done enough to satisfy any doubts they might have had.[51] Several Labour MPs talked of giving the Government the 'benefit of the doubt' or as one put it, putting one's 'trust and faith in the generals'.[52] Such MPs do not need substantial movement on an issue to feel that they have done enough.

Second, if the minister is prepared to negotiate, then most potential rebels feel the need to do the same. 'If the Government gives way, and yet we still rebel, then what is the incentive for the Government to give way in the future?'[53] As another put it, 'If you go saying [that] you are definitely going to vote against the Government, then what's the point of them talking to you?'[54] One left-wing MP put it more bluntly: if the minister gives way, 'you don't knock them in the bollocks', because further negotiations may be needed. 'It is a continuing process'.[55]

And third, the fact that ministers might be willing to negotiate on one issue helps dampen the extent to which MPs are willing to rebel on others. Most backbenchers choose their rebellions carefully, in order to avoid being seen as too troublesome. As one occasional rebel put it:

> I set myself a rule . . . If I am to be regarded as normally loyal, it would take quite exceptional circumstances for me to vote against . . . I try to keep the currency of dissent at its full value.[56]

An MP who led one of the larger rebellions during the Parliament confessed that he had not rebelled on one issue so that he would have more kudos with the whips ('I don't want to get a name as a serial campaigner'), a point he made explicitly to the whips in order to increase his bargaining power with them.[57] Another MP argued in terms of 'credit chips': every time an MP rebelled, he argued, they used up credit, giving them less bargaining power in future. Ministers, he claimed, would make time for him – because they knew that he was essentially a team player – in a way that they will not for the more rebellious MPs, who he said are seen as a 'joke'.[58] Another employed a different metaphor to make the same point: there were 'only so many bullets in the gun, so I don't fire them unnecessarily'.[59] Even one of the more rebellious MPs thought that the whips 'discount' MPs such as Alan Simpson and Dennis Skinner because they rebel so frequently.[60] And even amongst the most rebellious MPs there is a recognition that, 'If they know you are going to vote against the Government all the time you are discounted'.[61] 'Constant whingers' achieved little.[62]

An MP's apparent loyalty to the party line can therefore be far more tactical than is sometimes appreciated. The mere fact that the Government is prepared to engage with its backbenchers can be enough to limit backbench rebellion. Just listening and discussing – whilst beneficial – is not sufficient; some occasional concessions are also necessary. But those concessions can often be fairly small and have an impact on Parliamentary behaviour beyond the issue itself.

However, this tactic does not work with all MPs nor at all times. Some MPs – especially those more ideologically opposed to the New Labour 'project' or those with few 'credit chips' left – are not so easily persuaded by concessions. Similarly, on some issues the size of the concession necessary before MPs will be placated may need to be larger. And by their very nature, some issues give much less room for negotiation and manoeuvre. The Government's room of manoeuvre over NATS and jury trials (see Chapter 4), for example, was limited by the either/or nature of the issue. Room for negotiation on social security issues was also limited (see especially Chapter 3), both because concessions on social security have the potential to cost sizeable amounts of money and because of the Government's desire to move 'forward' on reform. (By contrast, Home Office matters tend to allow more flexibility, because concessions will not usually have large spending implications). But in general, and where possible, the tactic was normally employed throughout the Parliament and it worked well in damping down backbench discontent.

It is, of course, difficult to quantify the extent to which ministers were better at negotiating in the 1997 Parliament, compared to in the past; or, alternatively, the extent to which MPs in the 1997 Parliament were perhaps willing to be satisfied with smaller concessions compared to MPs in previous Parliaments (although given the strength of self-discipline discussed above, the likelihood has to be that Labour MPs after 1997 would be somewhat more likely to be persuaded by smaller concessions than might have been the case previously). The basic point, however, is clear: far from being autocratic and aloof, the Government was usually prepared to do deals with its backbenchers. These had the effect of reducing rebellions, over and above their immediate impact. Had the Government been as autocratic as is sometimes implied, the number (and size) of rebellions under Blair would have been far greater.

Conclusion

The overall picture of the PLP of this period, then, is far more complicated than the traditional image. It is certainly not of a Parliamentary party full of timid or acquiescent MPs. For one thing, the PLP was more rebellious than was often realized. After one of the first revolts of the 2001 Parliament (see Chapter 12), Peter Sissons said on the BBC News that it made 'all our poodle references look a little dated'.[63] But rather than having become dated, they had always been rubbish. As Part I showed, whilst Labour MPs were rebelling infrequently, when they did revolt they did so in sizeable numbers. The average revolt under Blair, for example, was larger than that by Government MPs in any post-war Conservative Government. And there were plenty of Labour MPs – around half the back-benchers – who were willing (if necessary) to break ranks and vote against the Government.

For another, as Part II has shown, the reasons for this cohesion were more complicated than they at first appeared. The Government certainly benefited from changes in the composition of the PLP. This PLP was younger than previous governing PLPs; it (probably) had more MPs who saw themselves as delegates of their party, at least when compared to more recent Parliaments; it was more right wing or 'Blairite' than before; and the factional organized opposition was weaker. There was also a sizeable group of newly elected women who – for reasons that are not entirely clear – were also much less likely to rebel. The Government also benefited from an overriding desire on the part of the vast majority of the PLP not to do anything that might make their party appear divided. Even when they were unhappy with the activities of their Government (and, as noted above, they were usually more happy than people realized), Labour MPs were, perhaps more than ever before, prepared to exercise a self-denying ordinance and bite their tongues.

But for all that, when they had concerns over policy and when the executive had not listened seriously to those concerns, they were still prepared to rebel and rebel in numbers. That was clearest over the lone parent, incapacity benefit and NATS rebellions. So the Government also deserves some credit. Despite its reputation as a Government that disdained Parliament and Parliamentarians, it was in fact far better at negotiating with its backbenchers than was widely realized. One Cabinet minister – never a Blairite and since sacked for his pains – drew a distinction between the institution of Parliament and its (Labour) Members. The Government was, he argued, distant from the former – hence all the complaints about the way it treated Parliament.[64] But it was very close to the latter. He described it as 'superb' at consulting with backbenchers.[65] This is, of course, not a view shared by all Labour MPs. One thought the Government had been 'Napoleonic' in nature.[66] Another claimed he had witnessed, 'an elected dictatorship preserved by patronage'.[67] Yet another claimed that it 'wasn't a listening Government'.[68] But these were the views of a minority (indeed, of a small minority) of Labour MPs. Even if the majority of Labour MPs would not go so far as to describe the Government as 'superb' (the scale of the vote against Clive Soley would not have occurred had the Government been superb at consulting) the majority view amongst the PLP was certainly that they enjoyed good access to ministers, even if the results of that access were sometimes less dramatic. But the fact that the Government was for the most part willing to negotiate helps explain the pattern of infrequent but occasionally substantial rebellions seen during the Parliament. As in most previous occasions when Labour has been in power, the formal mechanisms for backbench consultation may not have been great successes, but a more general willingness of ministers to consult with, and occasionally negotiate with, backbench critics, was enough to dampen down several potentially damaging rebellions – most notably over asylum and immigration – and to extinguish several other putative revolts altogether.

Seen in this light, the infrequency of rebellions is rather more positive. It was not that Labour MPs were too scared to defy their leaders; rather it was a result of agreement and consultation as much as of coercion. The pattern of selective, but large, rebellions shows that Labour MPs were not natural rebels, acting awkwardly for the sake of it. But pushed too far, they would revolt. Perhaps as importantly, seen in this light the blame for those rebellions that did occur – if blame there is – attaches not to the MPs who rebelled, but to the Government, for failing to sugar the legislative pill sufficiently.

---

[i]   Although Diane Abbott did claim that the whips would have 'no difficulty getting it through' (*Guardian*, 16 March 1999).

2   Interview, 28 March 2000.

3   Interview, 2 August 1999.

4   Interview, 28 March 2000. Or as even a Labour rebel of many years standing was willing to admit, 'There's a lot of things I'm happy with'. Interview, 13 February 2001.

5   Interview, 21 March 2001; also 4 May 1999, 21 March 2000, 28 March 2000.

6   Pippa Norris, 'New Politicians? Changes in Party Competition at Westminster', in P. Norris and G. Evans (eds), *Critical Elections*, London, Sage, 1999, p. 26.

7   Norris, 'New Politicians?', p. 26.

8   See David Baker, Andrew Gamble, and David Seawright with Katarina Bull, 'MPs and Europe', *British Elections and Parties Review*, 9 (1999).

9   Pippa Norris, 'New Labour, New Politicians?', in Andrew Dobson and Jeffrey Stanyer (eds), *Contemporary Political Studies*, Volume 2, Nottingham, PSA, 1998.

10   *New Statesman*, 5 July 1996.

11   Norris, 'New Labour, New Politicians?'

12   Norris, 'New Labour, New Politicians?', p. 776.

13   If anything, according to BRS, the newer MPs were more willing to rebel: 20 per cent of MPs elected before 1997 agreed that MPs should vote with the party regardless of their own beliefs, compared to 18 per cent of the newly elected. The figures for the question relating to the national interest were 13 and eight per cent.

14   Put charitably, this might be because they discover the confidence to vote independently of the party. Less charitably, it might be because they start to get pompous, and begin to believe that they are more important than their party.

15   The data on 1945 is less comprehensive; but what data exists points in the same direction. R. B. McCallum and Alison Readman, *The British General Election of 1945*, London, Frank Cass, 1964 (Second impression), p. 274.

16   The difference is especially stark with new MPs. Of newly elected MPs under 50, 20 per cent had rebelled. Those over 50, by contrast, were almost three times more likely to have voted against the party line (59 per cent).

17   See, for example, the two articles by Robert Dowse, 'The Left Wing Opposition During The First Two Labour Governments', Parts I and II, *Parliamentary Affairs*, 14 (1960).

18   In general see Jack Brand, 'Faction as its own Reward: Groups in the British Parliament 1945 to 1986', *Parliamentary Affairs*, 42 (1989). For Tribune in particular, see J. Richard Piper, 'Backbench Rebellion, Party Government and Consensus Politics: The Case of the Parliamentary Labour Party, 1966–1970', *Parliamentary Affairs*, 27 (1973–74).

19   Interviews, 16 May 2000, 6 February 2001. A classic Catch–22: one of the reasons people did not join the Campaign Group was because it was seen as marginalized. Yet one of the reasons it was marginalized was because it was so small.

20   Interview, 13 February 2001. Also, interview, 14 March 2000.

21   Interview, 14 March 2000.

22   Interviews, 6 February 2001, 13 February 2001. Although one said that he later came to see the shambles as a 'tonic', because it allowed them to discuss more generalised questions. Whatever they were, though, the meetings were not planning meetings.

23   Interview, 9 May 2000. Similar comments, interview, 14 March 2000.

24   Andrew Roth and Byron Criddle, *New MPs of 97*, London, Parliamentary Profile Services, 1997, vii.

25   Interview, 7 March 2000. Two other Labour MPs also spontaneously used the same phrase. Interviews, 6 February 2001, 13 February 2001.

26   'If control freakery means strong leadership, then I plead guilty', *Independent*, 20 November 1998.

27   Interview, 15 February 2000. Also, interview, 27 March 2001.

28   Interview, 23 October 2001. He added: 'The behaviour of the Conservatives after 1992 just reinforced that'.

29 Interview, 23 May 2000.

30 Interviews, 6 February 2001, 13 February 2001.

31 Interview, 15 February 2000.

32 Interview, 21 March 2000. Similar views, interview, 13 June 2000.

33 Interview, 13 June 2000.

34 Interview, 5–6 August 2000.

35 Interviewed by Sarah Childs, 13 June 2000.

36 HC Debs, 21 July 1998, c. 957.

37 Interview, 25 October 2001.

38 Interview, 15 February 2000. Or, as another put it: 'If the opposite of control freakery is absolute anarchy . . . ' (interview, 21 March 2000).

39 Interview, 25 May 1999.

40 Interview, 6 February 2001.

41 Interview, 29 February 2000. Given the identity of his constituency, it is unlikely to be nice at any time of the year.

42 Interview, 28 March 2000.

43 Ian Gilmour, *The Body Politic*, London, Hutchinson, revised edition, 1971, p. 269.

44 See for example, J. J. Lynskey, 'The Role of British Backbenchers in the Modification of Government Policy', *Parliamentary Affairs*, 27 (1970); Jack Brand, *British Parliamentary Parties*, Oxford, Clarendon Press, 1992.

45 Interview, 6 February 2001.

46 Interview, 13 June 2000. Philip Norton uses exactly the same phrase: *Dissension in the House of Commons 1945–1974*, London, Macmillan, 1975, p. 611.

47 *Guardian*, 3 November 1999.

48 Interview, 11 July 2000.

49 Interview, 30 March 2001.

50 Interview, 27 March 2001.

51 Interviews, 14 March 2000, 21 March 2000.

52 Interviews, 14 March 2000, 9 May 2000, 27, 23 May 2000, 27 June 2000.

53 Interview, 15 February 2000.

54 Interview, 6 March 2001.

55 Interview, 16 May 2000.

56 Interview, 25 October 2001.

57 Interview, 2 August 1999.

58 Interview, 29 February 2000.

59 Interview, 27 June 2000. Other military analogies came from the MP who said that he believed in the First World War concept of the 'fleet-in-waiting', being more effective than the one that actually attacks (interview, 7 March 2000), or from the MP who talked of keeping his 'powder dry' ('Week in Westminster', *The House Magazine*, 8 November 1999).

60 Interview, 7 March 2000.

61 Interview, 6 February 2001.

62 Interview, 11 April 2000.

63 BBC Ten O'Clock News, 16 July 2001.

64 As discussed in Philip Cowley, 'The Commons: Mr Blair's Lapdog?', in P. Norris (ed), *Britain Votes 2001*, Oxford, Oxford University Press, 2001, pp. 253–256.

65 Interview, 23 November 2001.

66 Interview, 7 December 1999.

67 Interview, 19 January 2000.

68 Interview, 7 March 2000.

Part III

The Opposition

10. Grandees and Guerrillas:

The Conservatives

One of the enduring myths of British politics is that it is excessively adversarial. That is, that the political parties routinely oppose everything each other does. In fact, as Richard Rose convincingly showed as far back as 1980, British politics is usually marked as much by consensus and harmony as by conflict and division.[1] Beneath all the bluster, British political parties do not disagree with one another half as much as is usually implied – or half as much as they often make out. Were adversarial politics the norm, then the Official Opposition would routinely vote against the Government when it came to the Second Reading (the vote on the principle of a bill) and/or the Third Reading (the vote on the bill as finally constituted) of government legislation. Yet Rose showed that in fact the Opposition rarely voted against more than a quarter of government bills. Even at the height of adversarial politics between 1979 and 1983, with the gulf between the two parties at its widest since the Second World War, the Official Opposition, then Labour, voted against just over a third of the Thatcher Government's legislation at Second or Third Reading.[2]

In Opposition for the first time since 1979, the Conservative frontbench during the 1997 Parliament came to be criticised by some of its own back-benches for not being adversarial enough towards the Government. Yet between 1997 and 2001, the Conservative frontbench opposed 41 per cent of the bills introduced by the Government (see Table 10.1), making it one of the most adversarial Oppositions of recent times.

There was an initial reluctance on the part of the Tory frontbench to oppose most aspects of the Government's constitutional reform agenda, especially those bills – involving Scotland, Wales and Northern Ireland – where referendums had been held in the countries concerned. But as the Government's agenda moved away from constitutional reform and away from legislation outlined in its election manifesto, so the Conservative front bench began to oppose a higher proportion of Government legislation, reaching a peak of 48 per cent in the second session and 45 per cent in the third. Even on Northern Ireland, traditionally a topic for cross-party agreement, consensus broke down from June 1998 onwards. Here, despite having supported the Second Reading of the Northern Ireland (Sentences) Bill, the Conservative front bench opposed the Bill's Third Reading, because they argued that the Government had failed to link the issue of prisoner release with the need for the IRA to begin weapons decommissioning. From then on, the Conservatives became more critical of the Government's Northern Ireland policy, while remaining broadly supportive of the overall 'peace process'.

Table 10.1 Conservative front-bench opposition to Government, 1997–2001

Session	Government Bills	Bills contested by Conservativ front bench	As % of Government Bills
1997–98	53	19	36
1998–99	31	15	48
1999–00	42	19	45
2000–01	28	10	36
Total	154	63	41

Notes: The figures show the Bills on which the Conservative front bench chose to divide the House at Second and/or Third Reading. They exclude Government bills where there were free votes, but include Reasoned Amendments on Second and Third reading.

But just like Labour, the Conservative Parliamentary Party did not always act as one. Throughout the Parliament, small groups of Conservative MPs refused to do the bidding of their whips and voted against their party line (usually also voting against the Government in the process when the Conservative front bench advice was to support the Government or abstain). In addition to sporadic issue-based rebellions by backbench MPs of the sort seen on the Labour benches there was also a small ginger group of Conservative MPs – dubbed the 'awkward squad' – who set out to cause trouble for the Government by throwing as many procedural spanners in the Parliamentary works as possible, often against the advice of their own front bench, and whose activities escalated as the Parliament progressed. Often the two forms of behaviour would coincide – some Conservative MPs rebelling because they felt strongly about an issue, others doing so to cause trouble – and sometimes they would exist in the same individual simultaneously, with MPs rebelling both because they felt strongly about an issue but also because they wanted to create problems for the Government. Clearly delineating the two, especially towards the end of the Parliament once the awkward squad's activities escalated, is difficult, if not impossible. This chapter therefore begins by detailing the issue-based dissent by Conservative MPs during the first three sessions, before examining the behaviour of the Conservative awkward squad and other rebellions in the final session.

Conservative backbench dissent

First session (1997–98). With the Conservative front bench largely acquiescent over the issue, the majority of Conservative backbench dissent during the first year of the Parliament came from Tory MPs unhappy about aspects of constitutional change. There were large rebellions over devolution to Scotland and Wales, with smaller but more frequent revolts over policy towards Northern Ireland, the latter establishing a pattern that would last throughout the Parliament.

The largest rebellion came over devolution. Five consecutive votes in June 1997 saw an average of 35 Conservative backbenchers oppose the Referendums (Scotland and Wales) Bill, establishing the rules of the devolution referendums. The first and largest occurred over the issue of who should be allowed to vote. An amendment by Bill Cash proposed that the Scottish referendum should encompass the whole of the United Kingdom rather than merely those resident in Scotland. This has been described elsewhere as a 'spoiling amendment', but Cash argued that the Bill, because of the tax-varying powers, put it in the category of 'the first constitutional status', similar to the European referendum of 1975 which was voted upon by the electorate of the United Kingdom as a whole.[3] In what was to be the largest Conservative rebellion of the Parliament, 82 Conservative backbenchers, a full half of the Parliamentary party, backed Cash's amendment. Twenty Conservatives then supported a Liberal Democrat amendment that would have consolidated the two separate ballot papers in the Scottish referendum into one, leaving just the question of whether the people of Scotland wanted a Scottish Parliament with tax-varying powers.[4] In a third division, 37 Conservative MPs supported an SNP amendment to replace the existing questions with a multi-option referendum, giving a choice between independence, devolution and the status quo.[5] In the fourth vote, 22 Conservatives voted against the details of the ballot paper in Scotland. And finally, nine Conservatives supported a Plaid Cymru amendment to insert a multi-option referendum, including full self-Government for Wales, into the Welsh ballot paper. In total, 94 Conservative MPs (listed in Appendix 7) defied their whips at some point during the Bill.

Conservative backbench opposition to the various Government bills that paved the way for the 'peace process' and devolved Government to Northern Ireland accounted for 21 out of the 34 Conservative rebellions in the first session. The Conservative front bench largely supported the Government in the early stages of the Northern Ireland 'peace process', but a small number of Conservative MPs rebelled on bills which variously established a Parades Commission to oversee sectarian parades, paved the way for elections, facilitated the release on licence of paramilitary prisoners whose organisations were observing a ceasefire, and which implemented the terms of the Belfast ('Good Friday') Agreement of April 1998.[6] These rebellions, though, were small, involving an average of just three MPs. Even the two largest rebellions of the first session, during the Northern Ireland (Sentences) Bill, involved only six Conservative MPs in both cases.[7] Table 10.2 lists the Conservative rebels on these, and all other Northern Ireland divisions, during the Parliament.

Table 10.2 Conservative rebels over Northern Ireland, 1997–2001

	Parades	Elections	Sentences	Good Friday	Victim Remains	NI Bill	Assembly Order	Disqualif-ications	Review	Flags	Police	Arms Decomm-issioning
David Atkinson	–	–	X	–	–	–	–	–	–	–	–	–
Richard Body	X	–	–	–	–	X	–	X	–	–	X	–
Peter Bottomley	–	–	–	X	–	–	–	X	–	–	–	–
Virginia Bottomley	X	–	–	–	–	–	–	–	–	–	–	–
Graham Brady	–	–	X	–	–	–	–	–	–	–	–	–
Ian Bruce	–	–	–	–	–	–	–	X	–	–	–	–
William Cash	–	–	–	–	–	X	–	X	–	X	X	–
Christopher Chope	–	–	–	–	–	X	–	X	–	–	–	–
Alan Clark	–	–	–	–	X	–	–	–	–	–	–	–
Michael Colvin	–	–	–	–	X	–	–	–	–	–	–	–
David Davis	–	–	–	–	–	X	–	–	–	–	–	–
Peter Emery	–	–	–	–	–	X	–	X	–	–	–	–
Michael Fabricant	–	–	–	–	–	–	–	X	–	–	–	–
Michael Fallon	–	–	–	–	–	–	–	X	–	–	–	–
Howard Flight	–	–	X	–	–	–	–	–	X	–	–	–

cont'd

	Parades	Elections	Sentences	Good Friday	Victim Remains	NI Bill	Assembly Order	Disqualif-ications	Review	Flags	Police	Arms Decommissioning
Eric Forth	–	–	–	–	–	X	–	X	–	–	–	–
Roger Gale	–	–	–	–	–	–	–	X	–	–	–	–
Edward Garnier	–	–	–	–	X	–	–	–	–	–	–	–
Christopher Gill	–	–	–	–	–	X	–	X	–	–	X	–
Teresa Gorman	–	–	–	–	–	–	–	X	–	X	–	–
James Gray	–	–	–	X	–	–	–	X	–	–	X	–
Douglas Hogg	–	X	X	–	X	–	–	X	–	–	X	–
Michael Howard	–	–	–	–	–	X	–	–	–	–	X	–
Gerald Howarth	–	–	X	–	X	X	–	X	–	–	X	–
Andrew Hunter	X	X	X	X	X	X	X	X	X	–	X	–
Bernard Jenkin	–	–	–	–	X	–	–	–	–	–	–	–
Edward Leigh	–	–	–	–	–	–	–	X	–	–	–	–
Dr Julian Lewis	–	–	–	–	–	–	–	X	–	–	–	–
David Maclean	–	X	–	–	–	X	–	X	X	–	–	–
Anne McIntosh	–	–	–	X	–	–	–	–	–	–	–	–
Michael Mates	–	–	–	–	–	–	–	X	–	–	–	–
Brian Mawhinney	–	–	–	–	–	–	–	X	–	–	–	X
Patrick Nicholls	–	–	–	–	–	–	–	X	–	–	–	–
Richard Page	–	–	–	–	–	–	–	X	–	–	–	–
Owen Paterson	–	–	–	–	–	–	X	–	–	–	–	–
Andrew Robathan	–	–	X	–	X	X	–	X	X	–	–	X
Laurence Robertson	–	X	X	X	–	X	–	–	X	X	X	–
Andrew Rowe	–	–	–	–	–	–	–	X	–	–	–	–
Nick St Aubyn	–	–	–	–	–	X	–	X	–	–	–	–
Jonathan Sayeed	–	–	–	–	–	–	–	X	–	–	–	–
Richard Shepherd	–	–	–	–	–	–	–	X	–	–	–	–
Michael Spicer	–	–	–	–	–	–	–	X	–	–	–	–
Desmond Swayne	–	–	X	X	X	X	X	X	X	X	X	–
Teddy Taylor	–	–	–	–	–	–	–	–	–	–	–	X
John Townend	–	–	–	–	–	X	–	–	–	–	X	–
Peter Viggers	–	–	–	–	–	–	–	X	–	–	–	–
Charles Wardle	–	–	–	–	–	X	–	X	–	–	–	–
John Wilkinson	–	–	X	X	–	X	–	–	–	–	–	–
David Wilshire	–	–	–	X	–	X	–	–	–	–	–	–
Ann Winterton	–	X	–	–	–	–	–	X	–	–	–	–
Nicholas Winterton	–	X	X	–	–	X	X	X	–	X	X	X

Note: X indicates that the MP voted against the party whip

Conservative back–benchers also opposed aspects of the Criminal Justice (Terrorism and Conspiracy) Bill (see Chapter 2). In the second largest Conservative rebellion of the session (and of the Parliament), 40 Conservative MPs (listed in Appendix 7) joined the 16 Labour backbenchers who objected to all the Bill's stages being completed in one day. With the exception of the Party's two front–bench spokesmen, every Conservative MP who spoke in the debate crit-icised the haste with which the legislation was being introduced. Echoing the views of critics on the Government benches, Alan Clark claimed that the Bill was 'an example of the contempt in which the Prime Minister holds the chamber' and that the House was being 'used simply as a rubber stamp'.[8] Later that day, three Conservative back–benchers supported Chris Mullin's amendment making the implementation of the Bill conditional on the audio recording of suspects.[9]

The only other issue to attract a significant number of Conservative rebels was the Second Reading of the rather obscure Supreme Court (Offices) Bill, which *inter alia* introduced compulsory retirement for the Permanent Secretary of the Lord Chancellor's Department at the age of 60, bringing the Department into line with all other Government departments. Seven Conservative backbenchers voted against the Bill.[10] The session also saw five rebellions by lone Conservative MPs.[11]

Second session (1998–99). During the second session Northern Ireland again dominated Conservative rebellions; and as the session progressed, so the number of Conservative MPs prepared to break ranks over the issue grew.

It began with a sole dissenting vote, when Laurence Robertson voted against a Government amendment to a Conservative Opposition Day Motion on decommissioning and prisoner releases. Then, in May 1999, nine Conservative backbenchers opposed the Second Reading of the gruesomely titled Northern Ireland (Location of Victims' Remains) Bill. In response to an IRA statement in March 1999 announcing that it knew the location of the graves of nine people, the British and Irish Governments had agreed to introduce legislation promising not to prosecute those responsible for the murders in return for information about the possible location of the bodies. Andrew Hunter spoke for many of his backbench colleagues when he described the Bill as 'obnoxious and dangerous'.[12] In July 1999 ten Conservative MPs opposed the Second Reading of the Northern Ireland Bill (the Anglo-Irish plan to revive the 'peace process'). Michael Howard, the former Home Secretary but now a backbench Conservative MP, argued that without a guaranteed timetable of IRA decom-missioning the 'Bill does not deserve the support of the House'.[13] Although Howard followed the Conservative front bench in abstaining on the Second Reading of the Bill, by Third Reading he too was willing to vote against the Government. The Third Reading vote that followed witnessed the largest Conservative backbench rebellion on Northern Ireland of the Parliament: 16 Tory MPs voted against the Bill, in defiance of the front bench line to abstain.

Just as on the Labour benches (see Chapter 3), there was a wide divergence of views on the Tory backbenches over whether to support the Anglo-American bombing of Kosovo in March and April 1999.[14] The Conservative front bench, though largely supportive of the Government, was unwilling to support the use of ground troops. During the main debate four backbench Conservatives MPs – Nicholas Soames, Sir Geoffrey Johnson-Smith, John Wilkinson and James Paice – made speeches in support of the Government, although Soames wanted to go further by committing ground troops.[15] Another six backbench Tories – Alan Clark, Sir Peter Tapsell, Douglas Hogg, Sir Peter Viggers, Crispin Blunt and Bowen Wells – urged that Britain stay out of the conflict.[16] And a third, much larger, group would later express growing unease about the possibility of British casualties.[17] But the Government's careful avoidance of votes on the Kosovo issue, coupled with the fact that the war did not drag on, ensured that Tory divisions were confined to interventions and speeches rather than formal votes. The illusion of Conservative party unity on the issue was therefore largely preserved.

The issue of immigration and asylum also caused discontent on the Conservative benches as well as on Labour's. There were three small rebellions by Conservative MPs during the session, all cast in a liberal direction. During the Report stage of the Immigration and Asylum Bill in June 1999, Peter Bottomley and Sir Peter Lloyd supported a Liberal Democrat clause repealing section 8 of the Asylum and Immigration Act 1996, and in November, Bottomley, Lloyd and Robert Jackson joined 16 Labour backbenchers in voting for a Lords amendment to the Bill that would have restored social security benefits to all asylum-sekers until the targets for processing cases had been met by the Home Office. In the following vote Michael Fallon supported a Liberal Democrat amendment forbidding the house arrest of an asylum seeker for more than ten days.

In July, four enterprising Conservative backbenchers – Christopher Gill, Douglas Hogg, Desmond Swayne and Nicholas Winterton – correctly spotted a potential flaw in the Food Standards Bill establishing a UK-wide Food Standards Agency. The Agency covered Scotland and yet the Scotland Bill had devolved power over food safety to the new Scottish Parliament. The four Conservatives therefore objected to a Ways and Means resolution that sought to charge English taxpayers in order to subsidise the Scottish component of the FSA. A further three rebellions in the session consisted of lone Conservative MPs.[18]

Third session (1999–2000). The issue of Northern Ireland again dominated Conservative divisions during the third session. At the beginning of the session in November 1999, four Tory backbenchers opposed the Order in Council that officially ended direct rule, conferring powers on the Northern Ireland

Assembly. In January 2000 13 Conservatives voted against the Second Reading of the Disqualifications Bill. The Bill dealt with the anomaly created by the Northern Ireland Act 1998 that permitted a member of the Irish Senate to be a member of the Northern Ireland Assembly but not of any other UK legislature. It ended the prohibition against members of the Irish legislature – both the Dail and the Senate – from being a member of any legislature in the United Kingdom, including the House of Commons, the Scottish Parliament, the Welsh Assembly and the Northern Ireland Assembly. The Conservative front bench stance was to abstain.[19] Many Conservative MPs disagreed. Eric Forth intervened during the speech of Ann Widdecombe, the Shadow Home Secretary, to complain about the equivocal stance of his front bench:

> Will my right hon. Friend reconsider the extraordinary philosophy that she outlined a moment ago? Apparently, we no longer oppose bills on Second Reading because we want to consider them later in detail. Surely it is possible – and, in the case of this measure, proper – to oppose a Bill in principle when it would affect so significantly the relationship between this legislature and others.[20]

Andrew Hunter described the Bill as 'just the latest obscene landmark in a process that ostensibly began as a peace process, but long ago became, in reality, a sordid, shabby process of appeasement'.[21] The Government had hoped to get through the remaining stages of the Bill the following day. But a group of Conservative MPs began a marathon session of filibustering (discussed further below). As the evening of the 25 January became the morning of 26 January, the quality of the debate inevitably plummeted. Five separate divisions throughout the night and into the following morning saw an average of 11 Conservatives support amendments and block Government motions that attempted to hasten the Bill's passage, with a total of 33 Conservative MPs voting against their front bench at some point.

In February 2000, in an attempt to derail the Belfast Agreement, six Tory back-benchers supported a rebel Ulster Unionist amendment that called upon the Secretary of State for Northern Ireland not to launch a review of the Belfast Agreement in the event of a suspension of the Assembly. In May, following the refusal of the two Sinn Fein Assembly ministers to allow the British flag to be flown over their departmental buildings, five Conservative backbenchers opposed giving the Secretary of State for Northern Ireland the power to set regulations for the flying of flags over Government buildings in Northern Ireland. In June six Tory backbenchers objected to the Police (Northern Ireland) Bill, which implemented most of the Patten Report into the reform of the Royal Ulster Constabulary (RUC). Andrew Hunter argued that the Bill was 'an affront to decency and democracy' and in what was becoming one of his favourite lines he concluded: 'One may speculate that the Bill may prove to be the British Government's final act of appeasement, but it is certainly one of the most sordid'.[22] A month later, ten Conservative MPs also opposed the Bill's Third Reading.[23]

Northern Ireland was, though, not the only issue to see discontent on the Conservative benches during the session. As the Government's focus shifted away from constitutional issues towards bills with implications for civil liberties, so Conservative backbenchers chose to oppose many of the measures before Parliament against the advice of their front bench. In December 1999 Douglas Hogg intervened six times during the Second Reading debate of the Terrorism Bill, before giving a speech that argued that the definition of terrorism in the Bill went far beyond the traditional definition.[24] Left to his own devices, he would have called a division on Second Reading, but acknowledging that he lacked sufficient support he instead backed the Liberal Democrat motion to refer the Bill to a Special Standing Committee for closer scrutiny. During the Bill's Report stage, Hogg then cast a further three dissenting votes, supporting amendments that would have limited the duration of the Act to five years and that would have excluded violence against property from the definition of terrorism.[25] During the passage of the Freedom of Information Bill, David Davis and Richard Shepherd (the latter a long-time exponent of greater freedom of information) each cast three dissenting votes in support of Liberal Democrat amendments that would have reduced the test of harm placed on the disclosure of public documents and would have increased the public's right to know about the investigations conducted by public authorities.

Conservative backbench opinion was also divided during the Second Reading of the Football (Disorder) Bill (see Chapter 4). Simon Burns and Sir Norman Fowler supported the legislation, both having been closely involved in previous attempts to legislate on the issue.[26] On the other side of the debate, libertarian Conservatives were concerned about the civil liberties implications of the Government's proposals, with Peter Lilley arguing that the thuggish behaviour of some England fans did not justify thuggish law.[27] Eric Forth disagreed with the Bill 'totally, entirely and in every respect', adding, in case anyone had failed to grasp the extent of his opposition, 'At every level, the Bill is wrong, defective, undesirable and unacceptable'.[28] When it came to the vote, the Conservatives split three ways. The official line – followed by the majority of MPs – was to abstain, but seven Conservative MPs opposed the Bill's Second Reading and two supported it. The largest Conservative rebellion on the Bill came when 13 Conservatives voted against the guillotine placed on the Bill's proceedings. Roger Gale compared the Bill with the ill-fated Dangerous Dogs Act 1989. Both pieces of legislation, he argued, were knee-jerk reactions, based on the 'do something' school of politics.[29] And the former Solicitor General and Attorney General, Sir Nicholas Lyell, said that it was 'quite wrong' to 'make a major attack on the civil liberties of people in this country'.[30] During the remainder of the Bill's passage, five Conservatives supported a Liberal Democrat amendment that would have removed the power of a police constable to stop someone from travelling abroad if they were likely to cause violence.[31] When the Bill reached its Third Reading, again with the front bench abstaining, Simon Burns supported the legislation, with Christopher Chope and Peter Lilley opposing it.

Several other diverse issues caused small numbers of Conservative MPs to break ranks with their party. On 27 March 2000 four Conservatives voted against increases in the rate of duty on tobacco products.[32] In May during the row over NATS (see Chapter 4), two Conservatives, David Davis and Richard Shepherd, supported the idea of the new private sector company being formally owned by the Crown. A month later the two Bottomleys – Virginia and husband Peter – voted with the Liberal Democrats after an Opposition Day debate on Britain's strategic interests. Later that month three Conservatives voted against the Third Reading of the Census (Amendment) Bill, the private members' Bill brought forward by the Conservative backbencher, Jonathan Sayeed, which amended the Census Act 1920 to enable a voluntary question on religion to be included in the 2001 census. Despite the Bill's private member status, the Conservative front bench took the rare step of urging their MPs to abstain. Sayeed defied the whips by voting in the aye lobby, while Eric Forth joined Douglas Hogg and Edward Leigh in the noe lobby. On 20 November 2000, three Conservative MPs – Peter Bottomley, Dr Julian Lewis and Sir Teddy Taylor – supported a Liberal Democrat prayer to revoke the £500 charge placed on immigrants who wished to appeal against the rejection of their visa application. Two Conservative MPs, David Davis and Eric Forth, joined the Government lobbies in opposing the prayer. Finally, near the end of the session, seven Conservative MPs voted against a statutory instrument relating to the privileges of European satellite television companies.[33] A further two rebellions saw a lone Conservative MP rebel.[34]

The 'awkward squad'

As well as these ad hoc rebellions by Conservative MPs, the Government also faced concerted opposition from a small ginger group of Conservative MPs. Whereas many Labour rebels did not like the labels given them by the media, many members of this group of Conservative MPs, formed around two former ministers, Eric Forth and David Maclean, revelled in their description as 'the awkward squad'. They engaged in a Parliamentary form of guerrilla warfare, with both their behaviour and their *raison d'être* likened by one of the group to that of the French resistance during World War Two:

> When France was invaded it was finished. Then two and a half thousand out of 40 million joined the *Maquis*. We can't defeat the Government in votes, we can't defeat them in argument, since no one ever listens, but we can tie them down in the same way that the *Maquis* tied down the Germans . . . it's only pot shots, but it's a form of opposition.[35]

Simon Hoggart drew a similar comparison: 'They are like guerrillas fighting in the forests and hills, the rag-taggle remains of a defeated army'.[36] It would be carrying the military analogy too far to suggest that they saw their front bench as quislings or like the leaders of Vichy France, but many members of the awkward squad certainly thought that their High Command was too conciliatory and too consensual towards the Government – that Conservative front benchers did not have 'the stomach for it'.[37] Singled out for criticism were the Chief Whip, James Arbuthnot, and the Shadow Leader of the House for most of the period, Sir George Young, both of whom many awkward squad members regarded as 'grandees'. 'Some of them learned their politics with cucumber sandwiches'.[38] These grandees wanted to play by the rules, accepting the norms of the House and saw anything else as *infra dig*. Eric Forth and his colleagues, by contrast, saw themselves as Parliamentary Clint Eastwoods, playing by their own rules. One described himself as 'a Parliamentary yob': 'It's in my nature to play party politics rough'.[39] Collectively, their aim was to cause what one of them called 'buggeration', 'to make life for the Government as miserable as possible'.[40] In some cases, this grew from a neo-liberal ideological objection to the idea of all but the most minimal of legislation ('What I want is institutional gridlock. I want it to be nearly impossible for Government to do anything') but it was just as likely to result from a belief in the value of confrontational politics, in which the point of Opposition was to oppose, and the role of the backbencher was to hold the Government to account.[41] As one said, 'It's not my job to cooperate with passing socialist legislation'.[42] If the Conservative front bench would not oppose the Government, then Conservative backbenchers would have to do it.

Despite the label, there was no formal organisation behind the awkward squad and its membership was both amorphous and variable. The inner core (see Table

10.3) was essentially just four Conservative MPs. Eric Forth and David Maclean organised most of the group's various activities, Forth acting as the unofficial whip, with Gerald Howarth and David Wilshire never far behind. Disliking e-mail, Forth would send dry little notes to his fellow conspirators: 'I am given to understand that the Powers That Be think that Wednesday's business will go through easily'.[43] Wednesday's business would then almost certainly *not* be going through easily. There were no formal meetings, although the core of the awkward squad were all members of the Thatcherite No Turning Back Group which met for dinner once a month, where they would all 'have a good whinge' about the activities of their own front bench and 'wish they were opposing things'.[44] Around a nucleus of Forth et al was an outer core, which comprised some 12 MPs, who were regularly to be found acting in concert with the inner core but who were less involved in organising their activities. And there was then another group of MPs, again around 12 in number, who would occasionally join in (especially once their activities escalated later in the Parliament), but whose involvement was less regular and depended at least in part on the particular issues involved and the tactics being employed. As one said 'Only the psychotic care enough to stay up all night'.[45]

Table 10.3 Conservative 'awkward squad'

Inner core	Outer core	Late converts
Eric Forth (1983)	Michael Fabricant (1992)	Peter Lilley (1983)
David Maclean (1983)	Douglas Hogg (1979)	Anne McIntosh (1997)
Gerald Howarth (1983)	Edward Leigh (1983)	David Ruffley (1997)
David Wilshire (1987)	James Gray (1997)	Patrick Nicholls (1983)
	Christopher Gill (1987)	Laurence Robertson (1997)
	Christopher Chope (1983)	Crispin Blunt (1997)
	Teresa Gorman (1987)	Ian Bruce (1987)
	Dr Julian Lewis (1997)	John Redwood (1987)
	Owen Paterson (1997)	Bill Cash (1984)
	Nick St Aubyn (1997)	John Hayes (1997)
	Desmond Swayne (1997)	Andrew Hunter (1983)
	John Wilkinson (1979)	Teddy Taylor (1964)

Note: the figure in brackets is the year the MP was first elected.

Initially, Forth and Maclean began by blocking Private Members' Bills, something that the procedures of the Commons makes relatively easy to do.[46] They believed that the Government was abusing private members' time by getting backbench MPs to introduce so-called 'handout' bills, Government bills in all but name.[47] By blocking Private Members' Bills, therefore, Forth and Maclean aimed to force the Bill to be reintroduced later, which would eat up Government time.[48] But they also shared an ideological objection to private members' legislation in general, believing that they were badly scrutinised, usually originated with single-issue groups, and nearly always imposed regulations and costs. In their view, it was possible to have 'good' Private Members' Bills, but they had to be totally non-controversial, consisting of just a few clauses. In practice 'precious few' were like this.[49]

As the Parliament progressed, so the awkward squad's activities increased, both in terms of frequency and in terms of the number of MPs involved. The slow start was partly due to the effects of the defeat of 1997 – a process that one MP described as 'getting over the shell shock'.[50] But Conservative MPs also had to adapt to being in opposition. By 1997 very few Tory MPs had been in the Commons when their party had last been out of Government, and it took time to adjust to the realities of being on the outside and to discover the more obscure Parliamentary procedures with which they could obstruct Government business.[51] But once they discovered them, and once they had tasted blood, they realised that causing trouble for the Government was 'fun'.[52] It 'gives me a purpose in life', said one, 'gets me up perkier in the morning. It's worth it to see their faces'.[53]

By the third session, the group had begun to object to otherwise non-contentious bills, such as the Sea Fishing Grants (Charges) Bill, and to call divisions and filibuster during their passage.[54] In just one day during the third session, they divided the House on four otherwise non-contentious bills.[55] Several other bills saw deliberate, and extensive, filibustering. On 14 March 2000, for example, 14 Conservative MPs filibustered and then voted against a supplementary estimate that granted the paltry sum of £1000 for the establishment of a Crown Prosecution Inspectorate.[56] The Report stage of the Royal Parks (Trading) Bill, which also saw considerable filibustering, contained a memorable rhetorical question by David Maclean during a discussion on the police's powers to seize perishable products: 'What advice does the Minister give to the policeman, or the chestnut seller, who finds that his hot brazier has been confiscated and then must find somewhere to put his hot nuts?'[57] No reply was recorded. The exemplar of this behaviour was the Disqualifications Bill, where opposition from Conservative backbenchers resulted in the deliberations of the Committee of the Whole House running from 5.43 pm on 25 January 2000 to 7.19 am on 26th. As a result, a full day's business, including Prime Minister's Questions, was lost.[58]

At times, the awkward squad's activities were in clear contravention of the Conservative whips. This was especially true of the Disqualifications Bill, where the Conservative front bench had hoped to embarrass the Prime Minister on his 1000th day in office at Prime Minister's Questions.[59] However, more often than not, the votes occurred late at night when the Conservative whips' line was that their MPs could go home, and very often there was no Conservative line to be rebelling against. Forth and co would instead stay around, looking for a fight, forcing divisions, often on otherwise non-contentious statutory instruments.[60] For example, on 19 July 1999, a small group of Conservative backbenchers divided the House over nine consecutive Government motions and statutory instruments beginning at 12.21am and ending at 1.52am. Each division takes between 12 and 15 minutes, itself wasteful of Government MPs' time, but more importantly the prospect of an unexpected division forces the Government whips to keep enough MPs in the precincts of the Commons to ensure victory, inconveniencing Labour MPs for hours more than the time taken for the votes themselves.[61] As Austin Mitchell noted in the *House Magazine*'s Commons Diary: 'I'd thought 10pm was now a guaranteed P.O.H (Push Off Home) time . . . Not so. Tonight 200 'volunteers' are kept back until 2.30 to vote down six of Forth's Freedom Fighters'.[62] Even more frustrating for Labour MPs were those occasions when Conservative backbenchers would keep a debate going into the early hours of the morning, only, at some ungodly hour, for the Tories *not* to force a vote.[63]

Perhaps because some of them secretly admired the awkward squad's activities (and perhaps because they could not do much to stop them even if they wanted to), the Conservative whips frequently turned a blind eye, even when the group's activities were in contravention of the Party's whip, and no disciplinary action was taken against any of its members. Several members of the awkward squad admitted that if their whips had ever asked them to desist, they probably would have done so.[64] But this attitude did not apply to the inner core. When a Tory whip tried to stop Forth filibustering during the Disqualifications Bill, he was given short shrift: 'Fuck off. Do you really think I've been here for 18 hours and I've got the chance of losing a day's business and I'm going to give it up now? Piss off'.[65]

Table 10.4 'Awkward squad' rebellions, 1997–2001

Session	Number of Bills opposed at Second/Third Reading	Number of divisions to see awkward squad rebellions
1997–98	0	1
1998–99	0	12
1999–00	4	17
2000–01	7	28
Total	*11*	*58*

By the beginning of the fourth session, the awkward squad's activities had escalated (see Table 10.4) to the point where it became very difficult to separate out their activities from the more issue-based rebellions. The fourth session saw the awkward squad force divisions on the principle of a full quarter of the Government's legislation, almost as much as the Conservative front bench objected to, and in some cases they were joined in the division lobbies by other Conservative MPs who had objections to the contents of the particular Bill.[66] The introduction of deferred divisions, something that all Conservative MPs had voted against when they had been proposed, complicated matters even further.[67] The very first vote using a deferred division – on European Union fish quotas – saw the Party formally instruct its MPs to spoil their ballot papers by voting twice, an act that provoked a reprimand from the Speaker.[68] And from then on, many deferred divisions saw small 'rebellions' by Conservative MPs. These were as much protests against the system – forcing votes on otherwise uncontroversial issues in order to slow down the process – as revolts over the issues themselves. The 29 'rebellions' ranged across a vast range of different issues – from fish quotas, to maternity leave, to family law, tax simplification, human rights, animal by-products, car registration plates, legal aid, local Government best value, mink keeping, broadcasting and Northern Ireland – and averaged just four MPs. Only four of the rebellions involved seven or more Conservative MPs, three of which related to measures introduced by the European Union.[69] The largest Conservative rebellion of the fourth session occurred over the funding of the Millennium Dome. With the front bench advising abstention, four Conservatives – including Michael Heseltine, a member of the Millennium Commission – voted for an extra infusion of cash for the Dome and nine back-bench Conservatives opposed.[70] These votes nearly all saw a combination of Conservative MPs with particular views on issues together with members of the awkward squad – almost two-thirds of the dissenting votes cast during the deferred divisions were cast by the MPs listed in Table 10.3.

There were only four non-deferred divisions to see issue-based dissent in the fourth session, averaging a total of three MPs. On 8 January 2001, Gerald Howarth and Jonathan Sayeed objected to the membership of the new Electoral Commission. A week later six Conservatives opposed a motion relating to the chairman of a tax simplification committee.[71] On 6 February David Atkinson, Peter Bottomley and Sir Peter Tapsell supported the programming motion for the House of Commons (Removal of Clergy Disqualification) Bill. Finally, on 6 March, Peter Bottomley was the only Conservative MP to support the money resolution of the International Development Bill.

If the aim of the awkward squad was to annoy Labour MPs, then they certainly succeeded. Their activities infuriated many Labour backbenchers. Some, especially those first elected in 1997, were annoyed at what they saw as the 'futility of Parliamentary games'.[72] Just as Billy Connelly says that because he had heard it so often he used to believe there was a football team called 'Partick Thistle Nil', so at times talking to Labour MPs it seemed there was a Conservative MP called 'Bloody Eric Forth'.[73] As one tired and frustrated MP complained in 2000: 'Here till four the other night, 250 of us, just for 20 Tories'.[74] But Labour annoyance just made the Conservatives more determined. As one Conservative MP said '[There is] nothing like seeing them rattled to make me want to do it again.'[75] The reaction he hoped for from Labour MPs was 'Fucking hell, it's you again, you bastard'.[76] And just as Labour MPs disapproved of the activities of the Conservatives, so the Conservatives disdained the approach of some of the Labour MPs, especially the new ones. Labour MPs, one claimed, disliked 'anything that made their personal life awkward'.[77] Another was more blunt. The New Labour MPs just wanted the rules of the Commons changed 'so that they can go home and change nappies. They think that they are here just to further the project, they see Parliament as an inconvenience, they just want to do what the Master wants'.[78]

Yet amongst some Labour MPs there was grudging admiration for Forth and his colleagues. Some longer-serving Labour MPs, especially the more rebellious, knew that they would have done the same in Opposition. During the 1970 Parliament a similar ginger group of Labour backbenchers had been set up by James Wellbeloved, which aimed, amongst other things, to 'knock a bit of stuffing out of the Government backbenchers'.[79] During the early 1980s, when the PLP was falling apart in organisational terms and MPs were beset by rese-lection battles, two Opposition MPs – Dennis Skinner and Bob Cryer – similarly took the fight to the Conservative Government by opposing legislation late into the night, prompting one experienced Labour backbencher to describe Eric Forth as 'Dennis Skinner in drag'.[80] A former Labour Chief Whip ('with a PhD in opposition') confessed that he frequently colluded with the activities of his backbenchers. 'There were many times when I did not have complete control over my backbenchers. There were even more times when I pretended not to have control over them and colluded with them in frustrating the Government of the day'.[81] Nor did all Labour MPs object to late nights: 'I worked nights in a steel factory, so if the Tories want to play silly buggers, I'll work nights again'.[82] The sneaking respect for Forth was shown when he was voted 'Opposition Politician of the Year' in the Channel 4 and *The House*

Magazine awards in 1999. The opposition to him, though, was equally clear when his name was put up for the House of Commons Commission to succeed Sir Peter Lloyd, and – after a heated debate – he was voted off.[83]

One of the effects of the awkward squad's activities was to increase the pressure on the Labour front bench to pursue yet further 'modernisation' of the Commons. The resentment their activities caused on the Labour benches was at least partly responsible for the decision to introduce deferred divisions and the programming of almost all Government bills in November 2000.[84] One Labour whip, Graham Allen, thought that 'by his antics over the past year or so', Forth had 'done more for the modernisation of this place than serious-minded reformers like myself managed in 14 years or more'.[85] This compounded Conservative feelings that the Government was progressively taking away the rights of Opposition backbench MPs properly to scrutinise the Government, so by the beginning of 2001 what one awkward squad member called a 'destructive cycle' had developed: 'They [the Government] antagonised us, we retaliated by using loopholes, so they closed the loopholes, which antagonised us'.[86]

Near the end of the Parliament one Conservative MP reflected that, for all their effort, the awkward squad seemed to achieved little. 'No minister has had a heart attack yet', he said ruefully.[87] Another thought that they had achieved 'no immediate tangible result . . . all we've done is keep people up late'.[88] But that was all most of them had wanted to do. They had not been aiming to defeat the enemy, just to take 'pot shots' at it and to cause 'buggeration'. And in that, they had been successful.

Conclusion

The behaviour of Conservative MPs between 1997 and 2001 was almost the mirror image of that of Labour MPs in the same period. Whereas Labour MPs rebelled infrequently but in quantity, Conservative MPs rebelled more frequently but – with the exception of the very large rebellions at the beginning of the Parliament over devolution – usually in small numbers. As Table 10.5 shows, there were 163 occasions when Conservative MPs voted against the advice of their party whips during the Parliament, 67 more than Labour. And although the awkward squad's activities account for a sizeable proportion of that number, there were still 111 rebellions, even once we discount the activity of Forth and his colleagues.[89] Even without the activities of the awkward squad, then, Conservative MPs voted against their party line more times than did Labour MPs. By the final session, the combination of the escalation of the awkward squad's activities, together with the introduction of deferred divisions, was producing a Conservative rebellion in over a quarter of all Parliamentary divisions. The average size of these rebellions, though, was small – just six MPs – and as Table 10.5 shows it became smaller as the Parliament progressed: from eight in the first session to seven in the second, to six in the third, down to five in the final session. And whereas only a minority of Labour MPs broke ranks – albeit a minority that was larger than most people realised – the Conservative backbench rebellions involved some 128 Conservative MPs, just over three-quarters of the Parliamentary party, and almost everyone who was a Conservative backbencher at some point in the Parliament. The most rebellious was, perhaps not surprisingly, Eric Forth, who voted against his party whip on 78 occasions.

Table 10.5 Frequency and size of Conservative rebellions, 1997–2001

Session	Number of rebellions	Average size of rebellion
1997–1998	35	8
1998–1999	24	7
1999–2000	43	6
2000–2001	61	5
Total	163	6

The issues to provoke rebellion amongst Conservative MPs ranged widely, but one was clearly dominant: Northern Ireland. It provoked 40 separate Conservative rebellions. Again, these tended to be small, averaging just five MPs, but their cumulative impact was considerable, involving the 51 different MPs listed in Table 10.2, almost a third of the Parliamentary party. Backbench unhappiness with the Government's policy towards Northern Ireland (and, concomitantly, with their front bench's stance towards the Government) clearly ran deep on the Conservative benches and may at least help to explain the Tory front bench shift on the issue in 1998. The most prominent Conservative dissenter on Northern Ireland was Andrew Hunter who cast 26 dissenting votes on that issue alone (and 47 in total, making him the second most rebellious Conservative in the Parliament). But because precedence in the debates is given to MPs from Northern Irish parties, even a vociferous opponent of the Government's policies like Hunter was restricted to relatively few speeches and interventions, and the Conservative divisions on the issue therefore went largely unnoticed.

Indeed, the same could be said of the whole Parliamentary party. When in Government, the media had picked over the Parliamentary party's divisions remorselessly. Out of Government, few people noticed and even fewer cared. Given what was happening on the Conservative benches, perhaps that was just as well.

[1]   Richard Rose, *Do Parties Make A Difference?*, London, Macmillan, 1980.

[2]   Dennis Van Mechelen and Richard Rose, *Patterns of Parliamentary Legislation*, Aldershot, Gower, 1986.

[3]   HC Debs, 3 June 1997, c. 252. See also David Denver et al, *Scotland Decides,* London, Frank Cass, 2000, pp. 46–48.

[4]   One Conservative MP, Piers Merchant, voted against the amendment. The Conservative line was to abstain.

[5]   Two Conservatives, Piers Merchant and Laurence Robertson, voted against the amendment. The Conservative line was to abstain.

[6]   The Public Processions (Northern Ireland) Bill, the Northern Ireland (Elections) Bill, the Northern Ireland (Sentences) Bill, and the Northern Ireland Bill.

[7]   In the second vote, five Conservatives voted in favour of the amendment; a sixth, Douglas Hogg, voted in favour of the Government.

[8]   HC Debs, 2 September 1998, cc. 720–721.

[9]   Crispin Blunt, Geoffrey Clifton-Brown and Dr Julian Lewis.

[10] Michael Colvin, Eric Forth, Dominic Grieve, Nick Hawkins, Gerald Howarth, Geoffrey Johnson-Smith and Ann Winterton.

[11] In June 1997, Alan Clark voted against the Second Reading of the Plant Varieties Bill implementing an international agreement on plant breeder's intellectual property, and in the next month Clark was again the lone rebel when backing a Liberal Democrat Opposition Day motion that accused the Government of diluting the role of Parliament. In July, Robert Jackson, the former Conservative Education Minister, twice voted in favour of the Government's plans to sell off student loan provision to the private sector, after the Second and Third Reading stages of the Education (Student Loans) Bill. Unlike his front bench, Jackson welcomed the Bill, believing that by privatising the debts of students to the new Student Loans Company, these debts could be increased without affecting the public sector borrowing requirement and the limits on public borrowing. Finally, in February 1998, John Wilkinson, a long-time opponent of the Child Support Agency (CSA) voted in favour of a Liberal Democrat Opposition Day motion calling for radical reform of the Agency.

[12] HC Debs, 10 May 1999, c. 56. Douglas Hogg was the sole Conservative MP to vote against the Bill's Third Reading.

[13] HC Debs, 13 July 1999, c. 210.

[14] See, for example, Patrick Wintour, 'Left and Right link up in odd alliances', *Observer*, 28 March 1999; Peter Riddell, 'Time for politicians to reveal their true aims', *The Times*, 31 March 1999; Donald Macintyre, 'The strange spectacle of the Tory right opposing a NATO war', *Independent*, 26 March 1999; Ewen MacAskill, 'Surprise condemnation from Tory backbenches', *Guardian*, 26 March 1999.

[15] HC Debs, 19 April 1999, cc. 593–594.

[16] Alan Clark, 'This way leads to the madness of all-out conflict', *Observer*, 28 March 1999.

[17] Simon Hoggart, 'Anxiety outweighs Tory rhetoric', *Guardian*, 20 April 1999.

[18] In February 1999, Peter Bottomley supported a Plaid Cyrmu amendment during the Report Stage of the Water Industry Bill that would have given the new National Assembly for Wales discretion on water policy in Wales; in June, Bottomley was again the only Conservative MP to support a Liberal

Democrat Opposition Day motion criticising the Government's failure to give adequate pensions to widows. During the spillover, on 8 November 1999, Desmond Swayne was the only Conservative MP to vote in favour of EU Working Time Regulations. Although he was against such regulations in principle, he believed that the specific regulation before the House might have improved the current situation (letter to author, 30 November 1999).

[19] The Conservatives were concerned about the release of paramilitary prisoners in the absence of decommissioning. So, although they abstained on the Bill's Second Reading, they put forward and supported Ulster Unionist amendments during the Bill's Committee stage that insisted that the Bill should not take effect until there had been substantial and verifiable decommissioning.

[20] HC Debs, 24 January 2000, c. 37.

[21] HC Debs, 24 January 2000, c. 66.

[22] HC Debs, 6 June 2000, cc. 228–229.

[23] Two Conservative MPs, Laurence Robertson and Nicholas Winterton, also voted against a group of Government amendments on the Bill immediately before Third Reading.

[24] HC Debs, 14 December 1999, c. 214.

[25] Hogg also opposed a Government Business motion that sought to carry the Bill on beyond 10pm.

[26] Sir Norman Fowler had tabled amendments to the Crime and Disorder Act 1998 that were very similar to the proposals under discussion two years later. Simon Burns had successfully introduced the Football (Offences and Disorder) Act 1999 as a private members' Bill but had been told by the Government at the time that stronger measures (which could have been added to his Bill) were not necessary.

[27] HC Debs, 13 July 2000, cc. 1231–1232.

[28] HC Debs, 13 July 2000, c.c. 1254–1255.

[29] HC Debs, 17 July 2000, c. 47.

[30] HC Debs, 17 July 2000, cc. 63–64.

[31] Peter Bottomley, Roger Gale, John Gummer, Edward Leigh and Peter Lilley.

[32] William Cash, Nigel Evans, Eric Forth and John Townend.

[33] Dr Michael Clark, David Davis, Eric Forth, Douglas Hogg, Peter Lilley, Laurence Robertson and Desmond Swayne.

[34] In July Christopher Chope voted against a Liberal Democrat amendment to introduce proportional representation for local elections in England and Wales; and in November Peter Bottomley was the only Conservative MP to vote in favour of a Liberal Democrat Opposition Day Motion that called for larger increases in the state pension for the over 75s.

[35] Interview, 13 February 2001.

[36] Simon Hoggart, 'Ragged remains of defeated Tory army fight on', *Guardian*, 20 March 2001.

[37] Interview, 6 March 2001.

[38] Interview, 6 March 2001.

[39] Interview, 6 March 2001.

[40] Interviews, 8 February 2000, 6 March 2001.

[41] Interview, 8 February 2000.

[42] Interview, 6 March 2001.

[43] Interview, 6 March 2001.

[44] Interview, 13 February 2001.

[45] Interview, 13 February 2001.

[46] See Holly Marsh and David Marsh, 'Tories in the Killing Fields', *Journal of Legislative Studies*, forthcoming.

[47] They were – but then so has every Government in recent years. See David Marsh and Melvyn Read, *Private Members' Bills*, Cambridge, Cambridge University Press, 1988.

[48] As happened with, for example, the Fur Farming Bill, when Forth and Maclean divided the House three times in March and May 1999. As well as talking out many bills, Forth (and usually Maclean)

often divided the House. In the first session, they divided the House on the Fireworks Bill, in the second, the Animal Welfare (Prohibition of Imports) Bill, in the third the Warm Homes and Energy Conservation Bill, the Age Equality Commission Bill, and in the fourth, the Outworking Bill, the Christmas Day (Trading) Bill and even the High Hedges Bill!

49   Interview, 8 February 2001.

50   Interview, 6 March 2001.

51   Just 36 Conservative MPs had been first elected at a general election before 1979. Byron Criddle, 'MPs and Candidates', in David Butler and Dennis Kavanagh, *The British General Election of 1997*, London, Macmillan, 1997, p. 202.

52   Interview, 6 March 2001. Or even 'great fun'. Interview, 30 October 2001.

53   Interview, 6 March 2001.

54   A future Leader of the House was to describe the Sea Fishing Grant (Charges) Bill as 'an unobjectionable, even tedious measure'. HC Debs, 28 June 2001, c. 821.

55   In four of these votes – on the Nuclear Safeguards Bill, the Sea Fishing Grants (Charges) Bill and the Social Security Contributions (Share Options) Bill – Peter Bottomley voted with the Government. Richard Shepherd also voted against the Social Security Contributions Bill. On 9 January 2001, Crispin Blunt, Dr Julian Lewis and Desmond Swayne voted in favour of a programming motion on the Armed Forces Bill.

56   During the debate, Stephen Timms, the Financial Secretary to the Treasury, pointed out that the sum of £1000 was purely a token amount. It was standard procedure to draw the House's attention to the intention that extra spending would be incurred on new services. There were 13 such votes in that year's spring estimates alone. HC Debs, 14 March 2000, c. 178.

57   HC Debs, 22 May 2000, c. 812.

58   It was the first time since 14 June 1988 that a sitting of the House had wrecked the next day's sitting. Then MPs sat from 2.30pm on Tuesday until 8.01 pm on Wednesday as they deliberated the Housing Bill. The *House Magazine*, 31 January 2000.

59   Michael White, 'Rebels ruin day 1000 showdown', *Guardian*, 27 January 2000.

60   For more on SIs, see Edward C. Page, *Governing By Numbers*, Oxford, Hart, 2001.

61   The following exchange took place during the Standing Committee on the Homes Bill. Tom Brake (who had just returned following the birth of his second son): 'At least my late nights have not been caused by the Hon Member for Bromley and Chislehurst [Forth]'. Brian Iddon: 'How can you be so sure?' *The House Magazine*, 12 February 2001.

62   *The House Magazine*, 15 January 2001. A Labour whip similarly described the awkward squad as the 'provisional wing of the Tory party'. HC Debs, 28 June 2001, c. 833.

63   Interview, 6 March 2001.

64   Interview, 13 February 2001.

65   Private information.

66   For example, on 22 January 2001, in addition to those members of the awkward squad, Sir Peter Emery and David Faber were in favour of banning tobacco advertising while Kenneth Clarke and Nicholas Soames were opposed to the Bill's Second Reading. On 13 February 2001, Sir Peter Emery also voted for the Third Reading of the Tobacco Advertising and Promotion Bill, while Kenneth Clarke voted against it along with Sir Richard Body and five awkward squad members.

67   Although one member of the awkward squad revealed that he was far less opposed than Forth to deferred divisions: 'Don't tell Eric, or he'll never speak to me again.' Interview, 13 February 2001.

68   Even here, though, there were some dissenters. Sir Geoffrey Johnson-Smith and Richard Spring voted with the Government, while five Conservatives – Christopher Chope, Eric Forth, Christopher Gill, Gerald Howarth and Richard Shepherd – voted against the Government.

69   On 13 December 2000, seven Conservatives – Christopher Chope, Eric Forth, Christopher Gill, Gerald Howarth, Geoffrey Johnson-Smith, Richard Shepherd and Sir Teddy Taylor – opposed the EU's budget proposals. Then, on 24 January 2001, with the official party line being to abstain, four

Conservative MPs supported EU documents that sought to deal with the issue of doping in sport, and five Conservatives opposed the measure. The four to support the measure were Howard Flight, John Gummer, Andrew Hunter and Sir Michael Spicer, with Douglas Hogg, John Redwood, Richard Shepherd, Sir Teddy Taylor and Nicholas Winterton opposing. On the same day, seven Conservatives – Angela Browning, Douglas Hogg, Andrew Hunter, John Redwood, Richard Shepherd, Sir Teddy Taylor and Nicholas Winterton – voted against a draft EU treaty on cooperation between EU customs officers.

[70] Humfrey Malins, Malcolm Moss and Nick St Aubyn joined Heseltine in voting for the measure, while Christopher Chope, Michael Fallon, Eric Forth, John Gummer, Douglas Hogg, Gerald Howarth, Andrew Hunter, Sir Teddy Taylor and Sir Raymond Whitney joined three Labour MPs in opposing it.

[71] Peter Bottomley, Christopher Chope, Eric Forth, Douglas Hogg, John Redwood and David Ruffley.

[72] Interview, 23 May 2000.

[73] Or, as Quentin Letts put it following Forth's elevation to Shadow Leader of the House (see Chapter 12): '"Go, Forth, and multiply" is what most Labour MPs think of the new Shadow Leader of the House'. *New Statesman*, 22 October 2001.

[74] Interview, 7 March 2000.

[75] Interview, 6 March 2001.

[76] Interview, 6 March 2001.

[77] Interview, 13 February 2001.

[78] Interview, 6 March 2001.

[79] Norton, *Dissension in the House of Commons, 1945–74*, p. 389.

[80] Interview, 13 March 2001.

[81] HC Debs, 28 June 2001, c. 825.

[82] Interview, 7 March 2000.

[83] HC Debs, 2 February 2000, cc. 1175–1176. He was, though, almost immediately put back on to the Commission, only to have to resign his place when he became Shadow Leader of the House following the 2001 Election (see Chapter 12).

[84] See Philip Norton, 'Parliament', in A. Seldon (ed), *The Blair Effect*, London, Little, Brown, 2001, p. 51.

[85] HC Debs, 28 June 2001, c. 834. One long-serving MP agreed: 'Forth played into the hands of those, particularly the women, who said: "If we can't change the hours now, we never will".' Interview, 25 October 2001.

[86] Interview, 13 February 2001.

[87] Interview, 6 March 2001. This might have been a joke. But perhaps not.

[88] Interview, 13 February 2001.

[89] The total of 163 does not equal the sum of the issue-based figure (111) with the awkward squad figure in Table 10.4 (58) because the two groups are not mutually exclusive.

11. Labour in Disguise?

The Liberal Democrats

In his seminal work *British Political Parties* Robert McKenzie allocated the Liberal Party just three pages out of a grand total of 678. To make matters worse, these three pages were considered material suitable for an appendix, tucked away at the back of the book along with other mind-numbing subjects like party finance. McKenzie justified this on the understandable grounds that at the previous election the Liberals had received just 2.5 per cent of the popular vote and just one per cent of the seats in the House of Commons. Despite its long and distinguished history, the party had no prospect of governing, and its arrangements were therefore 'of very limited interest'.[1]

The fragmentation of the party system from the late 1960s onwards has made it harder to dismiss 'other' parties on this basis. As a result, more recent works on political parties have tended to devote somewhat more than three pages to the centre party or parties. Yet their parliamentary wing remains almost entirely ignored. Philip Norton's 1983 study of the organisation and behaviour of the Liberal Parliamentary Party was described then – and not just by himself – as 'charting new ground', but any changes to that ground since have remained largely uncharted, with more recent studies notable by their absence.[2] P. G. Richards produced an early study of the SDP in Parliament in 1982, but Ivor Crewe and Anthony King's magisterial study of the SDP in 1995 examined the behaviour of its parliamentary party only occasionally, and then only in passing, whilst Don MacIver's 1996 collection of essays on the Liberal Democrats does not include one concentrating on the parliamentary party: the Party's parliamentarians have to make do with three pages in a chapter on the Party's organisation.[3]

Of course, just as McKenzie's dismissal of the Liberals was understandable (if brutal) given the circumstances, equally understandable (if brutal) has been the lack of any serious study of the party's Parliamentary wing. After all, there has not been all that much to study. The rise in the Liberal Party's share of the vote did not lead to a proportionate rise in the number of seats held by the Party. Even at the height of the SDP/Liberal Alliance – at the end of the 1979–83 Parliament, with their ranks bolstered by more than 30 defections from Labour – Alliance MPs accounted for just six per cent of the House of Commons.[4] Before the 1997 election, the Parliamentary Liberal Democrats amounted to just 26 MPs, no more than four per cent of the House.

The election in May 1997 of 46 Liberal Democrat MPs – the best third party performance since 1929 – means that this excuse no longer holds. There were (and are) still not all that many of them – the best third party performance since 1945 remains noticeably worse than the worst performance by either Labour or the Conservatives – but there were at least enough Liberal Democrat MPs to justify studying them. This chapter examines both Liberal Democrat cohesion (although as will become clear, it would be a very short chapter if that was its only purpose) and the direction of their votes. A common complaint during the 1997 Parliament – from the Conservatives, the media and even some Liberal Democrats – was that the Party had become a mere adjunct of Labour, ever willing to do the Government's bidding. William Hague claimed that the Liberal Democrats had been neutered; another senior Conservative politician argued that the Party was 'now so firmly in bed with the Labour Party that it has become little more than a shapeless lump under the Government's duvet'.[5] In his first conference speech as leader, Charles Kennedy felt it necessary to claim that the Liberal Democrats were 'nobody's poodles. But we are not rottweilers either. We don't savage on command. That is the old politics'.[6] The new politics were those of 'constructive opposition', but critics questioned whether the Liberal Democrat's policy of 'constructive opposition' contained all that much opposition.

A house united

There may not have been all that many Liberal Democrat MPs, but when they voted they voted as a block. On whipped votes at least, deviations from the party line were astonishingly rare. Throughout the entire 1997 Parliament there were just 30 occasions when one or more Liberal Democrat MPs voted against his or her party line. This compares to a figure of 96 for Labour (which, as shown in earlier chapters, was itself a very low figure) and 163 for the Conservatives. Given that there were 1,279 votes throughout the Parliament, this means that there was a Liberal Democrat rebellion only every 42 votes.[7] Indeed, for much of the 1997 Parliament, the Party's MPs were even more cohesive than this overall figure indicates. There were just four Liberal Democrat revolts during the very long first session, with just seven in both the second and third sessions. By the beginning of the fourth session, therefore, there had been just 18 rebellions, less than one in every fifty votes. The fourth session saw a small, but noticeable, increase in the number of rebellions to 12, which, because the session was shorter, represented just over one rebellion every 20 votes, and which helped increase the overall figures somewhat. Although this increase coincided with the introduction of deferred divisions (which led to increases in the rebelliousness of both Labour and Conservative MPs), this appears not to have been its cause, because just four of the 12 Liberal Democrat revolts in the fourth session took place on deferred divisions. And even the wild anarchic Liberal Democrats of the fourth session were less rebellious than either their Labour or Conservative peers. Nor is this a phenomenon unique to this Parliament. The 1992 Parliament saw just 35 Liberal Democrat rebellions – a rebellion in just three per cent of votes – but even this figure is exaggerated somewhat by the fact that 27 of the 35 took place during the passage of just one Bill, the Maastricht Bill, and 26 involved just one Liberal Democrat MP, Nick Harvey.[8]

Even when they did break ranks, Liberal Democrat MPs did not do so in numbers.[9] Two-thirds of the 30 rebellions in the 1997 Parliament consisted of just one lone MP. Another eight comprised between two and five MPs. Just two saw six or more MPs break ranks. The two largest Liberal Democrat rebellions of the Parliament occurred during discussion of the Finance Bill in the final session. The Government proposed a levy on the mining of limestone. While David Heath was in favour of such environmental levies, he was opposed to 'a crude levy' that did not give rebates to companies who implemented environmentally friendly extraction techniques.[10] And besides, as Heath admitted, his Somerton and Frome constituency was one of the largest producers of limestone aggregates. On 7 March 2001, five Liberal Democrats joined Heath in splitting from the majority of their party against the budget resolution introducing the levy.[11] Just over a month later, on 23 April, during the Committee stage of the Finance Bill, Ed Davey, the Liberal Democrat spokesman, tried to paper over the Party's splits on the issue by moving an amendment to make the Government's levy rebate scheme proportionate to the level of environmentally friendly measures implemented by extraction companies. But the Government's strict timetable on the Finance Bill prevented the Liberal Democrat amendment being voted upon. Instead, nine Liberal Democrats – all from rural constituencies – voted against clause 16, the clause introducing the levy.[12] The very next vote saw five Liberal Democrats vote against clauses 17 to 22, all consequential to the introduction of the levy.[13] Until the Finance Bill, the largest Liberal Democrat revolt of the Parliament had occurred during the Committee Stage of the House of Lords Bill in February 1999, when five MPs voted in favour of Bob Marshall-Andrews' amendment to exclude the use of patronage from any reshaped House of Lords (see Chapter 3).[14] Of course, because the number of Liberal Democrat MPs remained relatively small even after 1997, we should expect their rebellions to be small in absolute terms, and as a proportion of the Parliamentary Party, a rebellion of nine Liberal Democrat MPs is fairly substantial: had a comparable fraction of the PLP split away, it would have amounted to 46 MPs, almost exactly the same number of Labour MPs as rebelled over lone parent benefit (see Chapter 2). But large rebellions like this were rare; and so even allowing for the difference in size, it is clear that Liberal Democrat MPs did not hunt in packs.

Nor were there many persistent rebels. In total, 27 Liberal Democrat MPs (all listed in Appendix 8) broke ranks with their party at some stage in the Parliament, but most of them did so extremely infrequently. Thirteen of the 27 rebelled only once; another seven did so just twice. Table 11.1 lists the seven most rebellious Liberal Democrat MPs, but it is striking how the criteria for inclusion in this table is to have cast just three votes against the party line out of the 1,147 whipped votes during the Parliament. The most rebellious Liberal Democrat MPs, John Burnett and Mike Hancock, each voted against their party whips on seven occasions, which compared to either Jeremy Corbyn (64) or Eric Forth (78) is very small fry indeed.

Table 11.1 Most rebellious Liberal Democrat MPs, 1997–2001

Name	Number of dissenting votes
John Burnett	7
Mike Hancock	7
David Heath	6
Sir Robert Smith	5
Richard Livsey	4
Nick Harvey	3
Ray Michie	3

These occasional deviations aside, and it should be clear from the foregoing that they were very occasional, Liberal Democrat MPs were a cohesive bunch when the whips were on. Documenting this, though, is the easy part. Explaining it is far harder.

It is especially hard to explain because when it comes to free votes (those occasions when the whips are removed) we find exactly the opposite. Here, Liberal Democrat diversity was more common than uniformity, with the Party deeply divided on a number of issues. The sort of issues that see free votes are often said to be non- or cross-party. They are said to 'cut across party lines'. However, empirical research usually shows that the dominant cleavage remains that of party, with the issues more likely to cut down party lines than across them.[15] But with the Liberal Democrats, these issues really do have the potential to cause dramatic internal division in a way that they do not usually have with MPs of other parties. Votes in the 1997 Parliament – especially on gun control and on hunting but also on euthanasia and homosexuality – saw deep divisions amongst Liberal Democrat MPs. One vote on gun control saw the Parliamentary party split right down the middle.[16]

One obvious answer, therefore, would be that the Liberal Democrats are an attitudinally divided Parliamentary party, kept together by an extremely harsh disciplinary system. When the whips are on, discipline holds them together; but once let off the leash they go feral. Whilst this thesis may have some initial attractiveness, like most obvious answers it is almost certainly wrong. For one thing, there is little evidence that Liberal Democrat MPs are especially divided. Table 11.2 shows the standard deviations (that is, a measure of the extent of variation) of the responses to the BRS's basic scalar questions used in Chapters 6 and 7. It gives no sign that the party is any less cohesive than the other Parliamentary parties: the Liberal Democrats are the least cohesive party in none of the six areas.

Table 11.2 Standard deviation of MPs' views on BRS issue scales

	Left v Right	Jobs v Prices	Taxes v Spending	Nationali sation v Privati sation	Integr ation v Indepen dence	Equal v Home
Conservative	**1.50**	**2.31**	**1.86**	1.45	**2.55**	**2.91**
Labour	1.36	1.76	1.58	**1.63**	2.17	1.07
Lib Dems	1.18	2.10	1.18	1.54	2.11	.80

Note: Bold indicates the party most divided. Source: BRS, 1997.

The second reason this explanation is unlikely is that the Parliamentary Party does not have a strong whipping system. In fact, the opposite: the Liberal Democrats have a looser concept of party discipline than many other Parliamentary parties.[17] In other parties, for example, front benchers have to conform to the party line or face dismissal. The Liberal Democrats allow front benchers to vote against the party line, not least because they have historically lacked enough MPs to draw a real distinction between front and backbench.[18] As a result, figures for dissent by Liberal Democrats are not strictly comparable with those for Labour and the Conservatives; but since this should have the effect of increasing Liberal Democrat dissent, it merely makes the difference starker still.

The leader of the Liberal Democrats, even more than the other party leaders, also suffers from a distinct lack of carrots – such as ministerial office – to dangle in front of his (as yet, never her) MPs in order to induce cohesion in the voting lobbies. Becoming Liberal Democrat spokesman on, say, agriculture may be fun (if you like that sort of thing) but it is not a position for which one would sell one's soul in the division lobbies.[19] And the Leader's use of the stick is similarly hampered by the size of the Parliamentary party. The possibility of the sack from a portfolio would 'actually please many Members', as well as presenting problems for the Leader finding a replacement.[20] MPs from other parties might occasionally be kept quiet by the number of other MPs prepared to step into their shoes if they will not do as they are told. That can hardly be an explanation for the Liberal Democrats.

Nor does the answer appear to lie in Liberal Democrat MPs having a more party-centred concept of representation. Again, if anything, the opposite appears to be true. As part of the SPG survey used in Chapter 6, MPs were asked to rank the importance of representing the nation, representing the constituency and representing the party. Just one Liberal Democrat (out of the 22 who answered the survey) ranked representing the party as their most important role. This compared to no Conservatives and 13 per cent of Labour MPs. Nor is there any sign that Liberal Democrats rely on their party whips more than MPs from other parties. When the survey asked what factors strongly influenced MPs when deciding how to act and vote in Parliament, just 13 per cent of Liberal Democrat MPs said that they 'nearly always' relied on the advice of their party leadership, compared to 32 per cent of Conservative MPs and 46 per cent of Labour MPs (see Table 11.3).

And when the 1997 BRS asked MPs whether they should vote with their party regardless of conscience, just four per cent of Liberal Democrats agreed, compared to ten per cent of Conservatives and 19 per cent of Labour MPs.[21] Of the three parties, then, Liberal Democrat MPs are the least likely to say they are influenced by the advice of their party leadership or to claim that MPs should vote the party line. This too should have the effect of increasing rather than decreasing the amount of rebellion seen in the division lobbies.

Table 11.3 Sources of information when voting, by party (column %).

	Conservative	Labour	LibDem
Advice of party leadership	32	46	13
Personal opinions	62	42	81
Constituency opinion	5	9	6
Representations from interest or pressure groups	0	2	0
N	37	127	16

Source: SPG Socialisation Study, 1999.

The answer may therefore lie in the exact opposite explanation: that rather than being attitudinally divided the Liberal Democrats are an attitudinally cohesive party. For example, not only were the Liberal Democrats not the least cohesive party in any case in Table 11.2 but in four of the six cases they were actually the most cohesive. Yet the differences are not huge, and surely cannot explain the much larger difference in behaviour.[22] It may be part of the answer but it cannot be all of it.

The remainder may lie in the Party's policy-making structure. Liberal Democrats are proud of their policy-making process, comparing it favourably with the Conservatives' leader-centred approach and the fixes and stitch-ups that have sometimes characterised policy making in the Labour Party.[23] They claim, probably justifiably, to be the most participatory and inclusive of British parties when it comes to policy making.[24] The Party's conferences have delivered several embarrassing defeats to the leadership in recent years, proving themselves more troublesome than the conferences of the main two parties. In itself, the presence of a more inclusive policy-making process might be expected to make MPs feel less likely to vote against their party – because in doing so they would be voting against the entire party rather than just against the leadership – but in the case of the Liberal Democrats this effect is magnified because of the role that the Parliamentary Party plays in policy development. As one long-serving Liberal Democrat MP said:

> The policy process is theoretically the prerogative of the party policy committee out of the conference. But in fact, it is negotiated between the Parliamentarians and the policy

committee. At the end of the day, the policy committee has the say, but there's an intent to make sure that the MPs are in accord [with the policy]. We're the people that are going to have to deliver the message and if we don't believe it's credible, then it's wrong.[25]

One academic analysis describes this as a '*de facto* power of veto over the design of policy'.[26] Given such a veto, there will usually be little for MPs to rebel against. And given the MPs' views on the need (or lack of it) to stick to the party line, this might be just as well. Faced with a policy with which many of them disagreed, there would be little else to stop them rebelling.

The direction

But whom do they back? As Philip Norton noted in 1983, the practices of the House of Commons, being based on the assumption of two large opposing parties, have a problem with third parties; they are 'for all intents and purposes, an embarrassment'.[27] In practical terms, the organisation of the Parliamentary timetable predominantly revolves around the desires of the two main parties. This leads to a problem for third party MPs, as it often deprives them of an opportunity to vote for a distinctive policy platform of their own (assuming they have one). There are opportunities for other parties to establish stances of their own but such opportunities constitute a minority of the Parliamentary timetable. Instead, they are often forced to vote aye or noe on positions determined by the other parties.

Table 11.4 Liberal Democrat voting on whipped votes, 1997–2001

| | With Labour | | Against Labour | | Total | |
	N	%	N	%	N	%
With Cons	32	3	396	36	428	39
Against Cons	525	47	160	14	685	62
Total	557	50	556	50	1113	100

This is borne out by the data in Table 11.4, which shows the distribution of Liberal Democrat votes during the 1997 Parliament. Of the 1,279 votes, covering all legislation as well as non-legislative votes such as Opposition Day Motions, 132 were the subject of free votes (such as private members' legislation), where the parties issue no instructions to their MPs.[28] This leaves 1,147 votes which we can examine to measure the behaviour of the Liberal Democrats. On 34 occasions the Party abstained from voting. The Table shows the behaviour of the Liberal Democrat MPs in the remaining 1,113 votes.

The Liberal Democrats were able to take a stance independent of the two other main parties in only 14 per cent of votes. If we include the occasions on which they chose to abstain, the figure rises to 194 votes out of 1,147, or 17 per cent. (During the 1992 Parliament, the Liberal Democrats had managed to stand alone in just nine per cent of divisions, or 11 per cent if we include abstentions, probably indicating that the task of creating a uniquely Liberal Democrat position within Parliament becomes easier as the size of the party increases.) For the most part, they have instead to decide whether to back the Government or the Official Opposition. As the Table shows, between 1997 and 2001 they were slightly more likely to back the devil than the deep blue sea. Half of all votes (50 per cent) saw the Liberal Democrats vote with Labour; just over a third (39 per cent) saw them vote with the Conservatives. Just under half of the votes (525, 47 per cent) saw the Liberal Democrats voting with Labour against the Conservatives, compared to around a third (36 per cent) to see the opposite.

However, these overall figures mask some important differences. For the most part, the Liberal Democrats became noticeably less supportive of Labour as the Parliament went on. In the first session, they voted with Labour in 58 per cent of votes.[29] By the second session, the figure had fallen to less than half, 48 per cent.[30] The third session saw it fall yet further to 40 per cent. On Mrs Thatcher's first visit to China she asked a Chinese man what he thought of Stalin, and was told that Stalin was 60 per cent right and 40 per cent wrong.[31] On the basis of their voting in the first session, the Liberal Democrats appeared to take roughly the same view about Labour. The second session saw a slightly more critical tone, one that could be characterised as 50 per cent right, 50 per cent wrong. But the third session saw a complete reversal of that witnessed in the first: Labour was 40 per cent right, 60 per cent wrong. The short final session then saw a brief return to 56 per cent.[32]

At the same time, the Liberal Democrats also became noticeably more willing to vote with the Conservatives. In the first session, they voted with them in 27 per cent of divisions; the second session saw that figure rise to 40 per cent; the third saw it rise again to 44 per cent; and it rose yet again in the fourth, reaching 47 per cent. These data clearly give the lie to the accusation that the Liberal Democrats were merely Labour's poodles. As Figure 11.1 shows, by the third session they were more likely to vote with the Conservatives than with Labour, and for the whole Parliament – with the exception of the first session, when they were noticeably more likely to back the Government – the Liberal Democrats shared their favours roughly evenly between the two parties.

Figure 11.1 Liberal Democrat voting with Labour and Conservatives, 1997-2001, by session

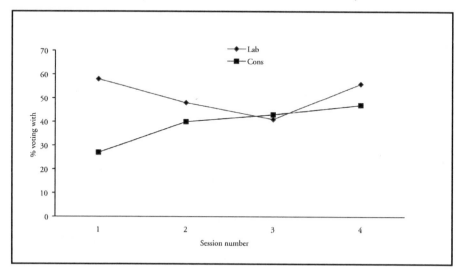

We find a slightly more complicated picture if we examine the Party's attitude to the legislation introduced by Labour. As noted in the last chapter, a useful (if somewhat crude) measure of the stance a political party takes on a bill is the way it votes at Second Reading (the vote on the principle of a bill) and/or Third Reading (the vote on the bill as finally constituted). Many bills pass uncontested, without votes at either Second or Third Reading. Other bills, such as the Firearms (Amendment) Bill and the various Sexual Offences bills, were contested, but were the subject of free votes. The remaining bills saw a total of 150 whipped Liberal Democrat votes at either Second or Third Reading (including reasoned amendments).

Table 11.5 Liberal Democrat voting at second and third reading, 1997–2001

	With Labour		Against Labour		Total	
	N	%	N	%	N	%
With Cons	10	7	35	23	45	30
Against Cons	92	61	13	9	105	70
Total	102	68	48	32	150	100

Ten of these votes (seven per cent) witnessed all three parties voting together. (Eight of these took place during five bills dealing with Northern Ireland or with terrorism; the remaining two occurred on the Second and Third Reading of the Elections Publications Bill). Another 13 votes saw the Party adopt an independent stance. Thirty-five saw the Liberal Democrats vote with the Conservatives against Labour. But the majority (92 votes, 61 per cent of the total) saw the Liberal Democrats vote with Labour against the Conservatives. As Table 11.5 shows, the Party was more than twice (indeed, nearly three times) as likely to vote with Labour against the Conservatives as *vice versa* when it came to the principle of a Government Bill. Throughout the Parliament, the Liberal Democrats voted against just 27 Government bills at Second or Third Reading, opposing the principle of just 18 per cent of the Government's legislation.

Liberal Democrat support for the Government against the Conservatives included – as might be expected – most of Labour's programme of constitutional reform, such as the Scotland Bill, the Government of Wales Bill, and the European Parliamentary Elections Bill. But it went further than that. As well as constitutional legislation, the Party supported the Government over legislation on health, educational standards, employment legislation, transport, regional development, the minimum wage, and independence for the Bank of England. In addition, the Liberal Democrats offered wholehearted and continuous support to the Government over Northern Ireland, even on those issues – such as decommissioning – where the Conservatives had opposed or abstained. As with the overall data, though, there are differences between the four sessions. In the first session, the Liberal Democrats voted with the Government in 75 per cent of votes on Second or Third Reading; in the second this figure had fallen to 52 per cent, before rising to 71 and 77 per cent in the third and fourth sessions.

The explanation of these differing trends in support – that is, overall support for the Government dipping in the second and third session, but support for Government bills rising – lies in the way the party votes on the fine print of legislation. It is one thing to support a Government Bill in broad terms, but that does not imply support for every line and sub-clause. Indeed, proponents of the Party's policy of constructive opposition would argue exactly this: that the Party should support the broad thrust of Government policy whenever possible – not opposing bills for the sake of opposing them – but then try to improve the detail by proposing and voting for amendments wherever possible.

For even when the Liberal Democrats supported the principle of a Bill, they were usually prepared to vote against the Government on some of the Bill's details. In the first session, all but four of the Government bills supported by the Liberal Democrats at Second or Third Reading saw the party vote against the Government at least once during Report, Committee (if taken on the floor of the House) or during consideration of Lords Amendments. This was true of a range of legislation, including most of the constitutional reforms. In the second session, the same was true of all but five bills; in the third it was true of all but six bills; and in the fourth seven.[33]

Table 11.6 Liberal Democrat voting on 'fine print', 1997-2001 on whipped votes during report, committee (on floor of House), and over Lords amendments, 1997-2001

	With Labour		Against Labour		Total	
	N	%	N	%	N	%
With Cons	3	1	174	35	177	36
Against Cons	234	47	87	18	321	65
Total	237	48	261	52	498	100

As Table 11.6 shows, when arguing over the fine print of legislation the Liberal Democrats were likely to vote with Labour in just under half (48 per cent) of all votes, and with the Conservatives in around a third (36 per cent). Again, however, these overall figures mask some real differences between sessions. The first session saw the Liberal Democrats vote with Labour on 59 per cent of these divisions; by the second session this figure had fallen to 44 per cent; and by the third, it had fallen yet further, to 35 per cent, before rising to 50 per cent in the final session. So on average the party was more likely to vote against the Government than for it and as the Parliament progressed the Liberal Democrats became increasingly more likely to vote against the detail of government legislation.

Figure 11.2 Liberal Democrat voting with Labour, by type of vote, 1997–2001

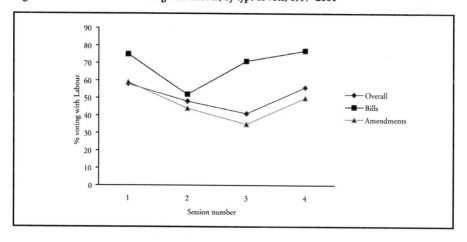

As shown in Figure 11.2, this is not because they became more obstructionist in general. On votes on the overall principle of legislation they were almost as supportive of the Government at the end of the Parliament as they were at the beginning. It is rather that as the Parliament progressed they became noticeably more likely to vote against the Government on the details of legislation. And because there are more votes on the detail of a Bill than there are on the principle (over three times as many), this has the effect of reducing the overall figures. To use the Party's own phrase of constructive opposition, the data appear to indicate that they began to stress the 'opposition', whilst still retaining the 'constructive'.

Conclusion

Given the size of their majority, the Labour whips will not have been losing too much sleep worrying about the way 46 Liberal Democrats were going to vote. A study of the Party's Parliamentary wing could therefore be dismissed on this basis. But this misses the important point. A party's Parliamentary wing is one of its most public manifestations. Having a voice in the Commons gives a party a platform and a legitimacy that is denied to those outside. Votes in the Commons are as much about putting on record the public stance of a party as they are about influencing legislation. The behaviour of a party's Parliamentarians is therefore important. And the larger a party's Parliamentary presence, the more important it becomes. When the entire Liberal Parliamentary party could (almost) fit into a taxi cab, they could be – and were – dismissed on the grounds that they were too slight a subject to be worthy of study. At 46 strong in the 1997 Parliament – and enough to fill a decent-sized coach – the Liberal Democrats could no longer be dismissed on this basis.

When voting on whipped votes they were a very cohesive grouping, one which began the Parliament voting strongly in support of Labour, on both the principle and detail of legislation. Despite sitting on the Opposition benches, they were more often than not to be found in the Government lobbies. However, Liberal Democrat support for Labour clearly waned.

As Figure 11.3 shows, for parts of the preceding (1992) Parliament, the Party's voting had been practically indistinguishable from Labour. In the second session of the 1992 Parliament, for example, the Party voted with Labour in almost 80 per cent of divisions. Figures for the third and fourth sessions were even higher (83 and 82 per cent). And voting with the Conservatives was then a rare thing indeed: in the 1995–96 session, the Liberal Democrats voted with the Tories in just five per cent of votes. It was perhaps just as well that the Liberal Democrats abandoned their policy of equidistance, because there was precious little that was equidistant about the way that they were behaving.

Figure 11.3 Liberal Democrat voting with Labour and Conservatives, 1992-2001, by session

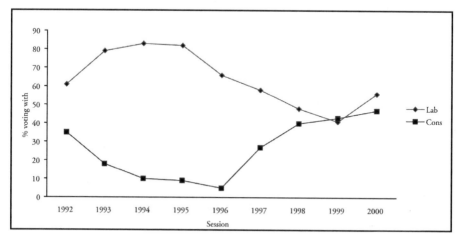

On winning the Liberal Democrat leadership contest in August 1999, Charles Kennedy put more emphasis than his predecessor, Paddy Ashdown, on the Party's independence, saying he wanted it to be 'confident enough to cooperate with the Government when we agree; independent enough to fight and win when we disagree'.[34] But the Party's support for Labour was already declining before Kennedy replaced Ashdown as leader. The Party's voting in the first session of the 1997 parliament was less pro-Labour than in the preceding parliament; their voting in the second session was less pro-Labour than the first; and their voting in the third was less pro-Labour than the second. The fourth session rather spoilt that neat trend, but the overall trend was still clear. Ironically, as the claims that the Liberal Democrats were becoming too close to Labour grew louder, so their voting in parliament became less supportive of the Government. If the Liberal Democrats ever were Labour in disguise, they are no longer.

[1] Robert McKenzie, *British Political Parties*, London, Heinemann, 1963 (2nd ed), 5.

[2] Vernon Bogdanor, 'Introduction', in V. Bogdanor (ed), *Liberal Party Politics*, Oxford, Clarendon Press, 1983, p. 4. Philip Norton's chapter in the same volume is 'The Liberal Party in Parliament'.

[3] P. G. Richards, 'The SDP in Parliament', *Parliamentary Affairs*, 35 (1982); Ivor Crewe and Anthony King, SDP, Oxford, Oxford University Press, 1995; and Don MacIver (ed), *The Liberal Democrats*,

Hemel Hempstead, Prentice Hall, 1996, which contains Stephen Ingle's chapter 'Party Organisation', pp. 122–125 of which focus on the Parliamentary party.

4   Philip Norton, 'The Parliamentary Terrier', *The House Magazine*, 19 September 1993.

5   *Guardian*, 21 January 1999; HC Debs, 13 May 1999, c. 492. Or see the cartoon by Peter Brookes, *The Times*, 24 September 1999.

6   Roland Watson and James Landale, 'Lib Dems not poodles, says Kennedy', *The Times*, 24 September 1999. For similar views, see for example Malcolm Bruce's letter to the *Telegraph* (11 April 2001).

7   Calculating the figure as a proportion of whipped votes (of which for the Liberal Democrats there were 1,147) gives one rebellion every 38 votes. Slice it how you like, the conclusion remains the same.

8   Also see Norton 'The Liberal Party in Parliament', p. 155.

9   Again, the same was true of the previous Parliament as well. Of the 35 revolts between 1992 and 1997, just three consisted of two or more MPs.

10   HC Debs, 7 March 2001, c. 378.

11   David Heath was joined in the noe lobby by Richard Livsey, Ray Michie, Sir Robert Smith, and Steve Webb. Thirty-seven Liberal Democrats supported the Government in the aye lobby.

12   Alan Beith, Colin Breed, John Burnett, David Heath, Archy Kirkwood, Ray Michie, Lembit Opik, Sir Robert Smith and Paul Tyler. Eighteen Liberal Democrats supported the Government in the aye lobby.

13   Alan Beith, David Heath, Ray Michie, Lembit Opik and Sir Robert Smith. Twenty Liberal Democrats supported the Government in the aye lobby.

14   Richard Allan, Tom Brake, Mike Hancock, David Heath and Adrian Sanders.

15   See for example Philip Cowley and Mark Stuart, 'Sodomy, Slaughter, Sunday Shopping and Seatbelts', *Party Politics*, 3 (1997); or Philip Cowley, 'Free Votes of Conscience: Taking Morality Policy Out of the Electoral Arena in the United Kingdom', in C. Z. Mooney (ed), *The Public Clash of Private Values*, Chatham, NJ, Chatham House, 2000.

16   Philip Cowley, Darren Darcy, Colin Mellors, Jon Neal and Mark Stuart, 'Mr Blair's Loyal Opposition? The Liberal Democrats in Parliament', *British Elections and Parties Review*, 10 (2000).

17   But not that loose. MPs who are unhappy about the whip are obliged to hear the Liberal Democrat position outlined in the House; they must try to resolve their difficulties with the relevant spokesperson; and if they then still feel they need to vote a different way, they are 'honour-bound' to speak to the Chief Whip. Jon Neal, '"Steering a Hundred Tonne Oil Tanker with a Rudder made of Blancmange". The Running of the Liberal Democrat Parliamentary Party – Past, Present and Future', unpublished undergraduate dissertation, University of Hull, 1999, p. 25.

18   Even after the 1997 election, the party initially continued with its policy that all MPs would have policy portfolios, although in practice some MPs were semidetached. Neal, '"Steering a Hundred Tonne Oil Tanker"', p. 9.

19   Perhaps not surprisingly, Liberal Democrat MPs tend therefore to be less ambitious than other MPs, although even so just over half of the Liberal Democrat MPs who responded to the BRS when asked 'Where would you most like to be in ten years?' replied 'in Government'.

20   Neal, '"Steering a Hundred Tonne Oil Tanker"', p. 25.

21   When the BRS asked whether they should vote with their party regardless of the national interest, the figures were four, eight and ten per cent respectively.

22   Unfortunately, the small number of cases involved (both in general and rebelling) means that it is not meaningful to attempt to link measures of dissonance with the party to individual acts of rebellion (as it was in Part II).

23   See, for example, Paul Webb, *The Modern British Party System*, London, Sage, 2000, pp. 209–210. Or see Ingle, 'Party Organisation'.

24   Critics, probably equally justifiably, argue that it is easy to have a participatory policy-making process when a party is rarely in a position to implement its policies.

25   From Andrew Russell, Edward Fieldhouse and Iain MacAllister, 'Dual Identities? The Organisation of the British Liberal Democrats', unpublished paper presented to the ECPR General Conference,

Canterbury, 2001, p. 4.

[26] Andrew Russell, Ed Fieldhouse and Iain MacAllister, *Neither Left nor Right but Forward? The Electoral Politics of the Liberal Democrats in Britain*, Manchester, Manchester University Press, 2002.

[27] Norton 'The Liberal Party in Parliament', p. 143.

[28] More accurately, 132 votes saw the Liberal Democrats allow free votes. One or more of the other parties may have been whipped, even if that whipping was occasionally somewhat covert.

[29] Philip Cowley and Mark Stuart, 'Mr Blair's Loyal Opposition?', *Parliamentary Brief,* 5 (1999).

[30] Cowley et al, 'Mr Blair's Loyal Opposition?'

[31] Mark Stuart, *Douglas Hurd*, Edinburgh: Mainstream, 1998, p. 100.

[32] Data drawn from the final session is distorted both by the short length of the session (see the note below) and by the fact that the session saw a relatively high number of deferred divisions (16) in which all three main parties voted together as a result of the activities of the Conservative awkward squad.

[33] These figures exclude programming motions. The figure for the final session is slightly misleading, simply because the short length of the session meant that there were so few votes on the details of legislation.

[34] *Telegraph*, 10 August 1999.

Part IV

Conclusion

12. That Was Then, This is Now

One of the most frequent complaints about the actions of the Blair Government was (and still is) that it marginalised parliament. One Conservative MP claimed that the 1997 Parliament would go down in history as the 'abused parliament'.[1]

First, there were Labour's reforms to the House of Lords, where the Government removed the hereditary peers who defeated it frequently, leading to the charge that it was emasculating the second chamber, weakening the one last significant check on its behaviour within parliament.[2]

Second, there were criticisms that Labour ministers were arrogant and dismissive of parliament. Changes to Prime Minister's Questions were presented to the House as a fait accompli, even before the Modernisation Committee had been established. Labour ministers were repeatedly accused of releasing information to the media before informing the Commons, provoking several complaints from the Speaker, including a formal complaint to both the Cabinet Secretary and the Leader of the House.[3] The Prime Minister was an infrequent participant in the Commons: Blair led his Government in fewer debates and participated in fewer divisions than any recent Prime Minister.[4] Even when the Prime Minister or other ministers were in the Commons, the complaint was that Labour backbenchers colluded with the Government. For example, three Labour MPs were suspended from the House for leaking Select Committee reports (see Appendix 2). Others were accused of asking patsy questions to ministers. As one Labour backbencher, Andrew Mackinlay, complained in a now famous question:

> Does the Prime Minister recall that, when we were in opposition, we used to groan at the fawning, obsequious, softball, well-rehearsed and planted questions asked by Conservative Members of [John Major]? Will my right hon. Friend distinguish his period in office by discouraging such practices – which diminish Prime Minister's Question Time – during this Parliament?[5]

And third, the massed ranks of Labour MPs meant that the Government enjoyed the largest majority of any single party since 1935. It was to be the first Government to last an entire Parliament undefeated in the House of Commons since that elected in 1966. This part of the marginalisation thesis was perhaps inevitable – the power of Parliament to influence the executive varies with the size of the Government's majority and because the Blair Government enjoyed an enormous majority Parliament's influence was therefore limited – but the problem was exacerbated by two factors.

There was the contrast between the Blair Government and its predecessor. For much of the 1992 Parliament the Conservatives had a majority that was in single figures or nonexistent. From April 1992 until May 1997, therefore, the outcome of Parliamentary votes was not always known before they took place and things were (almost) exciting. For the four years after 1997, by contrast, they were terribly predictable. In Parliamentary terms, the five years before 1997 were akin to a European Cup Final between, say, Manchester United and Juventus, complete with a disputed goal, some dreadful refereeing decisions, at least one sending off (perhaps also a couple of small fights), some wonderful goals, and ending 5–4, with the winning goal coming in the last minute. The Parliament of 1997, by contrast, resembled a Tuesday night fixture between Hull City and Hartlepool in the pouring rain, ending in a nil-nil draw, and without even the delight of a dog on the pitch to cheer things up.

And to make matters worse, there was the behaviour of Labour MPs. As has been shown throughout this book, there were complaints that too many Labour MPs gave unquestioning support to the Government. The new methods of whipping implemented just before the 1997 election – including tighter standing orders and the use of electronic message pagers to keep MPs informed of the party line – led to criticism that Labour MPs were too slavishly following the party line. The use of phrases such as 'Daleks', 'clones', and 'spineless' became common. Especially criticised were the new women MPs elected in 1997.

Yet if that is the case for the prosecution, then it does not take Perry Mason to construct the case for the defence.

The first problem with these criticisms is that they focus on peripheral matters, whilst overlooking the deeper, and more profound, challenges to Parliament. This is, essentially, the convincing case made by Peter Riddell in his *Parliament Under Blair*.[6] Most other institutions have, for example, come to terms better with Britain's integration into mainland Europe than Parliament. Parliament today also faces a judiciary that is increasingly assertive and – because of the Human Rights Act – increasingly empowered. Moreover, changes to the structure of Government, such as the development of agencies and regulatory authorities, undermine most of the traditional notions of accountability, whilst constitutional change, in particular devolution, has created alternative centres of power. Changes in the mass media have meant that increasingly little attention is paid to Parliament, and to cap it all, globalisation and rise of anti-politics (à la Seattle), has challenged both what Parliament could, and should, be doing. In short, Parliament is being 'squeezed out of the political debate'. Some of these problems may have been exacerbated by the actions or inaction of the Blair Government but most existed long before 1997. They are shifts in the tectonic plates of political life, and they have little to do with, and are more important than, whether Tony Blair turns up once or twice a week to answer questions.[7]

The second problem with most of the criticisms is not that they are necessarily wrong (because many of them are not) but that they pretend to be describing something that is somehow new. Most of the analysis of the behaviour of the Blair Government was profoundly, and depressingly, ahistorical. Tony Blair did attend Parliament infrequently, but the decline in prime ministerial participation in the business of the Commons is nothing new, having been declining since the mid–19th century. There were particularly steep declines in the 1980s and 1990s, under the Conservative premierships of Margaret Thatcher and John Major.[8] Labour backbenchers did frequently ask sycophantic patsy questions to ministers but it is a trick they perfected after years of watching Conservative MPs do the same.[9] Andrew Mackinlay's question (above) is frequently quoted as an attack on Labour MPs but the first part of the question refers to the 'fawning, obsequious, softball, well-rehearsed and planted questions asked by Conservative Members'.[10] Nor is the Blair Government the first to prefer to announce policy outside of the House of Commons. An earlier Speaker, Bernard Weatherill, frequently had to persuade a very reluctant Margaret Thatcher to come to the Commons to report on policy decisions. She used to complain that it was 'such a nuisance'.[11]

The final problem with many of the criticisms made of Labour's relationship with Parliament, though, is that they misunderstand or misrepresent what was taking place. This is true, for example, of complaints about the reform of the House of Lords. Far from Lords reform removing an independent check on the Government, the reforms created a more assertive and confident second chamber.[12] It is also true – and most relevant here – of the criticisms about the cohesion of Labour MPs. As this book has shown, the real reasons for the high levels of cohesion seen on the Labour benches between 1997 and 2001 are far more complicated than any instinctive bovine loyalty.

Labour MPs were rebelling infrequently but when they did break ranks they did so in sizeable numbers. And a full 50 per cent of Labour backbenchers voted against the Government at some point in the Parliament. Moreover, much of the cohesion that did exist did not result from any lack of backbone on the part of Labour MPs. Rather, it was caused by changes to the composition of the PLP (such as a shift in the Party's political attitudes), a broad agreement on the part of many MPs with much of the Government's programme, a lack of any sizeable factional opposition, a conscious desire on the part of many MPs not to appear disunited, and a Government which was, for most of the Parliament, and over most issues, prepared to consult, negotiate and do deals with its back-benchers in order to ameliorate discontent and lessen revolt.

Each of the chapters in Part I give examples of policy change produced in response to pressure from backbench Labour MPs. Of course, such influence was at the margins of policy. As was pointed out in Chapter 1, Parliament has long had a peripheral influence on policy making in Britain and it continued to have a peripheral influence under Blair. Backbenchers had effectively no say in the broad direction of policy. But it was ever thus. Blaming the Blair Government for this is about as sensible as blaming it for the loss of America.

Yet it could fairly be argued that many of the concessions were little more than the small change of political life. Moreover, Labour backbenchers were often not the only people pressurising the Government. When change came about, therefore, it was not solely because of the actions of backbench MPs. This was perhaps most clear in the case of pensions up-rating but it was also true in other cases as well. The role of the House of Lords was, for example, crucial in gaining a number of the concessions achieved. And pressure on the Government over issues such as incapacity benefit was strengthened by the lobbying of outside groups, especially those normally sympathetic to Labour (what one MP described as 'well-meaning *Guardian* readers').[13]

But the crucial thing is not the size of the concessions but that they were given at all. For a Government that was supposed to think Parliament an irrelevance, the Blair Government often went to great lengths to prevent rebellions taking place. Why did it continually offer these concessions to placate backbench Labour MPs if it did not care about their views or actions? Those occasions when Labour MPs would complain that the whips were being over-zealous were also proof of a concern on the part of the Party about the behaviour of its MPs. Similarly, when – as over Iraq – the whips resorted to procedural shenanigans in order to avoid a vote, or when – as over student grants – they attempted to minimise the expressions of dissent by swamping the debate – it is evidence of a concern, rather than a disregard, for Parliament. For a Government that supposedly ignored Parliament, it expended considerable energy trying to keep the visible signs of discontent to a bare minimum. Why bully, trick, persuade, cajole and negotiate if you do not care? One long-serving Labour MP, who had seen six different Labour leaders in his time in the Commons, thought that Blair was 'very sensitive' to rebellion, more so than any other leader that he had served under.[14] Of course, it was not usually, if ever, that the whips were worried about the eventual outcome of the vote – they knew they would win – but that, just like many other Labour MPs, the leadership were worried about the appearance of division. The symbolic value of Parliamentary behaviour was clear for all to see. For all the talk of the decline of Parliament, both before and after 1 May 1997, Parliament still clearly mattered.

Prospects for the new Parliament

The Parliament of 1997 ended with Labour enjoying an enormous, and impregnable, majority in the Commons; its successor began with Labour enjoying a majority just 12 lower. Even the MPs forming that majority were nearly identical.[15] A total of 560 sitting MPs were re-elected in 2001. Just 21 were defeated.[16] Eighty-five per cent of the Commons was therefore exactly the same after the election as it had been before – the lowest turnover since 1945.[17] The party composition remained almost identical. The number of Labour MPs fell by just five. The number of Conservatives rose by just one.[18] The party experiencing the largest rise in its numbers – the Liberal Democrats – saw their representation rise by just six. The Government's majority fell by 12, but remained an enormous 167. There was even a new Independent MP, Dr Richard Taylor, the victor in Wyre Forest, to replace the outgoing Martin Bell.[19]

Any visitor looking at the Commons from outside would therefore be hard pushed to see much evidence of change. Yet changes there were, even if they were not immediately obvious. For one thing, the growing perception that Parliament was being sidelined has created increasing pressure for reforms to strengthen the institution. This has, somewhat bizarrely, been strengthened by the low turnout in the General Election generating the perception that the public is dissatisfied with the institutions of representative democracy (as if strengthening select committees, say, will somehow make people in Liverpool Riverside happily troop out to vote). Shortly after the election, the Hansard Society's 'Commission on Parliamentary Scrutiny', chaired by Tony Newton, published its final report, *The Challenge for Parliament: Making Government Accountable*.[20] It was well received by commentators and practitioners, and added to a growing body of influential literature urging the reform of Parliament.[21] June 2001 also saw the formation of a cross-party group of MPs called 'Parliament First', whose opening act was a Commons motion stating that 'the role of Parliament has weakened, is weakening and ought to be strengthened'.

There were also some potentially significant changes in personnel, most obviously Robin Cook's move from Foreign Secretary to Leader of the House. Cook's predecessor, Margaret Beckett, was an executive-minded Leader of the House, largely uninterested in Parliamentary reform, except insofar as it could expedite the Government's programme. Not only is Cook temperamentally more Parliament-minded, he also now has the chance to enjoy a political Indian Summer in the post.[22] His early actions – including his appointment of reformist special advisers – were at least positive signs for those who want reform. The Government also created a new Cabinet post of Party Chairman. One justification for the position was that it would better enable the views of the Party, including the Parliamentary party, to be represented within Cabinet. It would also provide an obvious media spokesperson for the Party, saving Jean Corston – who replaced Clive Soley as PLP Chair soon after the election – from having to perform the sort of unsavoury media tasks that had so damaged Soley's reputation with the backbenchers.[23]

On the other side of the House, Iain Duncan Smith's election as Conservative leader meant the end of the Party's awkward squad. In a clear-cut case of poacher turned gamekeeper – indeed, poachers turned gamekeepers – Eric Forth was appointed Shadow Leader of the House and his sidekick David Maclean was made Conservative Chief Whip.[24] During the last Parliament many Labour backbenchers complained of the difficulty of achieving cross-party consensus on Parliamentary reform; the appointment of Forth and Maclean may now make that practically impossible. The slightly expanded Liberal Democrats also continued their voyage away from consensus with the Government. The early part of the Parliament (from the election to Christmas 2001) saw them vote against Labour in almost three-quarters of votes. They were now more than twice as likely to be voting with the Conservatives against Labour than *vice versa*.

There was also evidence that Labour's backbenchers may prove less cohesive in the new Parliament. For many, one sign of this came in their reaction to the proposed membership of the Commons departmental select committees when the Government attempted to remove Donald Anderson from the Foreign

Affairs Select Committee and Gwyneth Dunwoody from the Transport, Local Government and the Regions Select Committee, claiming that both had done their stint and the committees needed some fresh blood. Critics – of which there were plenty – saw it as an attempt by the Government to nobble two independent-minded Select Committee Chairs. But against the expectations even of those organising the opposition to the changes, the Commons refused to do the Government's bidding. The new composition of the Transport Committee was voted down by 308 to 221, that of the Foreign Affairs Committee by 301 to 232. Some 125 Labour MPs voted against the proposals in the first vote, with 118 doing so in the second. When Conservative whips tried something similar in 1992, they got away with it: fewer than 50 Conservative MPs voted against.[25]

The votes were widely described as evidence of an increasingly rebellious attitude amongst Labour backbenchers. This was almost universally contrasted with their behaviour in the previous Parliament, when they were supposed to have displayed what the *Guardian* described as 'rock hard discipline'.[26] This was said to be the point at which Labour MPs threw off their shackles and began to stand up to the Government. And this was almost universally portrayed as one of political life's Good Things, helping to shift the balance of power between the legislature and the executive.

Not only was the 'rock hard discipline' of the previous Parliament a myth but also, as Peter Riddell noted in *The Times*, much of the media coverage bordered on the hysterical, giving the impression 'we were back in the 1640s and Speaker Lenthall was defying Charles I over the arrest of the five members'.[27] The decision of the Commons to reject nominations for the membership of select committees may have marked a shift in the balance of power in the relationship between the executive and the legislature – but it was one that was very much at the margins.

Moreover, the votes were explicitly free votes. Of course, as one Conservative minister once admitted, there are 'free votes and free votes' – and plenty of ostensibly free votes have seen governments applying pressure behind the scenes.[28] On this occasion there was an informal payroll whip in operation (that is, members of the Government were expected to vote for the proposals but other Labour MPs had a free vote) but even that was not enforced.[29] Yet it is one thing to vote against the Government on a free vote and quite another to do so when the whips are on. Even before the select committee votes, Labour MPs had already shown themselves willing to vote against front bench advice on these sort of free votes. Throughout the 1997 Parliament, for example, the PLP had been divided over the City of London (Ward Elections) Bill.[30] As a private Bill, no whips were applied (hence its absence from analysis in the earlier chapters of this book) and one vote saw the PLP split almost down the middle (admittedly on a low turnout), 70 to 74. Divisions on free or semi-free votes like these therefore simply do not equate to divisions when the whips are on. As one of the MPs who organised the select committee 'rebellion' admitted: 'It's harmless. It won't do the Government any harm, but it'll send a message: don't take us for granted'.[31] The pressures placed upon MPs when the whips are on, though, will be of an entirely different magnitude. The two select committee votes were widely described as the first time the Blair Government had been defeated since 1997 but (at least at the time of writing) it remains undefeated on whipped votes.

Nor was it quite the peasants' revolt that some made it out to be.[32] To be sure, the rebels included some previously loyal MPs, such as Barry Gardiner, Diana Organ, Paul Truswell, and even the much-maligned Helen Brinton, and there were also some newly elected MPs (eight voted against the proposed composition of the Foreign Affairs Committee, three of whom also did so over the Transport Committee). Nevertheless, the vast majority of those who voted against the Government – 70 per cent in each vote – had form, having voted against the Government during the last Parliament. This was no slaughter of the innocents. The scale of the defeat was made all the more impressive by the involvement of those who had been loyal previously but the rebels alone were sufficient to defeat the Government.

The select committee 'rebellions' were essentially free votes on an issue that attracted widespread elite support (after all, few argue against 'strengthening Parliament'). Their significance for the rest of the Parliament is likely to be minimal.

That said, the Government almost certainly does face a potentially tougher ride from its backbenchers during this Parliament. From the election to Christmas 2001, there were almost 40 rebellions by backbench Labour MPs, more than in the entire first and second sessions of the 1997 Parliament put together. A full third of all votes saw a rebellion by Labour MPs. One of the reasons for this rise in dissent is obvious, if not entirely creditable: the backbenches now contain more disgruntled MPs, both those sacked from ministerial office or those passed over for promotion. If nothing else, the passage of time has meant that since the last election the median age of the PLP has risen to 50.[33]

But there are two other factors that are less commonly appreciated. The first is that the extraordinary self-discipline exercised by Labour MPs for much of the last Parliament will continue to decline. As time goes on, especially if the

Conservatives fail to make any obvious signs of electoral recovery, the pressure to be self-disciplined will continue to recede. There were signs of that even in the 1997 Parliament, with the outbreak in the third session of low-intensity rebellions, of MPs barking even when they knew they could not bite. This is confirmed by the pattern of dissent seen at the beginning of the 2001 Parliament. Most of the rebellions consist of small numbers of MPs. The average size of the Labour backbench rebellions to have taken place before Christmas 2001 was nine MPs. Moreover, many of those participating in the rebellions are the same people, rebelling repeatedly. It is not therefore that all Labour MPs have become more rebellious. Rather, it is that the previously rebellious are becoming even more rebellious. Indeed, one problem with the Government's tactic of not promoting those who rebel is that, after an MP has broken ranks once there is much less to prevent him or her doing so again. Exclusion may put off the initial rebellion but it merely encourages later rebelliousness.

The second reason for thinking that the 2001 Parliament will see more rebellions is the nature of the issues that are coming before the Commons. As shown in earlier chapters, the composition of the legislative agenda is an important determinant of Parliamentary behaviour.

The effect of the military action against Afghanistan and other aspects of the 'war against terrorism' will probably not be great. Parliament was recalled three times during the Summer recess to discuss the events of, and reaction to, 11 September, and each time it appeared that disquiet on the Labour benches was growing.[34] This resulted in a very public spat between Paul Marsden, the MP for Shrewsbury and Atcham, and the new Labour Chief Whip, Hilary Armstrong, after which Marsden gave what he claimed were verbatim transcripts of their conversation to the *Mail on Sunday*. This was then followed by an encounter between Marsden and some of the Labour whips in a Commons bar, during which Marsden claimed he was physically and verbally assaulted.[35] Although Marsden was presented as a hero in some quarters for daring to stand up to his whips, some of his complaints (such as expecting the Government to grant a free vote on military action) revealed some naivety on his part and the impact of his comments were anyway lessened once he defected to the Liberal Democrats on 10 December.[36]

The Marsden episode aside, the evidence from the previous Parliament was that discontent with foreign policy on Labour's benches was confined to a fairly small number of MPs. The votes on Iraq and Kosovo never attracted the support of more than two dozen Labour backbenchers. Similarly, revolts on civil liberties issues rarely drew more than 30 Labour MPs to their banners, and frequently far fewer. The Government initially tried to avoid a vote on the bombing in Afghanistan, only for opponents to force a vote on the adjournment of the House. Yet this merely revealed how few in number they were: just 11 voted against the Government.[37] Although the numbers rebelling on the subsequent Terrorism Bill were reduced by some Government concessions, it saw an average of just 11 MPs vote against the Government, peaking at 32 on the issue of judicial review of the Home Secretary's decisions. As Frank Johnson noted in the *Telegraph*:

> Behind [Blunkett], on the Labour backbenches, was every independent-minded libertarian in his party. Bearing in mind the size of the Parliamentary Labour Party, this is a tiny number. There are probably more Taliban in Tel Aviv. But when they are all together, and constantly interrupting the Home Secretary with their high-minded questions and observations, they seem to be a seething mass of rebellion.[38]

Larger revolts are likely on more bread-and-butter issues. The largest revolts in the 1997 Parliament were on social security reform and initiatives that involved the private finance of public services. Labour MPs began the 2001 Parliament making clear their opposition to reforms to incapacity benefit at a remarkably hostile Prime Minister's Questions on 4 July. Several meetings of the PLP have been similarly rumbustious.[39] If there is to be serious trouble from the backbenches in the 2001 Parliament, it is probably on these issues that it will occur. And from what we know about the Government's planned programme for the 2001 Parliament, it will see plenty of both types of issues, providing lots of opportunities for dissent.[40]

One thing is certain, though. If Labour MPs continue to rebel more frequently, and especially if they start to defeat the Government on whipped votes, the reaction from the media will not be positive. The Select Committee votes won widespread praise ('the rise of the House of Commons' and all that) but if it becomes a regular occurrence, things will be very different. The same commentators who spent the last four years moaning about the cohesion of Labour MPs will promptly start moaning about division within Labour's ranks.

[1] HC Debs, 27 February 2001, c. 726.
[2] See, for example, John Redwood, *The Death of Britain*, London, Macmillan, 1999, pp. 68–69.
[3] See Philip Norton, 'Parliament', in A. Seldon (ed), *The Blair Effect*, London, Little, Brown, 2001.
[4] Andrew Tyrie, *Mr Blair's Poodle*, London, Centre for Policy Studies, 2000, p. 31.
[5] HC Debs, 3 June 1998, cc. 358–359.
[6] London, Politico's, 2000.

[7] See also Richard Rose, *The Prime Minister in a Shrinking World*, Oxford, Polity, 2001.

[8] Patrick Dunleavy and George W. Jones, 'Leaders, Politics and Institutional Change: The Decline of Prime Ministerial Accountability in the House of Commons, 1968–1990', *British Journal of Political Science*, 23 (1993).

[9] See, for example, the entry in Gyles Brandreth's backbench diaries for 14 May 1992 when the Conservative whips give Brandreth a planted question for the Prime Minister which he himself describes as 'so cheap, so contrived, so graceless' but which he asked nonetheless. Gyles Brandreth, *Breaking the Code*, London, Weidenfeld and Nicolson, 1999, pp. 96–97.

[10] One study found that little difference between the behaviour of Labour MPs in 1997 and those of Conservative MPs in 1992. See R. C. V. Nash, 'New Labour and the Marginalisation of Parliament', unpublished dissertation, University of Hull, 2000.

[11] Private information.

[12] See Philip Cowley and Mark Stuart, 'Parliament: A Few Headaches and a Dose of Modernisation', *Parliamentary Affairs*, 54 (2001).

[13] Interview, 15 February 2000.

[14] Interview, 25 October 2001.

[15] For more on the composition of the Commons post–2001, see Philip Cowley, 'The Commons: Mr Blair's Lapdog?', in P. Norris (ed), *Britain Votes 2001*, London, Oxford University Press, 2001.

[16] One – Martin Bell – doing so in a different seat (Brentwood and Ongar) to the one (Tatton) he had been representing for the last four years.

[17] That is, excluding the two short Parliaments of 1950–51 and February-October 1974.

[18] Given that one of the Conservative gains was Tatton – a seat held by Martin Bell since 1997 but in which Bell was not standing in 2001 – the net gain from other political parties was effectively nil.

[19] The initial signs are that Taylor will have a much higher voting record than Bell's. He voted in 69 of the first 121 votes (57 per cent). It took Bell more than two years until his voting record exceeded 50 per cent (see Appendix 9). Taylor is also far less pro-Labour than was Bell. Almost two-thirds of his votes from his election until Christmas 2001 were cast against the Government. Bell, on the other hand, tended to vote with Labour more than against.

[20] London, Vacher Dod, 2001.

[21] Such as the report from the Liaison Committee entitled *Shifting The Balance* (HC 300, 1999–2000), or the report of the Conservative Party's Commission to Strengthen Parliament. The Commission was chaired by Philip Norton, and published its report – which was a sort of Philip Norton's Greatest Hits – in July 2000.

[22] 'Robin Cook's Revenge', *Economist*, 21–27 July 2001.

[23] Corston defeated Tony Lloyd in the election for the PLP chair by 183 votes to 167.

[24] Quentin Letts, 'HM Opposition: a user's guide', *New Statesman*, 22 October 2001.

[25] The Conservative whips tried to remove Nicholas Winterton from the Health Committee (to which four Conservative MPs objected) and Sir John Wheeler from the Home Affairs Committee (46 objected). See Gavin Drewry, 'Parliament', in P. Dunleavy, A. Gamble, I. Holliday and G. Peele (eds), *Developments in British Politics 4*, London, Macmillan, 1993, pp. 161–165.

[26] *Guardian*, 16 July 2001.

[27] *The Times*, 19 July 2001.

[28] HC Debs, 25 March 1996, c. 742.

[29] Colin Pickthall, Jack Straw's Parliamentary Private Secretary, voted against the proposals and several other ministers abstained.

[30] The Bill introduced a business vote, based on the rateable value of properties owned by companies in the City of London.

[31] Interview, 25 October 2001.

[32] See, for example, Michael Brown, 'Backlash from the Backbenches', *The House Magazine*, 23 July 2001, who talks of a 'peasants' revolt' and 'the week when the little people hit back'.

33 Cowley, 'The Commons', pp. 260–261. Byron Criddle, 'MPs and Candidates', in D. Butler and D. Kavanagh, *The British General Election of 2001*, London, Macmillan, 2001, p. 199.

34 See Frank Johnson, 'Disquiet on the Westminster front', *Telegraph*, 2 November 2001; Michael White, 'Rebels fail to dent support for action', *Guardian*, 2 November 2001; Simon Hoggart, 'Victory for the doom-mongers in a passionate war of words', *Guardian*, 2 November 2001.

35 Again, in the *Mail on Sunday*. 'He had his arm across my throat . . . he'd lost it', *Mail on Sunday*, 9 December 2001. It included a rogue's gallery of those said to have been involved (not all of them whips), including John 'Knuckles' Heppell, Gerry 'Fingers' Sutcliffe and Ivan 'Shorty' Henderson.

36 For Marsden as hero, see, for example, the *Guardian's* leader article ('Marsden's victory') of 23 October 2001 or its letters page the same day. For Marsden as naive fool, see the *Telegraph's* leader of 11 December ('Aboard the ship of fools'). As the *Telegraph* put it: 'Somebody should have warned him that knocking MPs into line is what Whips are for'.

37 The voting was 373 to 13, with the Conservatives and Liberal Democrats united in support of the Labour Government in the aye lobby. The ten Labour MPs were joined by three Plaid Cymru and two SNP MPs in the noe lobby. John McDonnell and another Plaid Cymru MP voted in the aye lobby to ensure that the division was forced.

38 Frank Johnson, 'Muesli-eaters fail to have Blunkett for breakfast', *Daily Telegraph*, 20 November 2001.

39 The first PLP meeting after the election, for example, saw criticism from several normally loyal MPs, such as Peter Pike (who spoke about conditions on council estates in his constituency) and Debra Shipley (who spoke passionately about the state of her local hospitals). Private information.

40 See Philip Cowley and Mark Stuart, 'Parliament: Mostly Continuity (but more change than you'd think)', *Parliamentary Affairs*, forthcoming, 2002.

Appendices

Appendix 1: By-elections, 1997–2001

The 1997 Parliament saw 17 by-elections (see Table A1.1), the majority of which were caused by the death of the incumbent MP. One was triggered by an elevation to the peerage (George Robertson *en route* to becoming Secretary-General of NATO) and a further five were caused by resignations. All of this was pretty much par for the course.[1] More unusual was the Winchester by-election, the first time since 1923 that an election petition had been successful on grounds of irregularities in the electoral process.[2] It did not alter the composition of the Commons one jot: in 1997 Mark Oaten had won the seat for the Liberal Democrats by just two votes; the resulting by-election saw him returned with a majority of 22,000. Equally unusually, the by-elections did not greatly change the party balance of the Commons. Only two seats changed hands. In 2000 the DUP gained South Antrim from the UUP, and – more surprisingly – the Liberal Democrats captured Romsey from the Conservatives. But these were all changes within the ranks of the Opposition. The Government held all of the eight seats they defended, as well as winning the Speaker's seat of West Bromwich West (previously a Labour seat).

Table A1.1 By-elections, 1997–2001

Constituency	Former MP	Cause	Date of by-election	Party holding seat	New MP	Result
Uxbridge	Sir Michael Shersby	Death	31 July 97	Con	John Randall	Hold
Paisley	Gordon McMaster	Death	6 Nov 97	Lab	Douglas Alexander	Hold
Beckenham	Piers Merchant	Resignation	20 Nov 97	Con	Jacqui Lait	Hold
Winchester	Mark Oaten	Election Petition	20 Nov 97	LD	Mark Oaten	Hold
Leeds Central	Derek Fatchett	Death	10 June 99	Lab	Hilary Benn	Hold
Eddisbury	Sir Alastair Goodlad	Resignation	22 July 99	Con	Stephen O'Brien	Hold
Wigan	Roger Stott	Death	23 Sept 99	Lab	Neil Turner	Hold
Hamilton South	George Robertson	Elevation to peerage	23 Sept 99	Lab	Bill Tynan	Hold
Kensington & Chelsea	Alan Clark	Death	25 Nov 99	Con	Michael Portillo	Hold
Ceredigion	Cynog Dafis	Resignation	3 Feb 00	PC	Simon Thomas	Hold
Romsey	Michael Colvin	Death	4 May 00	Con	Sandra Gidley	LD Gain
Tottenham	Bernie Grant	Death	22 June 00	Lab	David Lammy	Hold
South Antrim	Clifford Forsythe	Death	21 Sept 00	UUP	Dr William McCrea	DUP Gain
Preston	Audrey Wise	Death	23 Nov 00	Lab	Mark Hendrick	Hold
Glasgow, Anniesland	Donald Dewar	Death	23 Nov 00	Lab	John Robertson	Hold
West Bromwich West	Betty Boothroyd	Resignation	23 Nov 00	Speaker	Adrian Bailey	Lab Gain
Falkirk West	Dennis Canavan	Resignation	21 Dec 00	Lab	Eric Joyce	Hold

The by-elections did result in a small increase in the number of women MPs, up by two (one Conservative, one Liberal Democrat), as well as seeing two further MPs from ethnic minorities enter the Commons – although since one of the latter replaced the late Bernie Grant the overall number of ethnic minority MPs rose by just one.

Appendix 2: Ejections and Rejections

The 1997 Parliament was notable for the number of MPs suspended from the House, or who had the whip removed (either temporarily or permanently). There were also two defections and a further two MPs who became involved in court cases.

Five MPs (four Labour, one Conservative) were suspended as a result of rulings of the House. Robert Wareing was suspended in October 1997 for a week, having failed to declare certain (Serbian-related) business interests. In July 1999 Ernie Ross was suspended for ten sitting days and forced to resign as a member of the Foreign Affairs Select Committee, having leaked a draft committee report on Sierra Leone to the Government. The same month saw Don Touhig, the Chancellor's PPS, admit obtaining a draft copy of a Social Services Committee Report into child benefit from Kali Mountford. Touhig was suspended for three days, Mountford for five. All four of the above apologised for their actions, unlike the fifth person to be suspended: Teresa Gorman, suspended from the Commons for a month in March 2000 for repeatedly covering up her substantial property interests, remained unrepentant about her actions.

Labour also expelled three MPs during the Parliament. Tommy Graham was expelled in September 1998, having been found guilty by an internal Party Disciplinary Council on five counts, including two charges of offering compromising photographs of a homosexual trade union official in return for information on a rival. Both Dennis Canavan and Ken Livingstone effectively expelled themselves by standing against Labour in elections: Canavan in the Scottish Parliament, Livingstone in the contest for the London Mayor. One Conservative MP, Charles Wardle, lost his party's whip in April 2001, when he endorsed an independent candidate as his successor in preference to the candidate chosen by his local party. A further two MPs changed party. Peter Temple-Morris left the Conservatives in November 1997 to sit as an Independent One Nation Conservative, although it was reported even then that he regarded Labour's weekly whip as his 'guide'.[3] He formally crossed the floor, joining Labour, in June 1998. Shaun (most definitely not Sean) Woodward defected straight from the Conservatives to Labour. On 2 December 1999 Woodward was sacked as front bench Conservative spokesperson after refusing to accept the Party's line on the repeal of Section 28. Just 16 days later, he announced he had joined the Labour Party.

More remarkable still were the two high profile court cases, both involving newly elected Labour MPs. In February 1999, after a 40 day trial at the High

Court in Edinburgh, a jury took just three hours to acquit Mohammad Sarwar, the Labour MP for Glasgow Govan, of two charges of false declaration over election expenses and conspiracy to pervert the course of justice by offering a rival candidate £5000 to lie on oath. (Sarwar had been suspended from the PLP pending the outcome of the case; he regained the whip in March 1999). The following month Fiona Jones, the Labour MP for Newark, was found guilty in Nottingham Crown Court for knowingly making a false declaration of election expenses under the Representation of the People Act 1983. She became the first sitting MP to be convicted of breaking electoral law in 140 years, and was automatically disqualified from the House and sentenced to 100 hours of community service. However, in April 1999 the Court of Appeal overturned her conviction and later that month she was reinstalled as an MP.

When MPs lose the whip the most common reaction is not for them to vote against their former party; rather it is for them just not to vote. For example, prior to his suspension from the PLP (which preceded his suspension from the Commons), Robert Wareing had voted in 80 per cent of divisions. During his suspension he voted not once. Mohammad Sarwar voted just 50 times during the 516 votes when he was suspended from the PLP. As soon as Tommy Graham was suspended from the PLP his voting record dropped from 70 per cent to just 30 votes out of 1,201, and he voted in not a single vote in the final session of the Parliament. Dennis Canavan's voting record also dropped to 11 per cent in the second session, and to six per cent in the third session, at least in part because of his new duties in the Scottish Parliament, although the majority of the votes he did cast were against the Government. Ken Livingstone exhibited a similar pattern, voting on only 13 occasions out of a possible 483 and casting not a single vote for the Government on a whipped vote.

When MPs change parties, their voting changes too. Despite voicing criticism of his party, Peter Temple-Morris's voting behaviour prior to switching parties was that of a loyalist Conservative backbencher. He voted on 68 per cent of occasions, and cast no dissenting votes. As an Independent One Nation Conservative (sitting on the Labour benches), his voting record slumped to 28 per cent (in line with the other whipless MPs discussed above) but he cast no votes against the Government and all of his votes (apart from two free votes and those occasions where the Labour party was voting in the same lobby as the Conservatives) were cast against the Conservatives. As soon as he took the Labour whip, his voting record rose again, to 85 per cent, and he cast not a single dissenting vote against Labour. Shaun Woodward similarly underwent a Pauline conversion. Prior to his defection, he had cast only one dissenting vote against his front bench. After his defection, he did not vote against Labour. If one of those ever-present Martians had landed and examined the recent voting records of Shaun Woodward or Peter Temple-Morris (although we can safely assume that any Martian landing on Earth would have better things to do), they would find nothing to indicate that they had ever been anything other than loyal Labour backbenchers.

Appendix 3: Rebellious Labour MPs, 1997–1998

Table A3.1 Rebellious Labour MPs, 1997–98

	Lone parent benefit	Iraq	Student grants	Newspaper ownership	Criminal Justice (Terrorism and Conspiracy)
Diane Abbott	X	X	X	X	–
Irene Adams	–	–	–	–	X
John Austin	X	–	–	X	–
Harry Barnes	X	X	–	–	–
Tony Benn	X	X	X	X	X
Andrew Bennett	–	X	–	X	–
Roger Berry	X	–	–	–	X
Harold Best	X	–	–	X	X
David Borrow	–	–	–	–	X
Christine Butler	–	–	–	–	X
Ronald Campbell	X	–	X	–	–
Dennis Canavan	X	X	X	X	X
Jamie Cann	–	–	–	–	–
Martin Caton	X	–	–	–	X
David Chaytor	X	–	–	–	–
Malcolm Chisholm	X	–	–	–	–
Michael Clapham	–	X	–	–	–
Ann Clwyd	X	–	–	X	X
Harry Cohen	–	X	–	X	–
Frank Cook	X	–	–	–	–
Robin Corbett	–	–	–	–	X
Jeremy Corbyn	X	X	X	X	X
James Cousins	–	–	–	–	X
Ann Cryer	X	–	X	–	X
John Cryer	X	–	X	–	X
Lawrence Cunliffe	–	–	X	–	–
Tam Dalyell	–	X	X	–	X
Ian Davidson	–	–	–	–	X
Denzil Davies	–	–	X	–	–
Hilton Dawson	X	–	–	–	–
James Dobbin	X	–	–	–	–
Gwyneth Dunwoody	X	–	–	X	X
William Etherington	X	–	X	–	X
James Fitzpatrick	–	–	X	–	–
Paul Flynn	–	–	–	X	–
Maria Fyfe	X	–	X	–	X
George Galloway	-	X	-	-	-

cont'd

	Lone parent benefit	Iraq	Student grants	Newspaper ownership	Criminal Justice (Terrorism and Conspiracy)
Neil Gerrard	–	X	X	X	–
Ian Gibson	X	–	–	–	X
Norman Godman	X	–	–	X	–
Bernie Grant	X	X	X	–	X
David Hinchliffe	X	–	–	–	–
Kelvin Hopkins	X	–	X	X	X
Brian Iddon	X	–	–	–	X
Lynne Jones	X	–	X	X	X
Terry Lewis	X	–	X	X	–
Ken Livingstone	X	X	X	X	–
Andrew Mackinlay	–	–	–	–	–
Alice Mahon	X	X	X	–	–
John Marek	X	–	X	–	–
James Marshall	–	–	X	–	–
Robert Marshall–Andrews	–	–	–	X	X
John McAllion	X	–	X	X	X
John McDonnell	X	X	X	X	X
Kevin McNamara	X	–	–	–	X
Tony McWalter	–	–	–	–	X
Bill Michie	X	X	–	–	–
Austin Mitchell	–	–	X	–	–
Christopher Mullin	–	–	–	X	X
Kerry Pollard	–	–	X	–	X
Ray Powell	–	–	X	–	–
Gordon Prentice	X	–	–	–	X
Allan Rogers	–	–	X	–	–
Edward Rowlands	–	–	X	–	–
Brian Sedgemore	X	–	–	–	X
Jonathan Shaw	X	–	–	–	–
Alan Simpson	X	X	X	–	–
Dennis Skinner	X	X	X	–	X
Llewellyn Smith	X	X	X	–	–
Ian Stewart	X	–	X	–	–
David Taylor	–	–	–	–	X
Robert Wareing	X	X	–	–	X
David Winnick	X	–	–	X	–
Audrey Wise	X	X	X	X	X
Michael Wood	X	–	–	X	–
James Wray	–	X	–	–	–
Derek Wyatt	–	–	–	X	–

Note: X indicates that the MP voted against the party whip.

Appendix 4: Rebellious Labour MPs, 1998–1999

Table A4.1 Rebellious Labour MPs, 1998–99

	House of Lords Bill	Kosovo	Welfare Reform and Pensions Bill	Immig- ration and Asylum Bill	Access to Justice Bill
Diane Abbott	–	–	X	–	X
John Austin	–	–	X	–	–
Harry Barnes	X	–	X	–	X
Tony Benn	X	X	X	X	X
Andrew Bennett	X	–	X	–	–
Roger Berry	–	–	X	–	–
Harold Best	X	–	X	–	–
Christine Butler	X	–	–	–	–
Ronald Campbell	–	–	X	–	–
Jamie Cann	–	–	X	–	–
Martin Caton	X	–	X	–	–
David Chaytor	X	–	X	–	–
Malcolm Chisholm	–	–	X	–	–
Michael Clapham	X	–	X	–	–
Tom Clarke	–	–	X	–	–
Tony Clarke	–	–	X	–	–
Ann Clwyd	–	–	X	–	X
Harry Cohen	–	–	–	X	X
Iain Coleman	–	–	–	–	X
Michael Connarty	–	–	X	–	–
Frank Cook	–	–	–	X	–
Jeremy Corbyn	–	X	X	X	X
James Cousins	–	–	X	–	–
David Crausby	–	–	X	–	–
Ann Cryer	–	–	X	–	–
John Cryer	–	–	X	X	–
John Cummings	X	–	X	–	–
Tam Dalyell	–	X	X	X	–
Ian Davidson	–	–	X	–	–
Denzil Davies	X	–	X	X	–
Hilton Dawson	X	–	–	–	–
James Dobbin	–	–	X	–	–
Gwyneth Dunwoody	–	–	X	–	–
William Etherington	X	–	X	–	–
Frank Field	–	–	X	–	–
Mark Fisher	X	–	X	X	–
Paul Flynn	X	–	X	–	–
Maria Fyfe	–	–	X	–	–

cont'd

	House of Lords Bill	Kosovo	Welfare Reform and Pensions Bill	Immigration and Asylum Bill	Access to Justice Bill
George Galloway	–	X	–	–	–
Neil Gerrard	–	X	X	–	X
Ian Gibson	–	–	X	–	–
Norman Godman	X	–	X	–	X
David Hinchliffe	–	–	X	–	–
Kelvin Hopkins	X	–	X	X	–
Alan Hurst	X	–	–	X	–
Brian Iddon	–	–	X	–	–
Eric Illsley	–	–	X	–	–
Jenny Jones	X	–	X	–	–
Lynne Jones	–	–	X	X	X
Tess Kingham	–	–	X	–	–
Terry Lewis	X	–	X	–	–
Ken Livingstone	X	–	X	X	X
Andrew Mackinlay	–	–	X	–	–
Alice Mahon	X	X	X	X	–
John Marek	–	–	X	–	–
David Marshall	–	–	X	–	–
James Marshall	–	–	X	X	–
Robert Marshall–Andrews	X	X	X	X	–
John McAllion	X	–	X	–	X
Christine McCafferty	–	–	X	–	–
John McDonnell	X	X	X	X	X
Kevin McNamara	–	–	X	–	–
Bill Michie	X	X	X	X	–
Austin Mitchell	X	–	–	–	–
Julie Morgan	–	–	X	–	–
Denis Murphy	–	–	X	–	–
Kerry Pollard	–	–	X	–	–
Gordon Prentice	X	–	X	–	–
Edward Rowlands	–	–	X	–	–
Philip Sawford	X	–	–	–	–
Brian Sedgemore	X	–	X	–	–
Alan Simpson	–	X	X	X	X
Dennis Skinner	X	–	X	X	X
Llewellyn Smith	X	X	X	X	–
George Stevenson	–	–	X	–	–
Roger Stott	X	–	X	–	–
Desmond Turner	–	–	X	–	–
Robert Wareing	X	X	X	–	–
Betty Williams	–	–	X	–	–
David Winnick	–	–	X	–	–
Audrey Wise	X	X	X	X	X

cont'd

	House of Lords Bill	Kosovo	Welfare Reform and Pensions Bill	Immig- ration and Asylum Bill	Access to Justice Bill
Michael Wood	–	–	X	–	X
Tony Worthington	–	–	X	–	–
Tony Wright	X	–	–	–	–

Note: X indicates that the MP voted against the party whip.

cont'd

Appendix 5: Rebellious Labour MPs, 1999–2000

Table A5.1 Rebellious Labour MPs, 1999–2000

	Terrorism	Trial by jury	Pensions	FOI	Transport Bill	Football (Disorder)	Other issues
Diane Abbott	-	X	X	–	X	X	X
Harry Barnes	–	X	X	–	X	X	X
Tony Benn	X	X	X	X	X	–	X
Andrew Bennett	–	X	–	–	X	–	–
Joe Benton	–	–	–	–	–	–	X
Harold Best	–	X	–	–	–	–	X
Ronald Campbell	–	–	X	X	–	–	–
Martin Caton	–	–	X	–	–	–	–
David Chaytor	–	–	–	–	X	–	–
Michael Clapham	–	X	X	–	X	–	–
David Clark	–	–	–	X	–	–	–
Tony Clarke	–	–	X	–	–	–	–
Ann Clwyd	–	X	X	X	X	–	–
Harry Cohen	–	X	–	X	–	–	–
Michael Connarty	–	–	X	–	X	–	X
Frank Cook	X	–	X	X	X	–	–
Robin Corbett	–	–	–	X	–	–	–
Jeremy Corbyn	X	X	X	X	X	X	X
James Cousins	–	–	X	X	–	–	–
Ann Cryer	X	–	–	–	X	–	–
John Cryer	X	X	X	–	X	–	–
Tam Dalyell	–	–	–	X	X	–	X
Ian Davidson	–	–	X	–	X	–	–
Denzil Davies	–	X	–	–	X	X	X
Terence Davis	–	X	–	–	X	–	X
Hilton Dawson	–	–	–	–	X	–	X
Janet Dean	–	–	–	–	X	–	–
Andrew Dismore	–	–	–	–	X	–	–
James Dobbin	–	–	X	–	X	–	–
Brian Donohoe	–	–	–	–	X	–	–
David Drew	–	–	–	–	X	–	–
Gwyneth Dunwoody	–	X	–	X	X	–	X
William Etherington	–	X	–	–	X	–	X
Frank Field	–	X	X	–	X	–	X
Mark Fisher	–	X	X	X	–	–	–
Paul Flynn	X	X	–	–	X	X	–
Derek Foster	–	–	–	X	–	–	–
Maria Fyfe	–	–	–	–	X	–	–
George Galloway	–	–	–	–	–	–	X
Neil Gerrard	–	X	X	X	X	–	X
Norman Godman	–	–	X	–	X	–	X

cont'd

	Terrorism	Trial by jury	Pensions	FOI	Transport Bill	Football (Disorder)	Other issues
Llin Golding	–	–	–	–	X	–	X
Eileen Gordon	–	–	–	–	X	–	–
Patrick Hall	–	–	–	X	–	–	–
Fabian Hamilton	–	–	–	–	–	–	X
David Hinchliffe	–	–	–	X	–	–	–
Kelvin Hopkins	–	X	X	X	X	X	X
Alan Hurst	–	X	X	–	–	–	–
Brian Iddon	–	–	X	–	–	–	–
Eric Illsley	–	–	–	–	X	–	–
Jenny Jones	–	X	–	X	X	–	–
Jon Owen Jones	–	–	–	X	–	–	–
Lynne Jones	X	X	X	X	X	X	–
Alan Keen	–	–	–	–	X	–	–
David Kidney	–	X	–	–	–	–	–
Peter Kilfoyle	–	–	–	–	X	–	–
Oona King	–	–	–	–	–	–	X
Tess Kingham	–	–	–	–	X	–	–
Robert Laxton	–	–	–	–	X	–	–
David Lepper	–	–	–	–	X	–	–
Terry Lewis	–	–	X	–	X	–	–
Ken Livingstone	X	–	–	–	–	–	–
Andy Love	–	–	–	X	–	–	–
Andrew Mackinlay	–	X	–	X	–	–	–
Alice Mahon	–	X	X	X	X	–	X
John Marek	–	–	–	–	X	–	–
James Marshall	X	–	–	X	–	–	X
Bob Marshall–Andrews	X	X	X	X	X	X	X
John McAllion	–	–	–	–	–	–	X
Christine McCafferty	–	X	–	–	X	–	–
John McDonnell	X	X	X	X	X	X	X
Kevin McNamara	X	X	–	X	X	–	X
John McWilliam	–	–	–	X	–	–	–
Bill Michie	–	–	X	X	X	–	X
Austin Mitchell	–	X	–	X	–	–	X
Julie Morgan	–	–	X	X	–	–	X
George Mudie	–	–	–	–	–	–	X
Ian Pearson	–	–	–	–	–	–	X
Kerry Pollard	–	–	X	–	–	–	–
Gordon Prentice	–	X	X	X	X	–	X
Gwyn Prosser	–	–	–	–	X	–	–
Edward Rowlands	–	–	–	–	X	–	–
Martin Salter	–	–	–	–	X	–	–
Philip Sawford	–	–	X	–	–	–	–
Brian Sedgemore	–	X	X	–	–	–	–
Jonathan Shaw	–	–	–	–	X	–	–
Alan Simpson	X	X	X	X	X	X	X

cont'd

	Terrorism	Trial by jury	Pensions	FOI	Transport Bill	Football (Disorder)	Other issues
Marsha Singh	–	–	–	–	–	–	X
Dennis Skinner	–	X	X	X	X	X	X
Geraldine Smith	–	–	–	–	–	–	X
Llewellyn Smith	–	X	X	X	X	–	X
George Stevenson	–	–	X	–	X	–	–
Ian Stewart	–	–	X	–	–	–	–
Gavin Strang	–	–	–	–	X	–	–
David Taylor	–	–	–	–	X	–	–
Desmond Turner	–	–	–	–	X	–	–
Rudi Vis	–	–	–	X	X	–	–
Joan Walley	–	–	X	–	–	–	–
Robert Wareing	–	X	–	–	X	–	–
Betty Williams	–	–	X	X	X	–	–
David Winnick	–	–	–	X	X	–	–
Audrey Wise	X	X	–	–	–	–	–
Michael Wood	–	–	X	X	X	–	X
Tony (Dr) Wright	–	–	–	X	–	–	–
Derek Wyatt	–	–	–	X	–	–	–

Note: X indicates that the MP voted against the party whip.

Appendix 6: Rebellious Labour MPs, 2000–2001

Table A6.1 Rebellious Labour MPs, 2000–2001

	Terrorism Order	Other issues
Diane Abbott	X	–
Tony Benn	X	X
Michael Clapham	X	–
Jeremy Corbyn	X	X
Denzil Davies	X	X
Gwyneth Dunwoody	–	X
Frank Field	–	X
Mark Fisher	–	X
Neil Gerrard	X	–
Llin Golding	–	X
Jenny Jones	X	–
Tony Lloyd	–	X
James Marshall	X	–
John McDonnell	X	–
Alan Simpson	X	–
Dennis Skinner	X	X
Robert Wareing	X	–
Alan J Williams	–	X

Note: X indicates that the MP voted against the party whip.

Appendix 7: Rebellious Conservative MPs, 1997–2001

Table A7.1: Rebellious Conservative MPs, 1997–2001

	Devolution	Northern Ireland	Criminal Justice	Football (Disorder)	Other
David Amess	–	–	–	–	X
David Atkinson	–	X	–	–	X
Tony Baldry	–	–	X	–	X
John Bercow	X	–	–	–	X
Crispin Blunt	X	–	X	–	X
Richard Body	–	X	–	–	X
Peter Bottomley	–	X	X	X	X
Virginia Bottomley	–	X	–	–	X
Graham Brady	X	X	X	–	X
Julian Brazier	X	–	–	–	–
Peter Brooke	–	–	X	–	X
Angela Browning	X	–	–	–	X
Ian Bruce	X	X	–	–	X
Simon Burns	–	–	–	X	–
John Butterfill	X	–	–	–	X
William Cash	X	X	X	–	X
Christopher Chope	X	X	–	X	X
James Clappison	X	–	–	–	–
Alan Clark	X	X	X		X
Dr Michael Clark	X	–	–	–	X
Kenneth Clarke	–	–	–	X	X
Geoffrey Clifton–Brown	X	–	X	–	–
Tim Collins	X	–	–	–	–
Michael Colvin	X	X	–	–	X
Patrick Cormack	X	–	–	–	–
James Cran	X	–	–	–	–
Quentin Davies	–	–	–	–	X
David Davis	–	X	X	X	X
Stephen Day	X	–	–	–	–
Alan Duncan	X	–	–	–	–
Iain Duncan Smith	X	–	–	–	–
Peter Emery	–	X	X	–	X
Nigel Evans	X	–	–	–	X
David Faber	X	–	X	–	X
Michael Fabricant	X	X	X	–	X
Michael Fallon	X	X	–	–	X
Howard Flight	X	X	–	–	X
Eric Forth	X	X	–	X	X
Norman Fowler	–	–	–	X	X

cont'd

	Devolution	Northern Ireland	Criminal Justice	Football (Disorder)	Other
Dr Liam Fox	X	–	–	–	–
Christopher Fraser	X	–	–	–	–
Roger Gale	X	X	–	X	–
Edward Garnier	X	X	–	–	–
Nick Gibb	X	–	–	–	–
Christopher Gill	X	X	–		X
Teresa Gorman	X	X	–	–	X
James Gray	X	X	X	–	X
John Greenway	X	–	–	–	X
Dominic Grieve	X	–	X	–	X
John Gummer	–	–	–	X	X
Archie Hamilton	X	–	–	–	–
Philip Hammond	X	–	–	–	–
Nick Hawkins	X	–	–	–	X
John Hayes	X	–	X	–	X
Edward Heath	–	–	X	–	–
David Heathcoat–Amory	X	–	–	–	–
Michael Heseltine	–	–	–	–	X
Douglas Hogg	–	X	–	X	X
Michael Howard	–	X	–	–	–
Gerald Howarth	X	X	–	–	X
Andrew Hunter	X	X	X	–	X
Robert Jackson	X	–	–	–	X
Bernard Jenkin	X	X	–	–	–
Geoffrey Johnson–Smith	–	–	–	–	X
Robert Key	–	–	–	–	X
Julie Kirkbride	X	–	–	–	X
Eleanor Laing	X	–	X	–	–
Andrew Lansley	X	–	–	–	–
Edward Leigh	X	X	–	X	X
Dr Julian Lewis	X	X	X	–	X
David Lidington	X	–	–	–	–
Peter Lilley	–	–	–	X	X
Peter Lloyd	X	–	X	–	X
Tim Loughton	X	–	X	–	–
Peter Luff	X	–	–	–	X
Nicholas Lyell	–	–	–	X	–
John MacGregor	X	–	X	–	–
David Maclean	–	X	X	–	X
Anne McIntosh	X	X	X	–	X
Humfrey Malins	–	–	X	–	X
John Maples	–	–	–	–	X
Michael Mates	X	X	X	–	–
Brian Mawhinney	–	X	–	–	X
Piers Merchant	X	–	–	–	–
Malcolm Moss	X	–	–	–	X

cont'd

	Devolution	Northern Ireland	Criminal Justice	Football (Disorder)	Other
Patrick Nicholls	X	X	–	–	X
Archie Norman	X	–	–	–	–
Richard Page	–	X	–	–	–
James Paice	X	–	–	–	X
Owen Paterson	X	X	X	–	X
John Randall	–	–	X	–	–
John Redwood	X	–	–	–	X
Andrew Robathan	X	X	X	–	X
Laurence Robertson	X	X	X	–	X
Marion Roe	X	–	–	–	–
Andrew Rowe	X	X	X	–	–
David Ruffley	X	–	X	–	X
Nick St Aubyn	X	X	X	–	X
Jonathan Sayeed	X	X	X	–	X
Richard Shepherd	X	X	X	X	X
Keith Simpson	X	–	–	–	X
Nicholas Soames	–	–	–	–	X
Caroline Spelman	X	–	–	–	–
Michael Spicer	X	X	–	–	X
Richard Spring	X	–	–	–	X
Anthony Steen	–	–	–	–	X
Desmond Swayne	X	X	X	–	X
Robert Syms	X	–	–	–	–
Peter Tapsell	–	–	X	–	–
Ian Taylor	–	–	X	–	X
Teddy Taylor	X	–	X	–	X
John Townend	–	X	–	X	X
David Tredinnick	X	–	X	–	X
Michael Trend	X	–	–	–	–
Andrew Tyrie	X	–	–	–	X
Peter Viggers	X	X	–	–	–
Robert Walter	X	–	X	–	–
Charles Wardle	X	X	–	–	X
Nigel Waterson	X	–	–	–	–
Bowen Wells	–	–	–	–	X
Raymond Whitney	X	–	X	–	X
John Whittingdale	X	–	–	–	–
John Wilkinson	X	X	–	X	X
David Willetts	X	–	–	–	–
David Wilshire	X	X	–	–	X
Ann Winterton	X	X	–	–	X
Nicholas Winterton	X	X	–	–	X
Shaun Woodward	X	–	–	–	–

Note: X indicates that the MP voted against the party whip.

Appendix 8: Rebellious Liberal Democrat MPs, 1997–2001

Table A8.1: Rebellious Liberal Democrat MPs, 1997–2001

Name	Title of Bill/Issue	Date
Richard Allan	House of Lords Bill	16 Feb 1999
Jackie Ballard	Capital Allowances Bill (Business of the House)	13 Feb 2001
Alan Beith	Finance Bill	23 Apr 2001 (twice)
Thomas Brake	House of Lords Bill	16 Feb 1999
Dr Peter Brand	Referendums (Scotland and Wales) Bill	4 Jun 1997
	EC Documents (Equality in Employment)	25 Jul 2000
Colin Breed	Local Government Bill	5 Jul 2000
	Finance Bill	23 Apr 2001
John Burnett	Local Government Bill	5 Jul 2000
	EC Documents (Equality in Employment)	25 Jul 2000
	EU Budget	13 Dec 2000
	Armed Forces Bill (Programming Motion)	9 Jan 2001
	Budget Resolutions	13 Mar 2001
	Common Security and Defence Policy	21 Mar 2001
	Finance Bill	23 Apr 2001
Menzies Campbell	Post Office	15 Jul 1999
Edward Davey	Vote on Account (That the House Sit in Private)	27 Feb 2001
Ronnie Fearn	Capital Allowances Bill (Business of the House)	13 Feb 2001
Andrew George	Referendums (Scotland and Wales) Bill	4 Jun 1997
Donald Gorrie	EC Documents (Equality in Employment)	25 Jul 2000
Mike Hancock	Referendums (Scotland and Wales) Bill	4 Jun 2001
	House of Lords Bill	16 Feb 1999
	House of Lords Bill	10 Nov 1999
	Terrorism Bill	15 Mar 2000
	Football (Disorder) Bill	17 Jul 2000
	Freedom of Information Bill	27 Nov 2000
	Proscribed Organisations	14 Mar 2001
Nick Harvey	Finance (No. 2) Bill	28 Apr 1998
	Police (Northern Ireland) Bill	21 Nov 2000
	Christmas Adjournment	13 Dec 2000
David Heath	House of Lords Bill	16 Feb 1999
	House of Lords Bill	10 Nov 1999
	Disqualifications Bill	30 Nov 2000
	Budget Resolutions	13 Mar 2001
	Finance Bill	23 Apr 2001 (twice)
Simon Hughes	Homes Bill (Programming Motion)	8 Jan 2001
	Armed Forces Bill (Programming Motion)	9 Jan 2001
Nigel Jones	Referendums (Scotland and Wales) Bill	4 Jun 1997
	Sierra Leone	2 Mar 1999
Archy Kirkwood	Finance Bill	23 Apr 2001

Name	Title of Bill/Issue	Date
Richard Livsey	Finance Bill	16 Jul 1997
	Finance Bill	6 Jul 1999
	Post Office	15 Jul 1999
	Budget Resolutions	13 Mar 2001
Ray Michie	Budget Resolutions	13 Mar 2001
	Finance Bill	23 Apr 2001 (twice)
Lembit Opik	Finance Bill	23 Apr 2001 (twice)
Bob Russell	Commonwealth Development Corporation Bill	14 Jul 1999
Adrian Sanders	House of Lords Bill	16 Feb 1999
	EC Documents (Equality in Employment)	25 Jul 2000
Sir Robert Smith	Armed Forces Bill (Programming Motion)	9 Jan 2001
	Capital Allowances Bill (Business of the House)	13 Feb 2001
	Budget Resolutions	13 Mar 2001
	Finance Bill	23 Apr 2001 (twice)
Paul Tyler	Finance Bill	23 Apr 2001
Steve Webb	Budget Resolutions	13 Mar 2001
Phil Willis	House of Lords Bill	10 Nov 1999

Appendix 9: Martin Bell

Since industrialisation and the growth of the franchise in the 19th century, independent MPs have been rare beasts; since the abolition of the university seats in 1950 they were effectively extinct. Martin Bell, elected for Tatton in 1997, was the first mainland MP elected since 1950 to be entirely free of party ties. Immediately after Bell's victory, his defeated predecessor claimed that Bell had 'no opinions on anything', and that Tatton had elected a 'vacuum'. Neil Hamilton's (perhaps understandable) pique masked an important question: in a Parliament dominated by party, what role was there for an independent?

Enoch Powell once dismissed the idea of independent MPs as an 'irrelevant absurdity'. Powell's argument was this:

> A single imaginary question settles the point. Mr Candidate, if you find you have the deciding vote in an evenly balanced new House of Commons, will you use it to turn the Government out or to keep them in? The candidate cannot refuse to answer; when he does so, he ceases to be an independent candidate.[4]

Even if you do not agree with the logic – and Bell did not – the size of Labour's majority meant that he was never going to be faced with that decision. As a result the parties were not desperate for his vote and he was free to vote as he wanted.

The most striking feature about the way Martin Bell voted, though, is that more often than not he did not. In his four years in the House, he voted 621 times, some 49 per cent of all votes.[5] This was partly because he did not see voting as the most important thing he could do. He had, he claimed, better things to do with his time than add or subtract one to the largest Government majority since 1935. This applied especially late at night, when his participation would drop sharply ('I've got a wife and a life').[6]

But it is also because he faced the classic problem of any independent: the lack of information about how to vote and the lack of time to gather that information. For Bell, every vote was a free vote. With no whip to rely on, every vote required him to think. Vernon Bartlett, an independent MP from 1938 to 1950, solved this problem by hiding when a difficult vote came up. By contrast, Bell tried to vote on most of the main pieces of legislation, and he was more likely to vote on the principle of a Bill – at Second or Third Reading – than on the more detailed and abstruse amendments, which he confessed could be 'particularly tricky . . . I must have got it wrong sometimes'. When deciding how to vote, he would take advice from MPs of all parties, being particularly keen on what he described as 'the mavericks'. On two issues – fox hunting and the homosexual age of consent – where he had no strong views of his own, he was prepared to act more as a delegate for the perceived views of his constituents: as a result he voted against a ban on fox hunting and in favour of keeping the age of consent at 18.

Bell's voting record got better as time went on. In *Purple Homicide*, John Sweeney's enjoyable if rather one-sided account of the Tatton contest, Sweeney claimed he saw Bell grow as a politician as the campaign went on.[7] Something similar happened with Bell's relations with the House of Commons. The first few weeks were particularly difficult. To begin with, he was 'completely lost'. But as he became more confident, so his voting record improved. It averaged 28 per cent in the first 200 votes of the first session and grew to 36 per cent in the next 180. It reached 48 per cent in the second session and climbed to 62 per cent in the third, before falling away slightly to 56 per cent in the final session. Even at its peak, therefore, it was still lower than many other MPs but is probably the sort of voting record that most MPs would have achieved if they could not lean on their party whip.

When voting, Bell claimed that he sprayed his vote around. 'Sometimes I was left wing and sometimes I was right wing. Sometimes I was in the front line with the progressives and sometimes in the last ditch with the diehards . . . I am a democrat, a radical, a libertarian and a Blairite – Eric Blair, that is, not Tony'.[8] But his vote sprayed more in one direction than another. He voted with the Conservatives in just over a third of votes (35 per cent), with Labour in just over half (56 per cent) and with the Liberal Democrats on almost three-quarters of votes (71 per cent). But these overall figures hide some important variations. Bell began the Parliament working on the assumption that, if he was going to vote, he was inclined to give the Government the benefit of the doubt (saying in June 1999 that 'On the whole they are a good Government'). But as Figure A9.1 shows, as the Parliament progressed, he became increasingly critical of the Government.

During the first session, Bell voted with the Conservatives in just 21 per cent of votes but with Labour more than three times as often, in 68 per cent of votes. By the fourth session he was (slightly) more likely to vote with the Conservatives than with Labour. The percentage of his votes with the Liberal Democrats, though, never fell below 60 per cent. Bell, then, was no party clone merely masquerading as an independent. His voting was unlike that of any party's MPs – although he was consistently more likely to be found voting with the Liberal Democrats than with any other party.

Figure A9.1 Martin Bell's voting, 1997–2001

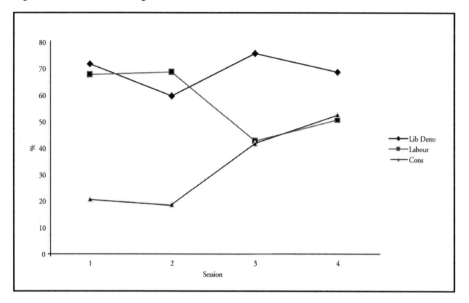

Appendix 10: Major Parliamentary Divisions, 1997–2001

First Session: 7 May 1997–19 November 1998

3 June. In the largest Conservative rebellion of the Parliament, 82 Tory MPs supported an amendment to the Referendums (Scotland and Wales) Bill that proposed that the Scottish referendum should encompass the whole of the United Kingdom rather than merely those resident in Scotland.

4 June. The Referendum (Scotland and Wales) Bill saw a further four rebellions by Conservative MPs. The largest saw 37 Conservatives support an SNP amendment favouring a multi-option referendum including independence.

11 June. The Bill extending the ban on handguns to all .22 weapons gained a Second Reading by 384 votes to 181.

28 November. Michael Foster's Wild Mammals Bill, a private members' Bill to ban hunting with dogs, was given its Second Reading by 411 votes to 151 on a free vote. The Bill later failed due to a lack of Parliamentary time.

10 Deecceemmbbeerr. In the first major Government backbench rebellion of the Parliament, 47 Labour MPs voted against the Government over plans to cut lone parent benefit. At least 20 Labour MPs also abstained.

17 February. Twenty-two Labour MPs voted against a Government motion that supported the use of 'all necessary means' to persuade Saddam Hussein to comply with UN weapons inspectors.

8 June. Thirty-four Labour MPs voted for an amendment to the Teaching and Higher Education Bill that would have retained maintenance grants for students from low-income families. A further 15 abstained.

22 June. In a free vote MPs voted by 336 votes to 129 in favour of an amendment to the Crime and Disorder Bill, moved by Ann Keen, which would have reduced the age of consent for homosexual sex between men to 16. The clause was later removed from the Bill following opposition in the House of Lords.

88 JJuullyy. Twenty-five Labour MPs voted for a backbench amendment to the Competition Bill that sought to bring predatory pricing in the newspaper industry within the remit of the Bill.

2 September. In the wake of the Omagh Bombing in August, Parliament was recalled in order for MPs to debate the Criminal Justice (Terrorism and Conspiracy) Bill. In four separate Labour rebellions, a total of 37 Labour MPs voted against the Bill's provisions against terrorist organisations. The largest Labour rebellion, on an amendment moved by Chris Mullin that would have required the audio recording of suspects, was supported by 29 MPs. In the second largest Conservative rebellion of the Parliament 40 Conservative MPs joined 16 Labour backbenchers who objected to all the Bill's stages being completed in one day.

Second Session: 24 November 1998–11 November 1999

25 January. In a free vote MPs voted by 313 votes to 130 in favour of the Sexual Offences (Amendment) Bill, which reduced the age of consent for male homosexuals to 16 but which also introduced safeguards against the abuse of trust by persons in authority for 16 and 17 year olds of both sexes. The Bill was later defeated in the House of Lords.

16 February. Thirty-five Labour MPs voted in support of an amendment moved by Bob Marshall-Andrews to the House of Lords Bill that would have removed the Government's right of patronage in appointing members of the reformed House.

19 April. Thirteen Labour MPs forced a closure motion to protest at the NATO bombing of Kosovo.

20 May. The largest Government rebellion of the Parliament saw 67 Labour MPs vote against the Government over the Welfare Reform and Pensions Bill. The rebels supported an amendment, moved by Roger Berry, that would have excised from the Bill the introduction of means-testing for incapacity benefit, as well as proposals to remove entitlement to the benefit from those who had made no national insurance contributions in the previous two years. Between 14 and 25 Labour MPs also abstained.

22 June. Twenty-one Labour MPs supported an amendment to the Access to Justice Bill moved by Bob Marshall-Andrews to restore legal aid for the disabled and the less well off in personal injury cases.

1133 JJuullyy. Ten Conservative backbenchers opposed the Second Reading of the Northern Ireland Bill – the Anglo-Irish plan to revive the 'peace process'. Sixteen Conservative MPs then opposed the Bill's Third Reading.

3 November. In six consecutive divisions as many as 54 Labour MPs voted in favour of Lords amendments to the Welfare Reform and Pensions Bill.

9 November. As many as 46 Labour MPs voted with the Lords on three amendments to the Welfare Reform and Pensions Bill which sought to ease the restrictions on incapacity benefit and which set the level of disability income guarantee. Sixteen Labour MPs also voted against a Lords amendment to the Immigration and Asylum Bill, which would have restored social security benefits to all asylum-sekers until the average Government targets for processing asylum cases had been met.

Third Session: 17 November 1999–30 November 2000

2244 JJaannuuaarryy 22000000. Thirteen Conservative backbenchers opposed the Second Reading of the Disqualifications Bill. In a remarkable display of filibustering throughout the night and into the following day, a further five divisions saw an average of 14 Conservatives oppose the Bill.

8 February. In two votes on the Second and Third Reading of the Northern Ireland Bill, a total of ten Labour MPs opposed the suspension of the Northern Ireland Assembly.

10 February. The Government reintroduced the Sexual Offences (Amendment) Bill, and the Bill was again passed at Second Reading, on a free vote, by 263 votes to 102.

28 February. Ten Labour MPs voted against the Government's Defence White Paper.

7 March. Twenty-nine Labour MPs voted for a reasoned amendment to the Criminal Justice (Mode of Trial) (No. 2) Bill moved by Bob Marshall-Andrews, which sought to retain the right of defendants to choose trial by jury for a range of offences.

15 March. Thirteen Labour MPs supported an amendment to the Terrorism Bill moved by Kevin McNamara that sought to withdraw the Government's definition of terrorism, replacing it with a definition where the public were put in fear or the democratic institutions of Government were coerced.

5 April. Forty Labour MPs backed an amendment to the Child Support, Pensions and Social Security Bill, moved by John McDonnell, to increase the basic retirement pension in line with earnings or the retail price index, whichever was the greater. On the same day there were a series of five rebellions involving between 18 and 36 Labour MPs on the Freedom of Information Act. The largest was on an amendment that would have removed the blanket exemption on the disclosure of purely factual information, as opposed to policy advice, used by Ministers when determining Government policy.

9 May. There were three rebellions over the Government's proposals for a public-private partnership for the National Air Traffic Services (NATS), contained in the Transport Bill. The two largest saw some 46 Labour MPs support amendments that ensured either that the new company would be owned by the Crown or that the transfer would be made to a 'not for profit' company.

11 July. Ten Conservative MPs opposed the Third Reading of the Police (Northern Ireland) Bill that sought to reform the Royal Ulster Constabulary (RUC).

17 July. Thirteen Conservatives (and two Labour MPs) voted against the guillotine placed on the Football (Disorder) Bill's proceedings. Eleven Labour MPs then supported an amendment to the Bill that would have removed the provision that a police officer had the power to detain someone at a port or airport for 24 hours if there was a reasonable likelihood that that person might cause disorder or violence.

25 July. Twenty-eight Labour MPs voted against the Third Reading of the Criminal Justice (Mode of Trial) (No. 2) Bill.

23 October. Michael Martin, the Labour MP for Glasgow, Springburn, and Deputy Speaker since 1997, was elected Speaker after 11 other candidates – two Liberal Democrats, six Conservatives and a further three Labour MPs – were all voted down. In the final vote, Martin was elected Speaker by 370 votes to 8.

15 November. Thirty-seven Labour MPs backed a Lords amendment to the Transport Bill that would have delayed the part-privatisation of NATS until after the general election. Another Lords amendment, which would have granted greater guarantees to NATS employees over their pension rights, was supported by 17 Labour MPs.

20 November. Seventeen Labour MPs backed a Liberal Democrat prayer that sought to revoke the £500 charge placed on immigrants who wished to appeal against the rejection of their visa application.

27 November. Twelve Labour MPs supported a Liberal Democrat amendment to the Freedom of Information Bill calling for greater disclosure of information by public authorities.

28 November. A proposal by the Lords to delay the NATS sell-off until after the general election was rejected by the Government for a second time but backed by 43 Labour MPs. An attempt to delay the sell-off by three months attracted 38 Labour MPs but was also rejected.

Fourth Session: 6 December 2000–11 May 2001

19 December. In a free vote, MPs voted by 366 to 17 in favour of human embryology regulations that authorised research to be conducted into degenerative diseases using embryonic stem cells.

17 January. In a free vote on a Government Bill, MPs voted by 387 to 174 in favour of a total ban on hunting with dogs in England and Wales. Alternative options – self-regulation and a licensing system (the so-called 'Middle Way') – were rejected by 155 votes to 399 and 182 to 382 respectively.

14 March. Twelve Labour MPs opposed a draft order outlining proscribed organisations under the Terrorism Act 2000.

22 March. MPs voted narrowly by 84 votes to 82 against an amendment that would have retained the open ballot system for the election of the Speaker. The election would now take place by secret ballot.

23 April. In the largest (and only substantial) Liberal Democrat rebellion of the Parliament, nine Liberal Democrat MPs opposed the introduction of an aggregates levy in the Finance Bill.

[1] Pippa Norris, *British By-Elections*, Oxford, Clarendon Press, 1990, p. 14.

[2] F. W. S. Craig, *British Electoral Facts*, Dartmouth, Parliamentary Research Services, 1989, p. 174.

[3] *Sunday Telegraph*, 18 January 1998.

[4] Enoch Powell, *Reflections*, London, Bellew, 1992, pp. 118–119. The remark was made in a speech in 1976.

[5] This includes five occasions where Bell went through both division lobbies to record abstentions. 'This was good for the voting record, and it considerably baffled the academics in Hull'. Martin Bell, *An Accidental MP*, London, Viking, 2000, pp. 202–203.

[6] All un-attributed quotes in this Appendix are from two interviews with Martin Bell, on 1 June 1999 and 6 March 2001.

[7] London, Bloomsbury, 1997.

[8] Bell, *An Accidental MP*, pp. 63–64.

Index